The Church of God and Its Human Face

The Church of God and Its Human Face

The Contribution of Joseph A. Komonchak to Ecclesiology

Martin Madar

⁌PICKWICK *Publications* · Eugene, Oregon

THE CHURCH OF GOD AND ITS HUMAN FACE
The Contribution of Joseph A. Komonchak to Ecclesiology

Copyright © 2019 Martin Madar. All rights reserved. Except for brief quotations in critical publications or reviews, no part of this book may be reproduced in any manner without prior written permission from the publisher. Write: Permissions, Wipf and Stock Publishers, 199 W. 8th Ave., Suite 3, Eugene, OR 97401.

Pickwick Publications
An Imprint of Wipf and Stock Publishers
199 W. 8th Ave., Suite 3
Eugene, OR 97401

www.wipfandstock.com

PAPERBACK ISBN: 978-1-5326-5745-0
HARDCOVER ISBN: 978-1-5326-5746-7
EBOOK ISBN: 978-1-5326-5747-4

Cataloguing-in-Publication data:

Names: Madar, Martin, author.

Title: The Church of God and its human face : the contribution of Joseph A. Komonchak to ecclesiology / by Martin Madar.

Description: Eugene, OR : Pickwick Publications, 2019 | Includes bibliographical references.

Identifiers: ISBN 978-1-5326-5745-0 (paperback) | ISBN 978-1-5326-5746-7 (hardcover) | ISBN 978-1-5326-5747-4 (ebook)

Subjects: LCSH: Church. | Komonchak, Joseph A.

Classification: BV600.3 .M32 2019 (print) | BV600.3 .M32 (ebook)

Excerpts from documents of the Second Vatican Council are from *Vatican Council II: Constitutions, Decrees, Declarations; The Basic Sixteen Documents*, edited by Austin Flannery, OP, © 1996. Used with permission of Liturgical Press, Collegeville, Minnesota.

Manufactured in the U.S.A. 06/04/19

For my teachers and those who taught them

Contents

Acknowledgments | xi
Abbreviations | xii
Introduction | xv

Chapter 1: Vatican II and the Shift in Catholic Ecclesiology | 1
    Ecclesiology Prior to Vatican II   3
        Beginnings of Formal Ecclesiology   5
        Counter-Reformation Ecclesiology   8
            Perfect Society Ecclesiology   10
        Ecclesiological Renewal Prior to Vatican II   16
            Möhler   17
            Mystical Body of Christ   22
            People of God   24
            Mystici Corporis   25
            The Church as Sacrament   26
            The Church and the Eucharist   27
            The Contribution of Yves Congar   29
    Ecclesiology at Vatican II   31
        Ecclesiology of Vatican II: An Overview   36
            The Church as Mystery, Sacrament, and Communion   36
            The Church as the Pilgrim People of God   39
            Ecumenism   41
            The Local Church   43
            Church and World   43

Laity   46
Collegiality of Bishops   48
Conclusion   49

Chapter 2: Life and Major Influences | 51
Life   51
Major Influences   55
Vatican II   56
Bernard Lonergan   57
Unexpected Influences   59
Influences from the Social Sciences   63

Chapter 3: Method in Ecclesiology | 65
Why Method?   66
Diagnosis of Deficiencies in Catholic Ecclesiology after Vatican II   68
Models Don't Go Far Enough   68
False Dichotomy between the Church as God's Gift and as Our Task   71
Theological Reductionism   74
The Central Challenge for Ecclesiology   75
What the Church Is   76
Congregatio fidelium   77
Community Constituted by Meaning and Mediated by Value   78
Human and Social Reality   79
Historical Subject of Its Self-Realization   80
Genesis of the Church   81
Ontology of the Church   84
Redemptive Community   87
God's Gift and Our Task   87
Solution of the Central Challenge for Ecclesiology   88
Vision of Systematic Ecclesiology   89
Theory as the Goal of a Critical, Systematic Ecclesiology   90
Methodological Shift in Ecclesiology   93
The Object of Ecclesiology   94
Ecclesiology as Theory about Practice   94
Social Sciences and Ecclesiology   95
Conclusion   98

Chapter 4: The Local Church | 102
    The Local Church at Vatican II   104
        The Issue of Terminology   106
        Three Key *Loci* of Vatican II's Treatment of the Local Church   107
            Bishop, Eucharist, and the Church   107
            Catholicity of the Church   110
            The Bishop and the Local Church   112
    Komonchak on the Local Church   115
        Theological Significance of Locality   116
            Descending Approach   116
            Ascending Approach   119
        Meaning of Catholicity   125
        Church Local and Universal   129
    Conclusion   150

Chapter 5: Authority in the Church | 152
    Authority as a Social Relationship   154
    Authority and Its Exercise   158
        Limits of Authority   158
        Authority and Conversion   159
        Magisterium and Obedience   161
    Conclusion   162

Conclusion | 164

Bibliography of Joseph A. Komonchak | 167
Bibliography | 179
Index | 193

Acknowledgments

With great joy, I take this opportunity to thank those who supported me professionally and personally throughout this project. My gratitude goes first to Fr. Joseph Komonchak whose life work of scholarship inspired this study and from whose teaching I continue to benefit tremendously. Since this book builds on my dissertation, I want to offer my sincere thanks to Drs. John Galvin (director), William Loewe, and Christopher Ruddy whose thoughtful critique and guidance improved my work immensely.

I want to give thanks to the administrators at Xavier University for granting me a semester-long research leave to work on this project. Many thanks are also due to my colleagues at the Department of Theology, especially Art Dewey, Anna Miller, and Kristine Suna-Koro.

I am grateful to my Pickwick Publications editors, Dr. Charlie Collier and Zane Derven, for guiding me through the publication process. Likewise, I cannot thank enough Andrew Buechel, James Nickoloff, and Fran and Peg Niehaus for their editorial support.

Throughout this project, I have been sustained by the encouragement of my friends and family whose presence and understanding made my work easier. I am especially thankful to Fr. Jerry Austin, OP, Fr. Mark Wedig, OP, Fr. Peter Haladej, Israel Diaz, and the Barbeite family. Last but not least, I am immensely grateful to my wife Anne whose enduring support accompanied me through the highs and lows of creating this book.

Abbreviations

Documents of the Second Vatican Council

AA *Apostolicam actuositatem*: Decree on the Apostolate of the Laity
AG *Ad gentes*: Decree on the Church's Missionary Activity
CD *Christus Dominus*: Decree on the Bishops' Pastoral Office in the Church
DH *Dignitatis humanae*: Declaration on Religious Freedom
DV *Dei verbum*: Dogmatic Constitution on Divine Revelation
GE *Gravissimum educationis*: Declaration on Christian Education
GS *Gaudium et spes*: Pastoral Constitution on the Church in the Modern World
LG *Lumen gentium*: Dogmatic Constitution on the Church
OE *Orientalium ecclesiarum*: Decree on the Catholic Eastern Churches
PC *Perfectae caritatis*: Decree on the Renewal of Religious Life
PO *Presbyterorum ordinis*: Decree on the Ministry and Life of Priests
SC *Sacrosanctum concilium*: Constitution on the Sacred Liturgy
UR *Unitatis redintegratio*: Decree on Ecumenism

Other Abbreviations

AS   *Acta Synodalia Sacrosancti Oecumenici Concilii Vaticani II*. 6 vols. in 32 parts. Vatican City: Typis polyglottis Vaticanis, 1970–1996.

CDF Congregation for the Doctrine of the Faith

CN   *Communionis notio*: CDF's Letter on Some Aspects of the Church Understood as Communion

ET   English translation

Introduction

THE TWENTIETH CENTURY WAS remarkably favorable to Catholic ecclesiology. This discipline, which attempts a theological understanding of the church, went through a renewal, long overdue, unleashing new vigor and creativity into the field.

Beginning in the 1920s, theologians turned to ancient and medieval theological sources, leading to a retrieval of ideas that were once at the center of theological reflection on the church, for instance, the church as the body of Christ, mystery or sacrament, people of God, and communion.

This work of *ressourcement* ("return to the sources") paved the road for the Second Vatican Council (1962–1965)—the most significant event in Catholicism since the sixteenth-century Reformation. Expected to do little more than rubber-stamp the theological theses of neoscholastic manuals, the council delivered a stunning surprise. While teaching in continuity with the larger tradition, it provided an ecclesiology that, by and large, drew on so-called *nouvelle théologie*, not on neoscholasticism—the theological system dominant at the time.[1] In its documents, the council incorporated

---

1. *Nouvelle théologie* (French, "new theology") was a theological movement among Catholic theologians mainly from France in the first half of the twentieth century, which wanted to overcome the limitations of neoscholastic theology. Among its most prominent representatives were Marie-Dominique Chenu, Henri de Lubac, Yves Congar, Jean Daniélou, and Henri Bouillard. One of the chief characteristics of this so-called "new theology"—a name given to it by its opponents and originally having a pejorative connotation—was the work of *ressourcement*, that is, a return to biblical, patristic, and medieval theological sources. The movement also advocated a dialogue with the contemporary world, incorporated experience into theology, and studied the development of dogma. Pius XII's encyclical *Humani generis* (1950) was critical of *nouvelle théologie* and was expected to end it. Although a number of the proponents of the "new theology" were disciplined at the time, many of their views were eventually espoused at the Second Vatican Council where they were some of the most influential

many of the insights that theologians had recently recovered and reintroduced them into the mainstream of Catholic ecclesiological consciousness.

After the council, the revitalization of Catholic ecclesiology entered a new stage as theologians began to interpret, develop, and advance the insights of the council. The renewed emphasis on the communal nature of the church, a dialogical stance toward the world, and an openness to ecumenism occupied the center of many ecclesiological projects. Ecclesiology became more complex, and efforts were undertaken in various parts of the world to apply and extend the teaching of the council to different local contexts. This was done not only by those whose scholarship made the council possible, but also by a new generation of theologians whose careers were just starting. In the postconciliar landscape of ecclesiology, the work of Joseph A. Komonchak stands out as one of the most distinctive contributions to date made by a theologian writing in English.

Komonchak is not only a premier US ecclesiologist, but also a leading English-language scholar of the history and theology of Vatican II. His expertise further includes the twentieth-century Catholic theology and the thought of John Courtney Murray. Educated in the US and in Italy, Komonchak spent the majority of his career as a teacher and scholar at the Catholic University of America in Washington, DC (1977–2009). He was the chief editor of *The New Dictionary of Theology* and the English-language editor of the five-volume *History of Vatican II*. He published primarily in the form of book chapters and articles in journals such as *Theological Studies, Cristianesimo nella Storia, Concilium, The Thomist, Chicago Studies, Method: The Journal of Lonergan Studies,* and *Revue d'Histoire Ecclésiastique*. Komonchak was a consultant to three committees of the United States Conference of Catholic Bishops (on Doctrine, Priestly Life and Ministry, and the Permanent Diaconate). He also served as a theological expert in ecumenical dialogues: the Vatican-sponsored Roman Catholic-Baptist International Dialogue (1984–1988) and the North American Orthodox-Catholic Theological Consultation. In recognition of his exceptional gifts, his theological accomplishments, and his dedicated service to the church and the theological profession, the Catholic Theological Society of America presented Komonchak in 2015 with its highest honor, the John Courtney Murray Award for distinguished achievement in theology.

When I applied to doctoral studies in systematic theology at the Catholic University of America, the prospect of taking courses with Komonchak was among the highest on the list of qualities that made the program attractive. I had the great fortune to attend Komonchak's doctoral seminar

---

periti ("theological experts").

on method in ecclesiology in the spring of 2009, the last time he taught it before his retirement. I realized at the time that Komonchak had developed a distinctive approach to theologizing about the church. I had not hitherto encountered in other theologians the sophistication with which Komonchak articulated the idea that God's church exists in history as a human and social reality—the point that inspired the title of this study. The genius of Komonchak's thinking about the church lies in the depth of his integration of the traditional understanding of the church as a *coetus hominum* ("a group of people") with the theological and spiritual conceptions of the church that were reintroduced into Catholic ecclesiology in the twentieth century. I found Komonchak's thinking about the church intellectually stimulating, which inspired me to explore it in more depth. I wrote my dissertation on Komonchak's contribution to the theology of the local church, upon which the current study builds.[2]

Komonchak's work is of significance not only for the discipline of ecclesiology, but also for envisioning church practice today. As regards the former, Komonchak has done a great service by laying the foundations for an ecclesiology that surpasses the level of images and models and reaches the level of theory. As regards the latter, the concreteness of Komonchak's ecclesiology and his theology of the local church have direct implications for current attempts to build a synodal church—advocated by Pope Francis—and for the exercise of authority in the church in general.

Komonchak has not produced a monograph that outlines his ecclesiology in one volume. His thinking about the church is instead spread throughout numerous journal articles and book chapters, which makes it a challenge to gain a comprehensive grasp of his ecclesiology. This study offers a synthesis of Komonchak's theology of the church, accompanied by analysis and critique. It is the first monograph offering a sustained engagement with Komonchak's thought on the church.[3] I hope that it will serve teachers and scholars by making the work of one of the finest contemporary ecclesiologists more accessible.

The book is laid out in five chapters. Chapter one establishes the context for Komonchak's engagement with questions of ecclesiology. It discusses the history of ecclesiology in the second millennium with a focus on the shift that Vatican II effected in Catholic ecclesiology from an overly institutional

---

2. See Madar, "Contribution of Joseph A. Komonchak." For my study of Komonchak's contribution to the interpretation of Vatican II, see Madar, "Alternative Middle Position," 643–69.

3. A *festschrift* in honor of Komonchak was published in 2015. While several essays engage Komonchak's ecclesiology, the contributors for the most part further their own scholarship on a particular topic. See Denny et al., *Realist's Church*.

view of the church to an ecclesiology that brings out the church's transcendent dimension. Chapter two gives a short biography of Komonchak and discusses major influences on his thinking about the church.

Chapter three explores Komonchak's most distinctive contribution to ecclesiology, which concerns his vision of ecclesiology as a critical, systematic theological discipline. The chapter presents Komonchak's decisive contribution toward overcoming the disjunction between the transcendent and the human dimensions of the church present in some post-Vatican II ecclesiologies. Here I argue that Komonchak's understanding of what the church is and of the task of ecclesiology offers the most coherent view of how to hold together the two sets of claims about the church, namely, that it is at the same time a transcendent reality and a human community.

Chapter four discusses Komonchak's theology of the local church. The focus is on three issues: the significance of locality for the theology of the local church, the meaning of catholicity, and the relationship of the local and universal church. Lastly, chapter five discusses Komonchak's understanding of authority in the church. Building on insights from chapter three with regard to the role of social theory in ecclesiology, the focus is on the notion of authority as a social relationship, the relation between authority and conversion, and the distinction between teaching and legislating.

My hope is that by highlighting Komonchak's distinctive contribution to ecclesiology, this study will also present a compelling argument as to why Komonchak's vision of ecclesiology as a critical, systematic theological discipline deserves greater attention.

1

Vatican II and the Shift in Catholic Ecclesiology

NO PREVIOUS ECUMENICAL COUNCIL can measure up to Vatican II in the scope and depth of its engagement with ecclesiology. Vatican II promulgated not one but two constitutions on the church. The theology of the church was not merely one issue among many on the council's agenda; it was at the center of the council's concerns and permeated its entire work. Among several shifts that Vatican II effected in Catholicism, one of the most important concerned ecclesiology. The shift was in the making for some time. Essentially, it consisted of moving away from an overly institutional view of the church to an ecclesiology that brings out the church's transcendent, spiritual dimensions. Vatican II thus created a new situation in Catholic ecclesiology, and after its close it became clear that one could not continue doing ecclesiology as before. Something changed; the pendulum swung in the opposite direction. From our current historical perspective, Vatican II can be seen as the end of one development and a beginning of another. No matter what one's assessment of the council is, it remains the case that Vatican II has had a greater impact on the Catholic Church in general and on its ecclesiology in particular than any other event since the sixteenth-century Protestant Reformation.

The Gregorian reforms of the eleventh century were decisive moments in the history of Western Christianity that also had vast implications for ecclesiology.[1] In contrast to the first millennium, when reflections on the church grew mainly out of sacramental practice and Christology, ecclesiology now came to be grounded more and more in canon law. Its focus shifted toward the institutional dimension of the church while the church's inner nature

---

1. See Schatz, "Gregorian Reform," 123–36.

became overshadowed. Over time, ecclesiology became "hierarchology."[2] In the nineteenth century, however, and even more strongly from the 1920s onward, theologians began to retrieve various insights from the ecclesiological tradition of the first millennium and reintroduce them into the Catholic consciousness. This brought more balance to the one-sidedness of Catholic ecclesiology and was an important factor in the overall theological renewal of the time. Yet this work of *ressourcement* was also met with suspicion of unorthodoxy and acquired the pejorative label of "new theology" (*nouvelle théologie*).[3] In its sixteen documents, however, Vatican II sanctioned many of the retrieved theological positions concerning the church and endowed them with magisterial authority. The council's validation of ecclesiological views that departed—at times significantly—from what had been the status quo for centuries effected a profound transformation of Catholic ecclesiology. During the first session of the council, Cardinal Giovanni Battista Montini (the future Pope Paul VI) noted the following during a speech he delivered in the conciliar aula:

> Yesterday, the theme of the church seemed to be confined to the power of the Pope. Today, it is extended to the episcopate, the religious, the laity and the whole body of the church. Yesterday, we spoke of the rights of the church by transferring the constitutive elements of civil society to the definition of a perfect society. Today, we have discovered other realities in the church—the charisms of grace and holiness, for example—which cannot be defined by purely juridical ideas. Yesterday, we were above all interested in the external history of the church. Today, we are equally concerned with its inner life, brought to life by the hidden presence of Christ in it.[4]

This seeming dichotomy between yesterday and today does not mean that Vatican II did not maintain clear lines of continuity with what preceded it. Nevertheless, the changes in content and the direction the council authorized are astonishing.

It would be difficult to appreciate the significance of the shift that Vatican II introduced into Catholic ecclesiology without a good grasp of the history of ecclesiology. The transformation that took place at the council becomes evident and rings with greater consequence in light of that history.

---

2. Congar, *Lay People*, 45.

3. See, for instance, Boersma, *Nouvelle Théologie and Sacramental Ontology*; Mettepenningen, *Nouvelle Théologie*; Flynn and Murray, *Ressourcement*.

4. Montini, "Il mistero della Chiesa," 6, quoted in Congar, "Moving toward a Pilgrim Church," 135.

Ecclesiology Prior to Vatican II

Ecclesiology as a distinct branch within theology is a relatively late development. It may come as a surprise that formal ecclesiological treatises appeared only toward the end of the Middle Ages, and that Catholic *systematic* ecclesiology did not emerge until several centuries later. This is not to say, however, that a theology of the church was absent until then. Theological reflection on the church has been coextensive with the phenomenon of the church. Neither the writers of the New Testament, nor the Fathers, nor the scholastics neglected to reflect on the church.[5] In fact, ecclesiology is unavoidable for Christians. It is implicit in most of their beliefs and practices. Yet it remains the case that while one can speak rightfully about an ecclesiology of Augustine, John Chrysostom, Peter Lombard, or Thomas Aquinas, to mention just a few, their writings do not contain a distinct treatise on the church, even though they often provide one, for instance, on the trinitarian mystery of God, on grace, or on the sacraments.[6]

Before separate ecclesiological treatises emerged, theological reflection on the church took place within already established fields of theology such as Christology, soteriology, or sacramental theology—as Yves Congar noted, "no other method was known."[7] Theologians of the patristic era had many profound things to say about the church.[8] Operating with a robust pneumatology, they connected the church intimately with the Holy Spirit.[9] In response to various challenges, they articulated a deep understanding of various ecclesiological topics: unity, holiness, catholicity, apostolicity, authority, ministry, episcopacy, and the connection between the church and the Eucharist. Pre-scholastic ecclesiology, like theology in general at the time, employed symbolic rather than technical theological language, and it focused on the church's interior reality mediated by the liturgy and sacraments. Many insights about the church from this period, however, became eclipsed in the course of the second millennium, when ecclesiological

---

5. The most comprehensive works on history of ecclesiology are found in the multi-language series on the history of dogma. See Dias, *Kirche in der Schrift*; Camelot, *Die Lehre von der Kirche*; Congar, *L'Église*.

6. While the well-known work of Cyprian *De catholicae ecclesiae unitate* may be seen as an exception in this regard, it can also be argued that it is more a polemic than an ecclesiology.

7. Congar, "Idea of the Church," 332.

8. For the development of ecclesiology from the post-biblical period to the reformation, in addition to the sources by Camelot and Congar (note 5 above), see, for instance, Plumer, "Development of Ecclesiology," 23–44, esp. 23–33.

9. See, for instance, Irenaeus, *Against Heresies*, 3.24.1.

reflection centered on articulation of the church's authority and focused primarily on its institutional dimension.

The scholastics of the twelfth and thirteenth centuries, who innovated by introducing into theology a more abstract language than was then common, continued in the practice of their predecessors and did not produce a separate treatise on the church. Their ecclesiology must be constructed from the pertinent remarks on the church throughout their writings. Peter Lombard (1100–1160), for instance, whose *Sentences* were the standard textbook for medieval students of theology and remained so (with some exceptions) until the beginning of the sixteenth century, treats the church within his Christology under the heading *de Christo capito*, and in this way offers commentators a point of entry into ecclesiology.[10] Thomas Aquinas (1225–1274), the most renowned of the scholastics, continued this trend and integrated his thoughts on the church into his treatment of grace, Christology, and the sacraments—especially the Eucharist. His commentary on the Creed provides perhaps his most sustained discussion of the church among his writings. The church plays a prominent role also in his commentaries on Scripture.[11] According to Yves Congar, the doctrine of the church as the Mystical Body is at the core of Aquinas's theology as a whole, giving everything in his thought an ecclesiological dimension.[12] Congar argued that the entire second part of Thomas's *Summa theologica*, which treats of the return of rational beings towards God, is ecclesiology.[13] Congar even surmised that Aquinas deliberately did not write a separate treatise on the church because it already suffused the entirety of his theology.[14]

While the scholastics had a high regard for the theologians of the patristic era and maintained patristic thinking on the church in many points, nevertheless their ecclesiology became discontinuous with their predecessors in several respects. The Gregorian reforms of the eleventh century were in large part responsible for this shift. The growing influence of secular princes on the ministry of bishops became an increasing concern at the time. In response, Pope Gregory VII (1073–1085) began to claim authority over all church offices, which strengthened papal authority to a degree previously unknown. Gregory's reforms led to the growth of canon law and

10. See Lombard, *Sentences* 3.13.

11. For a discussion of Aquinas's ecclesiology see, for instance, Congar, "Idea of the Church"; *L'Église*, 232–41; Dulles, "Church according to Thomas Aquinas," 149–69; Sabra, *Thomas Aquinas's Vision*; Rikhof, "Thomas on the Church," 199–223; O'Meara, "Theology of Church," 303–25.

12. Congar, "Idea of the Church," 358.

13. Congar, "Idea of the Church," 337, 339–40.

14. Congar, "Idea of the Church," 358.

became a decisive turning point in the history of the church. They also had a major impact on ecclesiology.[15] For instance, the Gregorian reforms gave rise to a new basis for understanding the church, namely, that of law and jurisdiction. The reforms also favored a universalistic ecclesiological framework. A century after Gregory's pontificate, it was the *modus operandi* for such major scholastic theologians as Alexander of Hales (1185–1245), Albert the Great (1200–1280), Bonaventure (1217–1274), and Thomas Aquinas. The starting point of their reflections on the church was the universal rather than the local church as had been the case in the first millennium. These scholastic theologians looked upon dioceses as administrative units of the whole or universal church, not as churches in the theological sense. Their ecclesiology was also pyramidal with a strong emphasis on the pope's *plenitudo potestatis*. They viewed the church's catholicity in its quantitative dimension as a geographical extension to all nations. The notion of catholicity as an integration of diversity within unity, prevalent with the theologians of the patristic period, became sidelined.

Beginnings of Formal Ecclesiology

Formal ecclesiological treatises, that is, writings which deal expressly with the topic of the church and approach it no longer within other fields but separately, began to surface at the dawn of the fourteenth century. James of Viterbo's *De regimine christiano* (1301–1302) is often identified as the first one, immediately followed by *De ecclesiastica potestate* of Giles of Rome (1302) and *De potestate regia et papalis* of John of Paris (1302–1303). The conflict between Pope Boniface VIII (1294–1303) and King Philip IV of France (1285–1314) provided the context for the composition of these earliest tractates, which naturally impacted the aspects under which the authors considered the church. The conflict raised anew the question about the relation of the temporal and the spiritual orders, specifically, the question of the pope's authority over that of a king. The initial treatises on the church were thus written to delineate that relationship. Drawing on the twelfth and thirteenth-century canonical commentaries on Gratian's *Decreta*, they discussed the powers in the church and in civil society and articulated a forceful argument for the superiority of the spiritual over the temporal realm.

The Avignon papacy (1309–1377) and especially the Great Western Schism (1378–1417) occasioned the second wave of treatises on the

---

15. For the impact of the Gregorian reforms on ecclesiology, see, for instance, Congar, *L'Église*, 102–12.

church.[16] The schism was devastating for the unity of the church in the West. For several decades there were two, and toward the end of the schism even three, claimants to the papacy. Naturally, questions of the church's unity and its means, and the structure of authority in the church became central ecclesiological issues. As Francis Oakley explains, the conception of the universal church as a single corporate entity akin to other legal corporations, which had been constructed by medieval canonists prior to the schism, lent itself to two different views of the church's unity.[17] On the one hand, there was the doctrine of absolute papal monarchy, according to which the church's unity could be preserved only by means of a complete subordination of all the church's members to a single head.[18] On the other hand, there was the conciliarist position whose advocates argued that the church's unity was grounded in the corporate association of its members who could exercise corporate authority even in the absence of the head.[19]

The key notion of conciliarist ecclesiology was that the whole assembly of the faithful was the locus of ultimate authority in the church. As Brian Tierney put it: "The whole Christian community was superior to any prelate, however exalted; the Pope was to be a servant of the Church rather than its master."[20] Consequently, conciliarists located ultimate authority in the church in the communitarian dimension of the entire church. They could thus argue that the whole church could elect and judge the pope. As regards the unity of the church, the conciliarist position was that the church's unity preceded and transcended its institutional unity.[21] While conciliarist ecclesiology was instrumental in ending the Great Western Schism and reached its apex at the Council of Basel (1431–1437), it faced strong opposition from the advocates of the absolute papal monarchy whose views eventually prevailed.

In this regard, John of Torquemada and his master work *Summa de ecclesia* were decisive. Torquemada was a member of the Order of Preachers or "Dominicans," as they are known popularly, and was educated at the University of Paris. He took part at the Council of Basel where he changed from being a centrist to being a papalist. His *Summa*, written between 1449 and 1453 and first published in 1480, stands out among the ecclesiological

---

16. For a comprehensive list, see Congar, *L'Église*, 270–71.

17. Oakley, *Western Church*, 159–64.

18. Its main proponents were Giles of Rome (1247–1316), Augustinus Triumphus (1243–1328), Alvarus Pelagius (ca. 1280–1352), and John of Torquemada (1388–1468).

19. For instance, Conrad Gelnhausen (ca. 1320–1390), Pierre d'Ailly (1351–1420), Jean Gerson (1363–1429), Francesco Zabarella (1360–1417), and Nicholas of Cusa (1401–1464).

20. Tierney, *Foundations of the Conciliar Theory*, 6.

21. See Haight, *Christian Community in History*, 1:378–81.

treatises of the time for its subsequent influence, especially after it was republished in 1560 at the height of the Counter-Reformation.[22] Thomas Izbicki calls it "the most comprehensive medieval synthesis of ecclesiological doctrines acceptable to Rome."[23]

Torquemada's *Summa* consists of four books: (1) the nature of the church, (2) Roman primacy, (3) councils, and (4) schism and heresy. He defines the church as "the entirety of the faithful who assemble on the basis of worship of the one true God and the profession of one faith."[24] Although he had an affinity for Aquinas and refers to the church as *congregatio fidelium*, the focus of Torquemada's ecclesiology is the visible institutional church. The chief aim of his *Summa* is to counter the claim that the whole church as a corporation is the subject of the power to govern the church. He argues that the pope as the successor of Peter, who alone was made a bishop directly by Christ, is the subject of absolute power in the church, which he then delegates to other bishops. Their jurisdiction is thus not proper to them but derived from the jurisdiction of the pope. Torquemada conceives the church as a monarchy, and even though he affirms that the unanimous agreement of a council in a matter of faith would carry higher authority than a pope who would contradict it, his ecclesiology generally subordinates the council to the pope.[25]

Torquemada's *Summa* is certainly more comprehensive than the first tractates on the church, but it is not yet a work of systematic ecclesiology. While it does not neglect the interior structure of the church as a sacramental mystery, its emphasis is rather on the church's canonical aspects. It can be seen essentially as a defense of the prerogatives of the pope over conciliarist claims.[26] It is this ecclesiology, however, that carried the day during the tumultuous times following the Council of Constance (1414–1418) and represented the direction in which the relationship of the pope and the council would develop—first with the bull *Execrabilis* of Pope Pius II (1460), which sought formally to end conciliarism and restore absolute papal authority, and culminating at Vatican I with the definition of papal primacy and infallibility (1870).[27]

---

22. For an account of Torquemada's ecclesiology, see, for instance, Izbicki, *Protector of the Faith*; Congar, *L'Église*, 340–44.

23. Izbicki, *Protector of the Faith*, 19.

24. Torquemada, *Summa de ecclesia*, 1.1. Unless otherwise noted, all translations are mine.

25. Prusak, *Church Unfinished*, 240.

26. Prusak, *Church Unfinished*, 240.

27. Papal primacy had already been defined at the Council of Florence (1439).

The conflicts over the relationship of the temporal and spiritual powers and over the role and authority of the council vis-à-vis the pope were major factors which caused that ecclesiology, from its inception, "became, to a large extent, a subset of canon law . . . a kind of ecclesiastical political science."[28] For the most part, this remained the case until the Second Vatican Council, which attempted to restore the notion of the church as a mystery or sacrament. Yet, as Richard McBrien has rightly noted, elements of the older juridical and legalistic approach to understanding the church have been influential in some quarters of the Catholic Church until the present.[29]

Counter-Reformation Ecclesiology

Following the Great Western Schism, ecclesiology continued to develop in the context of crisis. The attempt of conciliarism to reform the church did not succeed. Instead, the challenges of the Protestant Reformers, which had already been anticipated by the spiritualistic ecclesiologies of John Wyclif (1320–1384) and John Hus (1369–1415), greatly determined the direction Catholic ecclesiology would take from the sixteenth century onward. The Reformers attacked several institutional features of Western Catholicism such as the efficacy of the sacraments, the ministerial priesthood, and the authority of bishops and the pope. This resulted in their vigorous defense by Catholic theologians who began to treat explicitly the exterior aspects of the church and placed a strong focus on its visible hierarchical structure. As Richard Gaillardetz explains, "since it was the integrity of the visible and institutional church that was under attack, it was the visible, institutional integrity of the church that would receive a most spirited defense."[30] The context of the Counter-Reformation thus intensified the already juridical tone of ecclesiology and inserted a strong polemical and apologetic focus into what was now specifically *Catholic* ecclesiology.

Catholic theologians of the Counter Reformation understood the Reformers to teach that the true church was invisible, in the sense that only God knew who the members of the church were. Not concurring with the Reformers on this point, Catholic theologians maintained instead that the true church is a visible institution. This is perhaps best seen in the definition of the church articulated by one of the greatest Counter-Reformation figures, the Jesuit theologian and cardinal Robert Bellarmine (1542–1621). His definition of the church, which was used in theology textbooks well

28. McBrien, *Church*, 72.
29. McBrien, *Church*, 73.
30. Gaillardetz, *Church in the Making*, 1.

into the twentieth century, states: "Our view is that the church is only one reality, not two, and that this single and true reality is a group of people joined together by the profession of the same Christian faith and by communion in the same sacraments, under the governance of legitimate pastors and especially of the sole vicar of Christ on earth, the Roman Pontiff."[31] Bellarmine conceived of the church completely in terms of visible elements. In fact, he explicitly stated that "the church is a group of people as visible and palpable as a group of the Roman people, or the kingdom of France, or the republic of Venice.[32]

Bellarmine's understanding of the church suited well the apologetic climate of his day and was not an exception; others defined the church in a similar vein. For instance, Jacque Duperron (1556–1618), a French cardinal and archbishop of Sens, who was influenced by Bellarmine, defined the church as "those whom God has called to salvation through the profession of the true faith, sincere administration of the sacraments, and adherence to legitimate pastors."[33] Francis de Sales (1567–1622), another contemporary of Bellarmine, defined the church as "a holy universal community or general company of persons united and gathered in the profession of one and the same Christian faith, in participation in the same sacraments and sacrifice, and in obedience to one and the same vicar and general lieutenant of our Savior Jesus Christ and successor of Peter, under the charge of legitimate bishops."[34]

These definitions aimed at identifying the minimal requirements that make one a member of the church and were constructed deliberately in opposition to the view that the true church was invisible. While they did not deny the importance of inner virtues for a truly Christian way of life, they did not consider them necessary to establish someone in the church, which they conceived entirely in terms of criteria that can be empirically verified. Profession of the same Christian faith, communion in the sacraments, and submission to legitimate pastors are such criteria, which follow in the footsteps of Torquemada. As Bellarmine explains, on the basis of his definition,

> it is easy to determine who belong to the church and who do not. For there are three parts to this definition: the profession of the true faith, communion in the sacraments, and submission

---

31. Bellarmine, *De controversiis* 2.3.2:75.

32. Bellarmine, *De controversiis* 2:75.

33. Duperron, *Réplique à la réponse*, 36, quoted in Himes, "Development of Ecclesiology," 48n.

34. de Sales, *Opera omnia*, 1:43, quoted in Himes, "Development of Ecclesiology," 48n.

to the legitimate pastor, the Roman Pontiff. The first element excludes all unbelievers, both those who have never been in the church, such as Jews, Turks, and pagans, and those who once were in it but have withdrawn, such as heretics and apostates. The second element excludes catechumens and those who are excommunicated, since the former are not yet admitted to sacramental communion and the latter have been dismissed from it. The third element excludes schismatics, people who have the faith and the sacraments but do not submit to the legitimate pastor and therefore profess the faith and receive the sacraments outside. All others are included, even if they are reprobates, scoundrels, and impious.[35]

After non-Christians, heretics, apostates, catechumens, the excommunicated, and schismatics are thus excluded, Roman Catholics are the only ones who remain.

Bellarmine was aware of the limitations of defining the church externally, and to address this he employed the traditional conception of the church as a living organism consisting of a body and soul. The virtues of an individual pertain to the soul of the church, and the external criteria, which Bellarmine's definition identified, belong to the body of the church. Consequently, some belong both to the soul and to the body of the church. They are united with Christ both internally and externally and belong to the church most perfectly. Others, such as catechumens belong just to the soul of the church, and still others—sinners and heretics—belong only to its body.[36] Jerome Hamer contends that Bellarmine was aware of the dimension of the church as mystery, but omitted it for apologetic reasons. In the long run, this was an unfortunate move because Bellarmine's definition of the church later gained wide acceptance by theologians and canonists who advanced a view of the church reduced to what one's senses can perceive.[37]

Perfect Society Ecclesiology

Following the Council of Trent (1545–1563), the focus of Catholic ecclesiology on the church as a visible and hierarchical institution became conceptualized particularly in the notion of the church as a *societas perfecta*. Calling the church a perfect society did not mean that it was morally flawless, but that it was self-sufficient, complete in itself, and possessed all the means to

---

35. Bellarmine, *De controversiis* 2:75.
36. See Bellarmine, *De controversiis* 2:75.
37. Hamer, *Church Is a Communion*, 86.

achieve its end. The church was thus autonomous and not subordinate to any other society, especially the state. Although one finds an understanding of the church as a perfect society already in the writings of Bellarmine,[38] it did not become prominent until the eighteenth and nineteenth centuries. It reached its apex in the schemas on the church prepared for the First Vatican Council (1869–1870).

The term *societas perfecta* can be traced back to antiquity when it described "a desired integration and balance between civil power and ecclesiastical authority in a single, unified social system."[39] This unitary view of society existed until the late Middle Ages, when autonomous states and nations started to emerge across Europe, which created tensions in church-state relations and resulted in an understanding on the part of both the church and state that they were largely independent, separate, and self-governing entities.[40] In the late eighteenth century, the term *societas perfecta* resurfaced in response to nationalist movements such as Gallicanism, Febronianism, Josephism, and the *Kulturkampf*, which attempted to constrain the authority of the pope over local churches and transfer it in part to civil rulers. The ecclesial hierarchy perceived these movements as a threat to the freedom of the Catholic Church and was compelled to react. Jurists and theologians developed an understanding of the church as a perfect society, but they reversed the meaning the concept had in the past. While originally it referred to a harmonious coexistence of church and state, now it began to designate the church as completely self-sufficient and autonomous vis-à-vis civil society. Some elements of perfect society ecclesiology could be traced to the Gregorian reforms and the political categories of the scholastics. The key contributing factors in its emergence, however, had to do with the focus of Catholic ecclesiology on the institutional dimension of the church occasioned by the disputes with the Reformers, and by the eighteenth and nineteenth-century conflicts between the church and state.

Perhaps the earliest use of the term "*societas perfecta*" in the polemical and apologetic climate after the Council of Trent is found in a 1776 document by a Czech theologian and canonist Franz Stephan Rautenstrauch (1734–1785).[41] It spells out a set of rules for public debates in the Habsburg Empire, and with regard to the church it says: "The Christian society is of divine ori-

38. "The ecclesiastical state should be prefect, and self-sufficient in reference to its end. . . . Therefore it must have all the power necessary to obtain its end" (Bellarmine, *Controversies of the Christian Faith*, 1072–73).

39. Markey, *Creating Communion*, 32.

40. For a succinct study of the notion of a perfect society in Catholic ecclesiology, see Granfield, "Rise and Fall," 3–8.

41. Granfield, "Rise and Fall," 5.

gin. It is a perfect society."[42] Canonists developed the concept and employed it in disputes with Protestant counterparts who argued that the church was not a perfect society but a voluntary association (*collegium*) within civil society. Magisterial documents, especially in the latter half of the nineteenth century, and then less commonly during the decades leading to Vatican II, presented the church as a perfect society.[43] This designation of the church was also prominent in the neo-scholastic manualist tradition.

The schemas on the church prepared for the First Vatican Council (1869–1870), *Supremi pastoris* and *Tametsi Deus*, can be seen as a culmination in the genesis of *societas perfecta* ecclesiology. Vatican I took place in a climate of elevated tensions between church and state. Key to the council's aims was addressing the threat to the church's autonomy in general, and to papal sovereignty in particular. According to its original plans, the council was going to do this in a document on the church, but because of the approaching Franco-Prussian War and other factors, the plan changed. It was decided that priority be given to the questions of papal primacy and infallibility. A separate document was drafted, *Pastor aeternus*, and after deliberations it was approved on July 18, 1870. In September the Italian army began to occupy Rome and a month later Pope Pius IX adjourned the council, not allowing *Supremi pastoris* or *Tametsi Deus* to be discussed on the council floor.[44] Although these documents do not possess magisterial authority, they are of particular importance, for they epitomize an ecclesiology that conceives of the church primarily in societal terms. Drafted by eminent theologians of the time such as Giovanni Perrone, Clemens Schrader, and Joseph Kleutgen, these schemas represent the state of Catholic ecclesiology in the latter half of the nineteenth century, and importantly influence subsequent Catholic ecclesiology until Vatican II. If the council had not ended prematurely, it is likely that some of their affirmations would have become official Catholic teaching.

Both *Supremi pastoris* and *Tametsi Deus* espouse the notion of the church as a perfect society. For instance, in a chapter entitled "The Church

---

42. Rautenstrauch, *Synopsis iuris ecclesiastici*, 31, quoted in Granfield, "Rise and Fall," 5.

43. For a list of the documents, see, for instance, Congar, "Moving toward a Pilgrim Church," 132–33.

44. Initially, *Supremi pastoris* was the first schema on the church. After the bishops submitted written observations, it was decided that the schema be revised. The new schema became commonly referred to as *Tametsi Deus*. In the meantime, *Pastor aeternus* was designated to be the first schema on the church, and *Tametsi Deus* became the second schema. *Pastor aeternus*, however, does not use the notion of perfect society. For a study of *societas perfecta* ecclesiology at Vatican I, see, for instance, Granfield, "Church as *Societas Perfecta*," 431–46.

is a true, perfect, spiritual, and supernatural society," *Supremi pastoris* says: "The Church is not a member or a part of any other society; nor can she be confounded with or enter into partnership with any other society; on the contrary, she is so perfect in herself that, while being entirely distinct from all other human societies, she also far surpasses all of them."[45] One of the canons attached to *Supremi pastoris* states: "If anyone say that the Church is not a perfect society, but that it is a simple association [*collegium*], or that it is included within civil society or the national State in such a way that it is subject to secular power, let him be anathema."[46] *Supremi pastoris* argues that the church must be regarded as a perfect society, because otherwise its pastors would not possess absolutely complete legislative, judicial, and punitive power in the sense that it could not be exercised independently from the secular power, but would be subject to the latter's interference.[47] *Tametsi Deus* articulates the notion of the church as a perfect society by stating that the church is "a society, distinct from every other assembly of men [*sic*], which moves towards its proper end by its own ways and reasons; which is absolute, complete, and sufficient in itself to attain those things which pertain to it; and which is neither subject to, or joined as a part, or mixed and confused with any other society.[48] Canon 13 of the same schema states: "If anyone shall say that the Church is not a perfect society by its own right, but that it is subject to civil power, let him be anathema."[49]

One of the central affirmations of *societas perfecta* ecclesiology was that the church is an unequal and hierarchical society. The church was contrasted with democratic and representative societies from which it differed in that in the church there was a ruling class of clerics in whose hands the fullness of power was concentrated. *Supremi pastoris* communicated this clearly:

> But the Church of Christ is not an egalitarian society (*societas aequalium*) in which the faithful all enjoy the same rights: it is a hierarchical society (*societas inaequalis*), and that not only because of the fact that among the faithful some are clerics and others, laymen, but above all because there is in the Church a power divinely instituted, with which some have been graced to sanctify, teach, and govern, and which others do not possess.[50]

---

45. *Supremi pastoris*, no. 3, in *Papal Teachings*, 811. Latin original of *Supremi pastoris* can be found in Mansi, *Sacrorum conciliorum*, 51:539–53.
46. *Supremi pastoris*, canon 10, in *Papal Teachings*, 822.
47. See *Supremi pastoris*, no. 10, in *Papal Teachings*, 817.
48. *Tametsi Deus*, no. 9, quoted in Granfield, "Church as *Societas Perfecta*," 444.
49. Quoted in Granfield, "Church as *Societas Perfecta*," 444n89.
50. *Supremi pastoris*, no. 10, in *Papal Teachings*, 817.

Supremi pastoris echoes here the teaching of Gregory XVI (1831–1846), whose pontificate preceded that of Pius IX. In an 1843 bull he stated: "No one can be unaware that the church is an unequal society in which God has destined some to rule and others to obey. The latter are the laity and the former are the clergy."[51] Perhaps the bluntest articulation of the idea of the church as an unequal society is in an encyclical of Pius X (1903–1914):

> The Church is essentially an *unequal* society, that is, a society comprising two categories of persons, the Pastors and the flock. ... So distinct are these categories that with the pastoral body only rests the necessary right and authority for promoting the end of the society and directing all its members towards that end; the one duty of the multitude is to allow themselves to be led, and, like a docile flock, to follow the Pastors.[52]

Such an understanding of the church left little room, if any, for a theology of the laity. One could say the "church" even if one had only the clergy in mind.[53] The distinction between the ordained and the non-ordained notwithstanding, this view of the church as an unequal society completely obscured the notion that, based on baptism, all members of the church share an equality that preceded any distinctions. Vatican II would restore this latter understanding into Catholic ecclesiology.

Even though Vatican I did not refer to the church as a *societas perfecta* in the two documents it promulgated, it nevertheless became the dominant Catholic ecclesiology in the period between Vatican I and Vatican II. Magisterial documents employed the concept. Textbooks of ecclesiology which were used for the theological training of priests defined the church in those terms.[54] It would have been hard to find a bishop or theological expert at Vatican II who was not trained in this ecclesiology. Not surprisingly, it played a role in the preparatory schema for Vatican II's document on the church.

Canonists and theologians constructed a theoretical understanding of the church as a perfect society to establish the church's independence from the interference of the state. While this ecclesiology addressed that particular problem, in many other respects *societas perfecta* was a deficient

---

51. Quoted in Klostermann, "Desiderate zur Reform," 341.

52. Pius X, "*Vehementer nos*," no. 8, in Carlen, *Papal Encyclicals*, 3:47–48.

53. Cf. Congar, *True and False Reform*, 89.

54. For instance, the so-called *Spanish summa*, which was used widely for training of seminarians at pontifical universities, stated: "The Church is a perfect and absolutely independent society, with full legislative, judicial and coercive power" (Salaverri, "On the Church of Christ," 370).

ecclesiology. It did not maintain the balance between the church as a juridical and theological reality; it did justice only to the former. Although *societas perfecta* ecclesiology did not deny the divine aspect of the church, this was often reduced to the institution of the authority structure of the church, as Johann Adam Möhler remarked: "God had established the hierarchy and thus provided more than was necessary for the church until the end of the world."[55] The focus on the external and hierarchical elements obscured the understanding of the church in terms of mystery or sacrament. This resulted in an impression that the church as an institution was separate from the church as a community of faith and worship.

Furthermore, perfect society ecclesiology privileged the universal church and left little room for a theology of the local church. Since dioceses did not possess the fullness of legislative, juridical, and coercive power, they were not considered perfect societies. Consequently, they were not considered churches in the full sense. They were viewed as parts of the universal church, which was at times envisioned as a world-wide diocese whose bishop was the pope. Individual bishops were the pope's vicars.[56] Centralization and uniformity logically issued from such an ecclesiology. In perfect society ecclesiology there was a total identity between the church of Christ and the Roman Catholic Church, leaving no room open for ecumenical dialogue. Instead of ecumenism, this ecclesiology advocated a return of the heretics and schismatics to the one true church—the Roman Catholic Church.[57]

This conception of the church as an unequal society, coupled with the rigid distinction between the teaching church and the learning church, resulted in an ecclesiology in which the word "church" did not designate all the faithful, but primarily the clergy who formed the teaching church. The lay faithful were to accept what the clergy taught. Even though this ecclesiology never excluded the laity from the ecclesial reality, it had an effect of practically reducing the theology of the church to "hierarchology," as Congar unflatteringly observed:

> Whilst Protestants were reducing the Church to an inward Christianity, to salvation, and by so doing were dissolving ecclesiology, Catholic apologists were looking at her above all as the machinery of the means of grace, as the hierarchical mediation of the means to salvation. . . . The *de Ecclesia* was principally,

---

55. Möhler, "Review of *Des errsten Zeitalters*," 497.

56. See Granfield, *Limits of the Papacy*, 109–10; Prusak, "Theology of the Local Church," 302.

57. See, for instance, Pius XI, "*Mortalium animos*," no. 10, in Carlen, *Papal Encyclicals*, 3:317.

sometimes almost exclusively, a defense and affirmation of the reality of the Church as machinery of hierarchical mediation, of the powers and primacy of the Roman see, in a word, a "hierarchology."[58]

Congar also noted that because of the focus on the church's structures and neglect of its life, the impression was given that the laity were something like an appendage of the church, "at most necessary to her *bene esse*."[59]

Overall, the defensive atmosphere of the Counter-Reformation period further impacted the character of Catholic ecclesiology by narrowing down its focus almost exclusively to the church's institutional structures and hierarchical powers of mediation. Ecclesiology became ever more polemical and apologetic. The church became, to a large extent, identified with its institutional structures and was seen as "an objectively structured social phenomenon, a visible society with a structure of leadership, offices, a law, and customs."[60] While the proponents of this ecclesiology thought that it safeguarded the truth of the Catholic faith and protected the church from the usurpations of the state, it also led to "a desacralized and one-sided sociological view of the Church."[61] The Second Vatican Council would recognize these limitations and attempt to bring balance into Catholic ecclesiology. The recognition that a renewal was needed, however, did not happen suddenly during the council. It was preceded by a renewal in Catholic theology in the decades prior to Vatican II.

Ecclesiological Renewal Prior to Vatican II

Catholic ecclesiology went through an unprecedented revitalization during the decades leading up to the Second Vatican Council. This revitalization affected the whole of Catholic theology, and began in the later 1920s when the repressive atmosphere of the Modernist crisis abated.[62] In the aftermath of Pius X's encyclical *Pascendi dominici gregis* (1907), in which the pope condemned "modernist heresies," the theological climate was not favorable to constructive and innovative work. Many theologians instead turned to the study of ancient and medieval sources, which were not perceived as potentially controversial. This work of *ressourcement*, however, yielded unexpected

---

58. Congar, *Lay People in the Church*, 45.
59. Congar, *Lay People in the Church*, 51.
60. Haight, *Christian Community in History*, 2:283.
61. Kasper, *Catholic Church*, 64.
62. For a succinct account of the key dynamics of the revival, see Komonchak, "Returning from Exile," (1999) 35–48.

results. It recovered theological views, especially from the first millennium, that were once at the center of the Christian theological tradition, but had long since been sidelined, eclipsed, overshadowed, or forgotten. Ecclesiology was among the chief benefactors of this theological renaissance, which, when viewed in retrospect, paved the road for Vatican II.

The renewal of Catholic ecclesiology in the first half of the twentieth century cannot, however, be adequately accounted for without relating it to the pioneering work of Johann Adam Möhler and the influence he exerted on the key protagonists of the renewal.

Möhler

At the start of the revival in Catholic ecclesiology which culminated at the Second Vatican Council, stands nineteenth-century Tübingen scholar Johann Adam Möhler (1796-1838). Michael Himes considers him the founder of Catholic systematic ecclesiology; that is, a kind of theological reflection that explores the connections between the church and other central Christian doctrines (e.g., the Trinity, incarnation, Holy Spirit, creation, grace, salvation, and eschatology).[63] Möhler's presentation of the church was far richer than the apologetic and polemical ecclesiology of the Counter-Reformation period. At a time when the focus was on the visible, exterior dimension of the church, Möhler turned attention toward the church's interior life. From the perspective of the history of ecclesiology, his work appears something like an anomaly. It stands out as its own kind at the time.[64]

Romantic revival in Germany, of which Tübingen was a major center, had a strong impact on Möhler's thought. Möhler encountered it there in particular through his teacher and later colleague Johann Sebastian Drey (1777-1853), who was the founder of the Catholic Tübingen School and was himself strongly influenced by the work of Schleiermacher and Shelling.[65] As Himes explains, Möhler inherited a number of ideas associated with Schleiermacher which German Catholic theologians appropriated from him and adjusted to a Catholic framework among which were the notion of religious experience as the basis of theology, an understanding of the church less in terms of an institution than as a community of believers, and the view of the Holy Spirit as the soul of the church.[66]

63. Himes, "Development of Ecclesiology," 56, 45.

64. For a detailed study of Möhler's ecclesiology, see Himes, *Ongoing Incarnation*. For article-length studies, see, for instance, Riga, "Ecclesiology of Johann Adam Möhler," 563-87; Rosato, "Between Christocentrism and Pneumatocentrism," 46-70.

65. For an analysis of the influence of romantic idealism on German Catholic theology in nineteenth century, see O'Meara, *Romantic Idealism and Roman Catholicism*.

66. Himes, *Ongoing Incarnation*, 15-27.

Möhler's first major work was a patristic study investigating the notion of unity in the church, *Unity in the Church or the Principle of Catholicism,* in which he articulated an ecclesiology with strong pneumatological foundations.[67] In contrast to ecclesiological reflections of his time, which had the exposition of the church's juridical and structural aspects as their point of departure, the starting point of Möhler's ecclesiology was a reflection on the role of the Holy Spirit in the church. For Möhler, the key to ecclesiology was to think of the Spirit as generating the interior life of the church's members through their participation in community. Möhler considered the Holy Spirit to be the life-giving principle underlying ecclesial structures and envisioned the church as a dynamic organism journeying through history, growing and developing over time like other living organisms. While Counter-Reformation ecclesiology did not leave the Spirit out of ecclesiology, it envisioned its role mainly in terms of guaranteeing authority.[68] Möhler's strongly pneumatological conception of the church stood in contrast to the ecclesiology represented by Bellarmine. While he distinguished between the soul and the body of the church and identified the role of the Spirit with the former, overall Bellarmine's ecclesiology emphasized disproportionately the church's external nature, its body. One could see Möhler's turn to the invisible aspect of the church not only as an attempt to bring balance to an ecclesiology that was one-sided, but also as an acknowledgement that the Reformers were not entirely mistaken in their concern for the church's interior dimension.[69]

While Möhler's emphasis in *Unity* is on the role of the Holy Spirit in building up the church, it is not to the exclusion of seeing the church in connection with Christ. In fact, the image of the church as the Body of Christ is for Möhler the most adequate description of the church's deepest reality. According to it, the church is an organism whose inner unity is expressed externally in its life and structures. Roger Haight interprets Möhler's ecclesiology in *Unity* as elliptical, having two centers: Christ and Spirit.[70]

Unity showed Catholic theologians that they did not have to choose between the external and internal dimensions of the church. Möhler argued that the former mediate the latter in the sense that the external dimensions are built from and are an expression of the life of faith and working of the Spirit. Möhler could thus affirm the validity and necessity of visible ecclesial

---

67. See Möhler, *Die Einheit in der Kirche.*

68. Congar, *L'Église*, 382–83.

69. For a succinct analysis of Möhler's ecclesiology in *Unity*, see Haight, *Christian Community in History*, 2:336–55.

70. Haight, *Christian Community in History*, 2:340n83. See also Rosato, "Möhler's Ecclesiology," 59.

structures, such as episcopacy and papacy, without relativizing or negating them. He also held in tension unity and diversity within the church. He saw genuine growth and development of the church not being in opposition to the church's unity. Möhler thus rediscovered an organic understanding of the church's catholicity from the early church, which incorporated diversity into unity and went beyond merely geographic universality. He considered the Eucharist as the highest expression of the church's unity. One can recognize in these points the seeds of a theology of the local church.

Although Möhler's Spirit-focused ecclesiology did not find much following at his time, it became a major influence on the ecclesiology of Yves Congar and others a century later, whose work paved the way for Vatican II. Möhler, however, became dissatisfied with *Unity* and refused to revise it. Instead he wrote a new book which addressed what he came to perceive as the shortcomings of *Unity*: i.e., excessive subjectivism, exaggerated emphasis on the Holy Spirit resulting in accenting the divine element in the church almost to the exclusion of the human, and not doing justice to the Christological dimension of the church.

In his second major ecclesiological work, *Symbolism*, Möhler shifted considerably from a pneumatological to an incarnational and Christocentric approach to ecclesiology.[71] Following the model of the Christological doctrine of the hypostatic union, he articulated an understanding of the church as one reality, which is a union of two separate elements: human and divine. He coined a phrase which became a shorthand for his ecclesiology in *Symbolism*; namely, the church as a "continual/permanent/ongoing incarnation" (*andauernde Fleischwerdung*):

> The visible Church, from the point of view here taken, is the Son of God himself, everlastingly manifesting himself among men in a human form, perpetually renovated, and eternally young—the permanent incarnation of the same, as in Holy Writ, even the faithful are called "the body of Christ." Hence it is evident that the Church, though composed of men, is yet not purely human.[72]

With this notion of "continual incarnation," Möhler left himself open to misunderstanding. It could be seen as equating Christ and the church. Philip Rosato argues, however, that it is questionable whether such an understanding is warranted by a close reading of *Symbolism* since Möhler there wanted to correct exaggerations present in *Unity*, such as the identification of God and human being and not leaving enough room for human freedom. In light

71. See Möhler, *Symbolik*.
72. Möhler, *Symbolism*, 259.

of this, Rosato suggests that Möhler should be read not as equating Christ and the church, but as proposing an analogy between them, namely, that like Christ, the church consists of a human and a divine component. Rosato explains that "when Möhler uses the words 'continuing,' 'is being continued' and 'remaining,' he does not mean that Christ is to be identified totally with any particular *form* of the Church at any period in its development, but he is insisting that Christ works through the visible institution of the Church as well as he works in individuals."[73] Nevertheless, one may question whether the notion of hypostatic union is an adequate conceptual tool, even analogically, to express the two aspects of the church: divine and human. There is no personal union between the church and any of the persons of the Trinity.

Möhler's ecclesiology in *Symbolism* also demonstrated an ecumenical concern. As the subtitle indicates, Möhler was interested in comparing doctrinal differences between Catholics and Protestants. He believed that a clear articulation of the differences might lead them toward a better understanding of one another and toward a level of synthesis out of which unity might emerge. Möhler wanted to find balance between more pneumatic Protestant and more incarnational Catholic ecclesiologies.

Möhler died prematurely at the age of forty-two, but he made a great impact on Catholic ecclesiology. By theologizing about the church in conversation with pneumatology, Christology, and theological anthropology, he transformed ecclesiology into a systematic theological discipline. While this transformation was appreciated only in a limited way in the nineteenth century and was largely overshadowed in the period following the First Vatican Council, it was noticed more substantially when his work received renewed attention in the first half of the twentieth century. Through Möhler's influence, "ecclesiology grew from being primarily concerned with questions of institutional polity to treating the Church's inner nature and external mission as a dimension of the economy of salvation."[74] Theologians came to understand the church as an aspect of the mystery of faith and not merely as its bearer.

One aspect of Möhler's ecclesiology that received immediate attention from his contemporaries was his view of the church as a continual incarnation. It influenced the first generation of theologians of the so-called Roman school and was a key factor in the recovery of the notion of the church as the body of Christ. The theologians of the Roman School were all Jesuits and taught at the Gregorian University in Rome after it was returned to their

---

73. Rosato, "Between Christocentrism and Pneumatocentrism," 64.
74. Himes, "Development of Ecclesiology," 59.

control in 1824.[75] They were exponents of so-called manualist theology and had significant influence on official magisterial theology. At the origin of the school were Giovanni Perrone (1794–1876), Carlo Passaglia (1827–1887) and their students Johann Baptist Franzelin (1816–1886) and Clemens Schrader (1820–1875). Like Möhler, they were interested in studying the Church Fathers and investigating the church in relation to other topics of theology. They adopted Möhler's view of the church as a continuation of the incarnation in history, which gave ecclesiology a more theological grounding than was common in the writers of the Counter Reformation. Yet, their tendency to interpret *incarnatio continua* in overly literal terms, at times suggesting an equation between Christ and the church, made it difficult to account for the church's human failings.[76]

Several Roman school theologians were theological experts at the First Vatican Council. Perrone and Schrader were among the drafters of the schema *Supremi pastoris*. Although *societas perfecta* was the prevalent ecclesiology in the schema, its opening chapter presented the view of the church as the mystical body of Christ. The notes enclosed with the schema explained that this image of the church was chosen for several reasons: it had a strong scriptural basis, it expressed the church's divine essence, and it was expedient to answer Protestant criticisms that Catholics emphasize only the external dimensions of the church.[77] Many bishops, however, were critical of describing the church in terms of the body of Christ. Some opposed it for being too abstract and mystical; others questioned the prudence of using the image since it was popular with the Jansenists. Still others did not deem it helpful in combating the threats the church was experiencing at the time.[78] In spite of the criticisms, the view of the church as the mystical body of Christ was incorporated into the revised draft of *Supremi pastoris*, whose name changed to *Tametsi Deus*. Joseph Kleutgen, who was commissioned to re-write *Supremi pastoris*, was convinced of the theological importance of the image of the body of Christ, even though he modified the overall approach. As noted above, because the council ended prematurely, *Tametsi Deus* was neither discussed by the bishops nor promulgated. This is quite unfortunate. One is inclined to agree with Granfield that Catholic ecclesiology "might well have taken a different direction

---

75. The university was founded in 1551 by Ignatius of Loyola. From 1773 until 1824 it was under the control of the diocesan clergy of Rome, because from 1773 to 1814 the Jesuit order was suppressed.

76. For a study of manualist ecclesiology through the lens of church authority and its exercise, see Sanks, *Authority in the Church*.

77. See Granfield, "Church as *Societas Perfecta*," 434.

78. See Granfield, "Church as *Societas Perfecta*," 434.

earlier in the twentieth century, if the Body of Christ theology of Möhler, Passaglia, Schrader and others had been incorporated comprehensively into the council documents, or even if the societal theme had been used in the more spiritual sense of the early Church Fathers."[79] Instead, following Vatican I and throughout the modernist crisis, *societas perfecta* ecclesiology continued to dominate Catholic ecclesiology. The view of the church as the body of Christ was far less prominent.[80]

While institutional and juridical approaches to ecclesiology continued to exercise dominance until the eve of Vatican II, especially in seminary manuals, during the decades leading up to the council various streams of renewal began to revitalize Catholic ecclesiology. Stemming from the fertile ground of the biblical, patristic, liturgical, and ecumenical movements, they exposed the church's interior dimension and brought some balance to the one-sidedness of the institutional approach.[81]

Mystical Body of Christ

First among the streams of renewal was mystical body of Christ ecclesiology, which began to develop in the 1920s. Inspired by the writings of Möhler and Matthias Joseph Scheeben (1835–1888),[82] it flourished within the patristic *ressourcement* and the liturgical movement and was particularly prominent among theologians writing in French.[83] It culminated with Pope Pius XII's encyclical *Mystici corporis* in 1943. While the understanding of the church as the body of Christ is one of the oldest ecclesiologies on record, going back to the Pauline corpus,[84] the designation of the church as the *mystical* body of Christ is of late medieval origin, when the designations of the church as the

---

79. Granfield, "Church as *Societas Perfecta*," 445.

80. It played a minor role, for instance, in Leo XIII's encyclical *Satis cognitum* (see Leo XIII, "*Satis cognitum*," nos. 3–5, 10, in Carlen, *Papal Encyclicals*, 2:388–91, 395–96).

81. For a succinct account of the developments in Catholic ecclesiology from the nineteenth century to the eve of Vatican II, see McNamara, "From Möhler to Vatican II, 9–35.

82. Scheeben studied at the Gregorian (1852–1859) under Passaglia and Perrone, who exposed him to Möhler. Scheeben developed his theology of the mystical body in *Die Mysterien des Christentums*.

83. See Scully, "Theology of the Mystical Body," 58–74. For an annotated bibliography of publications in various languages on the subject of the mystical body of Christ during this period, see Bluett, "Mystical Body of Christ," 261–89.

84. See 1 Cor 10:17; 12:27; Rom 12:4–8; Eph 1:22–23; 2:16; 4:1–6; Col 1:18; 1:24; 2:19; 3:15. A continued scholarly interest in the body of Christ imagery in Paul can be seen, for instance, in a recent exegetical study on this theme in Ephesians. See Feník, *Given to the Church*, 83–217.

real body of Christ and of the Eucharist as the mystical body of Christ got reversed. Tracing this shift was one of the many significant contributions of Henri de Lubac to ecclesiological renewal prior to Vatican II.[85]

The work of Belgian Jesuit Émile Mersch (1890–1940) was among the most influential in the revival of the theology of the mystical body. First he produced a historical study investigating the notion of the body of Christ in Scripture and the Church Fathers, in which Mersch concluded that understanding the church as the mystical body of Christ ought to be considered a central truth of Christianity.[86] Then he pursued more synthetic work that bore fruit in his second major text, which was published posthumously.[87] In it, Mersch wanted to present an alternative to the neoscholastic view of the relationship of Christ to the church expressed in terms of efficient causality, which he found inadequate. Focusing on the interior dimension of the church, he presented a view of Christ at work in the church from within. Like Möhler and others before him, Mersch thought of the church as a prolongation of Christ. Without denying the importance of the institutional view of the church, he distinguished it from the mystical body, which he understood as the communion among the followers of Christ.[88]

Another key figure in the revival of the theology of the mystical body was the Dutch Jesuit Sebastian Tromp (1899–1975). Because of his leading role among the minority at Vatican II, which opposed the council's direction, his contribution to the renewal of Catholic ecclesiology tends to be overlooked. His theology of the mystical body, however, was regarded highly in neoscholastic circles, and as professor at the Gregorian University from 1929 until 1967, Tromp also had influence on the theological positions taken by Pope Pius XII. Tromp's views of the mystical body were in large part enshrined in the encyclical *Mystici corporis*; in fact, Tromp is believed to have been its principal writer. Tromp represented a different approach to the theology of the mystical body than Mersch, Karl Adam, or Romano Guardini, who emphasized the personalist and communitarian aspects of the doctrine. Tromp's approach was to harmonize the ancient body of Christ ecclesiology of the Fathers with the ecclesiology of a perfect society.[89] He argued that it is not legitimate to oppose the views of the church as the

---

85. See de Lubac, *Corpus Mysticum*.
86. See Mersch, *Le Corps mystique du Christ*.
87. See Mersch, *La thélogie du corps mystique*.
88. For a detailed study of Mersch's theology of the mystical body, see Malanowski, "Christocentrism of Émile Mersch."
89. See Tromp, *Corpus Christi quod est ecclesia*.

mystical body of Christ and as the hierarchical institution, since the Fathers insisted on the visible unity of the body of Christ.

People of God

Another stream of renewal, which began to flow alongside the theology of the mystical body, was the idea of the church as the people of God. It became a corrective voice to a number of weaknesses alleged of theology of the mystical body. Critics of mystical body theology argued that it left unclear the relationship between the visible and the invisible aspects of the church. They also contended that envisioning the church in terms of a living organism, like a human body, resulted on occasions with a false identification of an individual Christian with Christ and led to an erroneous mysticism, which obscured the distinction between Creator and creature.[90] German Dominican theologian, Mannes Koster, argued that the idea of communion with Christ was too vague to be a basis on which one could construct an ecclesiology.[91] Koster considered the very starting point of mystical body ecclesiology problematic, for it began with an individual's relationship with Christ. For Koster, however, the church was first and foremost a social reality that came to be from the sum of individuals. More importantly, he thought that the ecclesiology of the mystical body did not account adequately for the visible structures of the church, which he thought were indispensable for an adequate ecclesiology. He considered the doctrine of the mystical body to be more suitable for Christology than for ecclesiology and argued that for the latter, the idea of the people of God was more suitable as its basis. Koster also thought that the designation "people of God" expressed what the church really is and considered it a more comprehensive description, while the idea of the mystical body was no more than a metaphor. Most contemporaries of Koster did not share the severity of his criticism of the theology of the mystical body.

The idea of the church as the people of God introduced a certain dynamism into the concept of the church. It communicated the notion that the church was more than the institution possessing all the means of grace; namely, it was made of people who heard God's call and answered it. This view of the church also enriched the understanding of the church's continuity with the chosen people of Israel and expressed the idea that the church is a people on a journey. In connection with the idea of the church

---

90. An extreme example is the work of Karl Pelz, who compared the union of Christ and Christian to transubstantiation. See *Der Christ als Christus*. In 1940, the book was put on the Index.

91. See Koster, *Ekklesiologie im Werden*.

as the people of God, the notion of the *pilgrim* church, common among the Church Fathers, was also retrieved.⁹² It highlighted the church's historical and eschatological dimensions. It allowed one to distinguish between the church as the people on a journey and the kingdom of God, which is their destination. This distinction became a key presupposition in discussions about the possibility of reform in the church.

Mystici Corporis

At the time when criticisms of the mystical body of Christ ecclesiology were increasing, Pope Pius XII's encyclical *Mystici corporis* (1943) gave it warm approval and proved to be decisive against any efforts to displace it with the idea of the church as the people of God.⁹³ *Mystici corporis* was the most comprehensive magisterial pronouncement in the area of ecclesiology from the anti-Modernist crisis at the beginning of the twentieth century to the start of the Second Vatican Council. The encyclical represented the first significant shift since the Counter-Reformation in the way a magisterial writing addressed the church theologically. It adopted the approach of Tromp and attempted to integrate *societas perfecta* ecclesiology and the newly recovered theme of the mystical body of Christ. Although the institutional understanding of the church permeates the encyclical, taken as a whole, it was a welcome advancement beyond the *status quo* of the ecclesiological manuals. *Mystici corporis* signaled an openness on the side of the magisterium that something different than a merely juridical approach to understanding the church was welcome. It marked an important transition point in Catholic ecclesiology and to some extent prepared the way to Vatican II, even though the council did not follow all of its positions.

The chief contribution of *Mystici corporis* to the development of Catholic ecclesiology was the recovery of the communal dimension of the church that emphasized the interdependence of its members. The encyclical articulated an understanding of the church that was more inclusive of all the church's members than was the case in the ecclesiology of a perfect society. While the encyclical did not mention "people of God" by name, it did incorporate some of the criticisms its advocates raised against the theology of the mystical body, such as the overly biological terms in which the doctrine had been interpreted and its tendency to downplay the visible structures of the church; the encyclical warned against exaggerations in these areas. As a

92. Robert Grosche's collection of essays *Pilgernde Kirche* was among the first Catholic contributions in this area.

93. Pius XII gave cautious approval also to the biblical and liturgical movements in his encyclicals *Divino Afflante Spiritu* (1943) and *Mediator Dei* (1947) respectively.

result of this document, theologians began to integrate the concepts of the mystical body of Christ and the people of God into a single view and began to speak of the church as the new people of God existing under the form of the body of Christ.[94]

Among the main limitations of *Mystici corporis* was its exclusive identification of the mystical body of Christ with the Roman Catholic Church (no. 13). By denying the inclusion of all the baptized into the body of Christ, the encyclical effectively put baptized non-Catholics in the same theological category as non-Christians. In spite of its incorporation of a dynamic metaphor of the body into ecclesiology, the encyclical presented a "top-down" ecclesiology, which did not take into consideration the church's concrete historical existence. The overall juridical framework of *Mystici corporis* continued the universalistic ecclesiology and did not lend itself to a theology of the local church. These limitations gave rise to intense discussions among Catholic theologians who saw the need for new approaches and models in Catholic ecclesiology.

The Church as Sacrament

The notion of the church as sacrament was another fruit of the *ressourcement* of the tradition, contributing to the renewal of Catholic ecclesiology prior to Vatican II. Like the "people of God," it attempted to address the relation of the visible and the invisible aspects of the church and express it with more clarity than was the case in most theologies of the mystical body. While the interpretation of the mystical body by Tromp and by *Mystici corporis* affirmed the visibility and institutional integrity of the church, they gave the impression that the institutional structures of the church were ends in themselves. A new basis for affirming the necessity of church structures was needed.

Several theologians proposed to think of the church not primarily as the administrator of the sacraments but as the primordial sacrament itself (*Ursakrament*), that is, a sign of God's saving love before the world.[95] They employed the notion of sacrament in relation to the church in order to underline its mystery. They argued that the church was not a sacrament alongside the seven sacraments, but rather it was the basic sacramental reality that actualizes itself through those seven sacraments. As Henri de Lubac put it, "the Church is a mystery; that is to say that she is also a sacrament.

---

94. McNamara, "From Möhler to Vatican II," 23, 29.

95. See, for instance, de Lubac, *Catholicisme*; Semmelroth, *Die Kirche als Ursakrament*; Schillebeeckx, *De Christusontmoeting*; Rahner, *Kirche und Sakramente*.

She is 'the total *locus* of the Christian sacraments,' and she is herself the great sacrament that contains and vitalizes all the others."[96]

As a primordial sacrament, the church was portrayed as the sacrament of Christ, who in his humanity was the sacrament of God. Again, as de Lubac explains:

> The Church, the only real Church, the Church which is the Body of Christ, is not merely that strongly hierarchical and disciplined society whose divine origin has to be maintained, whose organization has to be upheld against all denial and revolt. That is an incomplete notion and but a partial cure for the separatist, individualist tendency of the notion to which it is opposed; a partial cure because it works only from without by way of authority, instead of effective union. If Christ is the sacrament of God, the Church is for us the sacrament of Christ; she represents him, in the full and ancient meaning of the term, she really makes him present. She not only carries on his work, but she is his very continuation, in a sense far more real than that in which it can be said that any human institution is its founder's continuation.[97]

This understanding of the church as sacrament envisions ecclesial structures not as an end in themselves but as a means. Their *raison d'être* is to mediate God's saving action. In addition to being able to better account theologically for church structures, the concept of the church as sacrament had another advantage over that of the mystical body: it avoided too close of an identification between Christ and the church. Understanding the church in terms of a sacrament allowed theologians to express the unity between the sign and its referent, while at the same time maintaining a distinction between them.[98]

The Church and the Eucharist

Yet another fruit of the *ressourcement* that strongly impacted the renewal of Catholic ecclesiology prior to Vatican II was the rediscovery of the connection between the church and the Eucharist. A central figure in this regard was the Jesuit theologian Henri de Lubac (1896–1991). A similar development also took place in Russian Orthodoxy where several theologians, who immigrated to France after the Russian Revolution of 1917, developed what

---

96. de Lubac, *Splendor of the Church*, 147.
97. de Lubac, *Catholicism*, 76.
98. See Wood, "Continuity and Development," 155–61.

became known as the "eucharistic ecclesiology."[99] Their work of patristic *ressourcement* lent insights to Catholic theologians into the relation of the church and the Eucharist.

De Lubac's chief significance for the renewal of Catholic ecclesiology is in connecting closely the social character of the church and the Eucharist. This was already one of the key points of his first major work, *Catholicism* (1938), and was later refined in *Corpus Mysticum* (1944) where de Lubac argued for a return to a more Eucharistic understanding of the church. He traced in detail the shift in the use of the term "mystical body" (*corpus mysticum*) in medieval theology of the Eucharist and piety. He showed that during the first millennium the term "mystical body" designated the Eucharist and the term "real body" (*corpus verum*) designated the church. He showed that during that time there existed a close link between the sacramental and ecclesial communion. The Eucharistic controversies of the eleventh century, however, disrupted this close connection. They were responsible for the reversal in terminology: "real body" came to designate the Eucharist and "mystical body" came to designate the church.[100]

In addition to showing how the church and the Eucharist were linked closely in the first millennium, *Corpus mysticum* mounted a challenge to the neoscholastic understanding of both the church and the Eucharist. De Lubac argued that neoscholastic theologians conceived the Eucharist primarily through the lens of transubstantiation. The Eucharist was seen as a miraculous intervention unconnected to the life of the church. As Lisa Wang explains,

> [de Lubac] shift[ed] the emphasis of the sacramental significance of the eucharist from the consecrated elements to the communal context of the sacrifice. This ha[d] the effect of changing the focus of the sacrament from the body of Christ on the altar to the body of Christ which partakes of that offering. This body is a community, a society, and it is to this body that the body on the altar is given for nourishment, not to an individual in isolation.[101]

De Lubac thus could assert that while the church makes the Eucharist, it is equally the case that the Eucharist makes the church.[102]

---

99. For instance, Alexei Khomiakov (1804–1860), Nicholas Afanasiev (1893–1966), and his students John Meyendorff (1926–1992) and Alexander Schmemann (1921–1983).

100. See de Lubac, *Corpus Mysticum* [ET], 13–119.

101. Wang, "*Sacramentum Unitatis Ecclesiasticae*, 146.

102. For a detailed study of de Lubac's understanding of the connection between

The Contribution of Yves Congar

No single theologian made a more significant contribution to the renewal of Catholic ecclesiology in the decades leading to Vatican II than the French Dominican Yves Congar (1904–1995). He was a leading figure of the *ressourcement* movement. By retrieving the biblical and patristic sources of theology, he wanted to "reclaim for ecclesiology the experience of the first millennium."[103] Congar was profoundly influenced by the work of Möhler who inspired many of Congar's ideas concerning the church and became the most important source in his approach to ecclesiology.[104] As several of his contemporaries, Congar reintroduced Möhler's ideas into the landscape of Catholic ecclesiology. He also shared Möhler's aspiration "to develop a vision of the Church that was more vital, synthetic, communal, and pneumatologically based."[105]

Congar's contribution to the renewal of Catholic ecclesiology prior to Vatican II is immense. It includes theologies of the laity, the local church, ministry, church reform, and the church's missionary activity to mention a few.[106] With a number of other Catholic theologians at the time, Congar sought to move Catholic ecclesiology beyond the juridical approach of the neoscholastic manuals and recover the sense of the mystery of the church. He sought to develop an understanding of the church that would avoid both clericalism and "hierarchology." Among those who influenced the revival of Catholic ecclesiology in the decades leading to Vatican II, Congar stands out eminently as someone whose thinking on the church was deeply rooted in, and could not be disassociated from, his ecumenical concerns. Personal encounters with Russian Orthodox theologians impacted Congar in the way he began to think about the connection between the Trinitarian mystery of God and the church and between the Eucharist and the church. Russian theologians also introduced Congar to the notion of the qualitative understanding of the church's catholicity, all of which led him to a greater appreciation of the local church.

In his first book, *Divided Christendom*, Congar presented principles of Catholic participation in the ecumenical movement.[107] In addition to a well-disposed presentation of the distinctive features of Orthodoxy,

---

the church and the Eucharist, see, for instance, McPartlan, *Eucharist Makes the Church*.

103. Dulles, "Half-Century of Ecclesiology," 425.

104. See Puyo, *Une vie pour la vérité*, 48.

105. Markey, *Creating Communion*, 45.

106. For a detailed study of Congar's ecclesiology, see, for instance, MacDonald, *Ecclesiology of Yves Congar*; Flynn, *Yves Congar's Vision*; Beal, *Mystery of the Church*.

107. See Congar, *Chrétien désunis*.

Protestantism, and Anglicanism, the book already contained several of Congar's seminal ecclesiological insights that would become hallmarks of Vatican II's ecclesiology. It recognized Protestant Christians as "separated brethren," articulated the notion of the "elements of the church" that Protestants preserved, spoke of "degrees of communion" existing among various Christian churches, and affirmed the salvific presence of the Holy Spirit among them.[108] Congar's contribution to the renewal of Catholic ecclesiology prior to Vatican II also includes an exploration of the idea of reform in the church. In his second major work, *True and False Reform in the Church*, he articulated the criteria for the church's reform without schism.[109] In the 1950s the very idea of the church's reform triggered a perplexed reaction from a majority of Catholics. Congar argued, however, that the notion of a continual reform in the church was not only a valid theological position for a Catholic to hold, but also that it was a presupposition of any ecumenical progress. For Congar, the church should permanently strive for an institutional and communal renewal. He considered the church's structures to be subordinate to its mission.

Congar also produced a path-breaking study in the theology of the laity, *Laity in the Church*, that had a profound impact on Vatican II's understanding of the church and on the development of communion ecclesiology.[110] The subject of the laity was virtually invisible in the institutional and juridical approaches to ecclesiology that dominated Catholic understanding of the church since the time of the Reformation and still had the upper hand in manuals of ecclesiology when Congar wrote this text. The laity were seen as the multitude that should follow the pastors and allow themselves to be led.[111] The novelty of Congar's work was that it departed from the traditional way of doing ecclesiology. Instead of starting with the hierarchy, his starting point was the laity and the communal life of the whole church. He emphasized that both the hierarchical and the communal functions of the church are foundational to its life. He also departed from the canonical approach to ecclesiology which defined the lay faithful as those who are not ordained. Congar instead defined a lay person as a baptized Christian who participates in the priestly, prophetic, and kingly missions of Christ. In *Laity in the Church*, Congar also undertook a study of the history of ecclesiology. He showed that perfect society ecclesiology contained an impoverished understanding of the church and argued for richer notions of the church such

---

108. Doyle, *Communion Ecclesiology*, 46.
109. See Congar, *Vraie et fausse réforme*.
110. See Congar, *Jalons pour une théologie*.
111. Cf. Pius X, "*Vehementer nos*," no. 8, in Carlen, *Papal Encyclicals*, 3:47–48.

as mystery and people of God. After Vatican II, Congar revised some elements of his theology of the laity; in particular he modified what he came to perceive as too sharp of a distinction between the ordained and lay present in his original edition of *Laity in the Church*.[112]

Congar sought to develop an ecclesiology that would integrate the various streams in the renewal of ecclesiology in the first half of the twentieth century: the mystical body of Christ, people of God, and sacrament. In addition, he sought to develop an understanding of the church that was strongly rooted not only in Christology but also in pneumatology, which became a distinctive feature of his ecclesiology. Inspired by Möhler, Congar envisioned a robust role for the Spirit in guiding the people of God through history, and he thought of the Spirit as inspiring the structural reform of the church. Many of the views on the church that Congar developed from 1930s to 1950s became enshrined in the documents of Vatican II. As many have pointed out, the council could have hardly been what it was without Congar's scholarship.[113]

The Second Vatican Council was the culmination of the developments outlined in the previous pages. The council departed notably from the ecclesiology of the neoscholastic tradition and in large part reflected instead the ideas of various theologians whose writings attempted a renewal of Catholic ecclesiology.

Ecclesiology at Vatican II

In October of 1958, when Pope Pius XII died and Angelo Roncalli succeeded him as John XXIII, there were two kinds of treatises on the church in Catholic ecclesiology: the old apologetic, which presented the church as a perfect society; and the new, dogmatic one whose focus was on the church as the mystical body of Christ. A typical seminary curriculum reflected this situation. The course in ecclesiology, which would typically comprise two semesters, consisted of an apologetic part (*pars apologetica*) and a dogmatic part (*pars dogmatica*).[114] The church was also treated in fundamental theology, which too was a year-long course, functioning in the curriculum as a foundation for courses in dogmatic theology. The key topics of fundamental theology

---

112. For Congar's own account of how his thought developed, see Congar, "My Pathfindings," 169–88.

113. See, for instance, Komonchak, "Return of Yves Congar," (1983) 402; Doyle, *Communion Ecclesiology*, 38; McBrien, *Church*, 140.

114. Textbooks from which seminarians studied ecclesiology were typically divided into those two parts. See, for instance, Zapelena, *De ecclesia Christi*; Van Noort, *Dogmatic Theology*.

were divine revelation and the teaching authority of the church. The course culminated with a demonstration of the institution of the church, particularly of the Magisterium entrusted with the deposit of faith. This was the status quo on one level, but the actual state of Catholic ecclesiology was more complex. The *ressourcement* theologians, who for several decades studied patristic and medieval sources, uncovered ideas that once were in the theological mainstream but became eclipsed in the course of the second millennium. They brought those ideas to light and used them to construct interpretations of the church that focused on its interior dimension. In hindsight, one can see that those theologians set in place the building blocks for a renewal of Catholic ecclesiology. Their scholarship, however, awaited reception beyond a limited circle of specialists. The Second Vatican Council was around the corner, and as startling as it must have seemed at the time, the council took it upon itself to be the agent of renewal.

Pope John called the council unexpectedly on January 25, 1959, less than three months into his pontificate. He envisioned three main goals: renewal, adaptation or updating of the church, and the reunion of Christians.[115] After a period of preparation, during which various preparatory commissions drafted texts for bishops to deliberate on and approve, the council began on October 11, 1962.[116] From the moment of its announcement, Vatican II came to be seen as an opportunity to remedy the incomplete treatment of the church at Vatican I. This created an atmosphere of high expectation for the schema on the church (*De ecclesia*). It was drafted by the Preparatory Theological Commission and was ready prior to the council's opening, but because of some organizational glitches, the bishops did not receive it until November 23. The drafters of the schema assumed that the pope had charged them to simply repeat and reinforce the ecclesiological vision of the neoscholastic manuals. The schema thus focused on the institutional dimension of the church and presented its mission principally in terms of opposing Protestantism, secularism, modernism, and other evils of the day. The schema consisted of eleven chapters.[117] The first two chapters treated the nature of the church, its necessity for salvation, and its membership. They were followed by two chapters on the episcopate, which also contained one paragraph on the presbyterate. Evangelical perfection and the laity were the topics of chapters five and six. The following two chapters were on the magisterium and on authority and obedience in the church. The

115. See the pope's speeches on the occasions of announcing, convoking, and opening the council. They can be found in Anderson, *Council Daybook*, 1–2, 6–9, 25–29.

116. For a detailed discussion of the council's preparatory period see, for instance, Komonchak, "Struggle for the Council," (1995) 167–356.

117. It can be found in AS 1.4:12–91.

last three chapters discussed the themes of church and state, the church's missionary rights, and ecumenism.

The title of the schema's first chapter, "The Nature of the Church Militant," reflected both the tone of the document and its overall approach to understanding the church. At the forefront was attention to the church's visible structures. The schema generally followed *Mystici corporis* and restated several of its affirmations: the Roman Catholic Church is the mystical body of Christ; that only Catholics are true members of the mystical body, while all others—whether Christian or not—relate to it only by desire; and that bishops receive the power of jurisdiction by delegation from the pope, not through ordination, which meant practically that bishops were essentially vicars of the pope. As regards the relationship between church and state, the schema presented the traditional Catholic position, which averred that in those places where Catholics were in the majority, the civic authority should grant full freedom and support to the practice of Catholic religion and constrain other religious expressions. In places where Catholics were in the minority, the civic power should tolerate the practice of other religions. On a few points, the schema ventured beyond the treatment in the manuals, as in chapter six, which contained a rather encouraging presentation of the theology of the laity. Based on the positive experience of the Catholic Action movement in the previous several decades, the chapter affirmed that the laity's vocation is not only in the secular realm but also within the church. In chapter eleven, the schema made a small step forward by going beyond the so-called "ecumenism of return" of Pope Pius XI's encyclical *Mortalium animos* (1928). The chapter acknowledged that salvific elements can be found in other Christian communities, and it also cautiously affirmed the ecumenical movement.[118]

While some bishops had a favorable view of this initial schema on the church, most bishops found it disappointing, for it reflected only minimally the developments in ecclesiology that were taking place within the biblical, liturgical, patristic, and ecumenical movements. The bishops also thought that the schema's openness to ecumenism was insufficient. The schema was thus severely criticized. It was perhaps the speech of Bishop Émile-Joseph de Smedt of Bruges (Belgium) that most aptly expressed the schema's most significant shortcomings. De Smedt denounced it for its triumphalistic tone, for the clericalism imbedded in its pyramidal view of the church, and for its excessively juridical approach to understanding the church.[119] As a

118. Gaillardetz, *Church in the Making*, 8–12.

119. For a discussion of this draft at the first session of Vatican II see, for instance, Ruggieri, "Beyond an Ecclesiology of Polemics," 281–357, esp. 328–40.

result of these and other criticisms, it was evident that the schema needed to be fundamentally reworked. The first session of the council ended on December 8, 1962 without a vote being taken on whether or not the schema *De ecclesia* should be withdrawn and a new one prepared.

In the early days of December, when the schema on the church was discussed in the conciliar aula, the bishops were already somewhat experienced in raising opposition to conciliar draft documents. Several days earlier, they subjected the schema on the sources of revelation (*De fontibus revelationis*) to criticisms so devastating that, on the pope's order, it was removed from consideration and assigned to a Mixed Commission for a major revision.[120] It was becoming clearer and clearer that through their criticisms of the initial schemas the bishops were in effect questioning whether the neoscholastic, manualist way of theologizing was adequate to address the vision of the council as Pope John had articulated it and to which most of the bishops were warming up.

During the intersession between the first and the second sessions, a sub-commission for the schema on the church was formed, and it decided that as a way of proceeding forward it would use a draft on the church that Gérard Philips had composed earlier. Philips was a theological expert at the council (*peritus*) and himself a member of the sub-commission. He excelled in bringing together opposing views. When the new schema was presented at the second session of the council in the fall of 1963, one could not miss how different it was from the initial schema. It was much shorter, only four chapters long. The title of its first chapter, "The Mystery of the Church," was particularly striking. Instead of starting with the notion of the church as a society, the new schema began by relating the church to the mystery of God's self-revelation. This theme resurfaced in a section of chapter three on the church as the people of God. The new schema incorporated robustly the notions of the church prominent in the ecclesiological renewal that was taking place in the decades leading up to the council. The schema became significantly less dependent on the language of the neoscholastic theological manuals and instead showed preference for language closer to Scripture, the Church Fathers, and the liturgy. It contained such descriptions of the church as mystery, sacrament, the people of God, the body of Christ, and communion. This new schema was greeted favorably by most of the bishops and marked a new starting point for conciliar deliberations on the church. In hindsight, one can see that a shift in Catholic ecclesiology was underway. The status quo was not holding up. What would later be called an "ecclesiology of communion" was

---

120. See Ruggieri, "First Doctrinal Clash," 233–66.

gaining more and more ground. As a result of further deliberations and bishops' proposals during the second and the third sessions of the council, the schema on the church underwent another significant refashioning. It was approved on November 21, 1964 with 2,151 yes and 5 no votes as the Dogmatic Constitution on the Church (*Lumen gentium*).[121]

Vatican II did not limit its treatment of ecclesiology to its Dogmatic Constitution on the Church. The more the bishops desired to realize Pope John's vision for the council, the more it became evident that issues pertaining to ecclesiology were at the forefront, directly or indirectly, of other topics they wanted to address. It became clear, for instance, that the principles for renewal they wished to inscribe in the constitution on the liturgy (*Sacrosanctum concilium*) were rooted in a particular understanding of the church—a vision that was in tension with preconciliar ecclesiology. Similarly, the vision of ecumenism the bishops were considering, and to which they decided to dedicate a separate document ("Decree on Ecumenism," *Unitaits redintegratio*), rested on an ecclesiology that did not treat the nature and structures of the church in all-or-nothing terms. The council was thus engaged with ecclesiological questions on several fronts simultaneously, which created a demand for consistency in the treatment of the church across multiple documents.

What further stands out about the place of ecclesiology at Vatican II is not only that it was central to multiple topics the council addressed, but also that the council issued two different constitutions on the church. Originally the plan for the council included only one document specifically on the church. In the last stages of the council's preparation, in order to better organize its work, Archbishop Leo Suenens from Belgium (soon to be cardinal) proposed to the pope and a small group of cardinals that the council consider the church from two perspectives: in its inner life (the church *ad intra*) and in its relationship to the world (the church *ad extra*). Near the end of the first session, Suenens presented his proposal to the conciliar assembly where it was received favorably. A mixed commission was created and charged with preparing a second schema on the church which, by addressing the church's relationship to the world, would complement the Dogmatic Constitution on the Church. The drafting of "The Pastoral Constitution on the Church in the Modern World (*Gaudium et spes*)"—as this second schema on the church was eventually named—was particularly complicated, but

---

121. For a discussion of this draft and its modifications at the second and third sessions of the council, see Melloni, "Beginning of the Second Period," 1–115; Komonchak, "Toward an Ecclesiology of Communion," (2003) 1–86; Tagle, "'Black Week' of Vatican II," 387–95, 417–52.

it became one of the greatest achievements of Vatican II.[122] *Lumen gentium* and *Gaudium et spes* can be seen as the two pillars of Vatican II's ecclesiology, although ecclesiological concerns permeated all of council's work.

Ecclesiology of Vatican II: An Overview

In the documents of Vatican II, one finds an ecclesiology that in its scope and richness is unparalleled on the magisterial level. Generally, by following insights from the *nouvelle théologie* rather than those of neoscholasticism, the council ratified the move Catholic ecclesiologists had been making for several decades. The move consisted of returning to the language of Scripture, the Church Fathers, and the liturgy in order to articulate an understanding of the church that accounted better for the breadth of the Christian theological tradition.

The following overview of the council's ecclesiology will focus on those key affirmations which illustrate the shift that occurred in Catholic ecclesiology at Vatican II.[123]

The Church as Mystery, Sacrament, and Communion

A central affirmation of Vatican II's ecclesiology is that the church is more than its structures and laws. In its innermost reality, the church is a participation in the triune life of God, on whom its very existence depends. This key point is made most clearly by describing the church as mystery and sacrament, and by envisioning its interior dimension as communion. From the outset, *Lumen gentium* relates the church to the Trinitarian mystery of God and defines it as an aspect of that mystery.[124] The Constitution presents the church not as an autonomous entity but as dependent on its relationship to God. It describes the church in trinitarian terms as "a people brought into unity from the unity of the Father, the Son and the Holy Spirit."[125] To address the charges of triumphalism and juridicism, Christ, not the church, is said to

---

122. For the history of *Gaudium et spes* at the council, see, Grootaers, "Drama Continues between the Acts," 412–29; Vilanova, "Intersession (1963–1964)," 402–15; Tanner, "Church in the World," 270–386; Routhier, "Finishing the Work Begun," 122–77. For a shorter account, see, for instance, Lawler et al., *Church in the Modern World*, 13–41.

123. For a more comprehensive treatment of Vatican II ecclesiology see, for instance, Kloppenburg, *Ecclesiology of Vatican*; Gaillardetz, *Church in the Making*; Tanner, *Church and the World*.

124. LG 1–4.

125. LG 4.

be "the light of the nations"; whatever light shines on the face of the church is his.[126] With the idea of the church as mystery, the council retrieved a deeply biblical and patristic way of thinking about the church.[127]

The term "mystery" is applied to the church in a theological sense. Mystery is thus not the same thing as a problem that awaits a solution, or a riddle that needs to be deciphered. Something is a mystery, theologically speaking, not merely because of human limitations, but because it is ineffable and inexhaustible. God is a mystery in an absolute sense, which means that "no words can ever adequately express his reality, and that he remains greater than our best ideas about him. . . . God remains always 'incomprehensible,' in the sense of being beyond all definition and limitation, greater than the knowledge which any creature can have of him."[128] Calling the church a mystery means, as Pope Paul VI aptly put it, that the church "is a reality imbued with the divine presence and, for that reason, she is ever susceptible of new and deeper investigation."[129] The church shares in the mystery of God insofar as it participates in God's work of salvation. The church can be seen as an ineffable reality that cannot be grasped adequately by considering only its visible appearance.

Nevertheless, the church is also a visible, tangible reality. To keep the visible and invisible aspects of the church together, Vatican II employed the notion of "sacrament."[130] The church is said to be a kind of sacrament (*veluti sacramentum*)—a sign and instrument of intimate union with God and of the unity of all humanity.[131] The church is thus a mediator of salvation, not only its recipient. The church mediates salvation insofar as it is "an effective and graced sign before the world of God's saving love."[132]

The council saw clear advantages to describing the church as a sacrament over the idea of the church as a perfect society. The latter has been used in post-Reformation Catholic ecclesiology as a way to communicate that the church is a visible reality. For various reasons, however, perfect society ecclesiology communicated very poorly that the visible aspects of the church signified its invisible interior dimension. In addition, since the

126. LG 1.

127. The term *mystery* is used for the church in the title of the first chapter of *Lumen gentium* and again in articles 5, 39, 44, and 63.

128. Gleeson, "Mystery," 692.

129. Paul VI, "Opening General Congregation," 148.

130. The term sacrament is applied to the church in LG 1, 9, 59; SC 5, 26; GS 42; AG 5. The church is referred to as "a universal sacrament of salvation" in LG 48; GS 45; AG 1.

131. LG 1; GS 42.

132. Gaillardetz, *Church in the Making*, 43.

concept of sacrament maintains both unity and difference between the sign and the signified, the understanding of the church as a sacrament is better equipped to uphold the proper distinction between the church and Christ than mystical body of Christ theologies. The understanding of the church as a sacrament also has an important pastoral ramification; it calls the whole church to holiness. This is articulated in *Lumen gentium* not only in chapter five, which speaks of the universal call to holiness of all the baptized, but also in the description of the church as both holy and in need of purification, always following the path of penance and renewal.[133]

To articulate what the church is in its innermost reality, in addition to "mystery" and "sacrament," Vatican II also used the term "communion." In its attempts to express the organic reality of the church, the council showed preference for the notion of communion over that of the body of Christ, even though the conciliar documents contain strong Christological affirmations in continuity with the teaching of *Mystici corporis*.[134] "Communion" designates the inner life of God and the church's participation in it. Communion is the name for what the visible dimensions of the church are supposed to signify, namely, God's saving presence. The notion of communion includes both vertical and horizontal dimensions—the former having to do with God and the latter referring to the relationships among the church's members. The council presents the horizontal dimension of communion as having several forms. First, communion refers to the bond between the church's members regardless of distinctions between the laity and the clergy, as seen, for instance, in *Lumen gentium* 13: "All the faithful scattered throughout the world are in communion with each other in the Holy Spirit."[135] Second, the idea of communion grounds Vatican II's teaching on the collegiality of bishops—the notion that all bishops together, including the pope, rule the universal church.[136] The council presents episcopal collegiality as a form of (hierarchic) communion and sets it over against "the preconciliar notion of the Church as an absolute monarchy with the pope at the top of the structural pyramid."[137] Third, envisioning the college of bishops in terms of communion and taking into consideration what the council also teaches about the connection between the Eucharist and the church,[138] the universal church is seen as a communion of local churches. Lastly, communion is the framework

---

133. McBrien, *Church*, 165–66. See LG 8.
134. See LG 7.
135. See also LG 4; DV 10; UR 2; GS 32.
136. LG 22–23.
137. McBrien, *Church*, 172.
138. LG 7 and 26.

within which Vatican II discusses the divisions among Christian churches and ecclesial communities in the Decree on Ecumenism. The divisions are seen as a separation from full communion,[139] and the goal of ecumenism is envisioned as its reestablishment.[140]

To set out the mystery of the church, *Lumen gentium* further employs a variety of images taken from Scripture, the Church Fathers, and the liturgy. The church is said to be a sheepfold, God's farm, God's building and temple, Jerusalem which is above, mother, and spouse.[141] These images are just listed, however; the council did not attempt to construct a synthesis of them.

The Church as the Pilgrim People of God

Vatican II further articulated the point that the church is more than its structures and laws by describing it as the people of God. "People of God" is the title of the second chapter of *Lumen gentium*. The chapter discusses the mystery of the church as lived in history, between the ascension and the Parousia. Initially, in the second draft of the schema on the church, "people of God" appeared in the title of the third chapter.[142] Cardinal Suenens suggested, however, that the chapter be divided and the material on the people of God be moved before the second chapter, which treated the hierarchical structure of the church. This editorial change actually marked a profound shift in the council's vision of the church. The change communicated the point that "the church is not first the clergy; it is first of all the whole people of God," and that "believers share a oneness and baptismal equality that precedes the distinctions among different roles in the community."[143] "People of God" is thus not a designation of the laity or of the clergy but of all the faithful (the *christifideles*). Describing the church as the people of God and insisting that it refers to *all* the baptized addressed the charge of clericalism in the initial schema *De ecclesia*. It created a contrast with the tendency of preconciliar ecclesiology to identify the church primarily with the ordained and religious.

Vatican II developed the idea of the church as the *whole* people of God simultaneously in *Lumen Gentium* and in the Constitution on the Sacred Liturgy (*Sacrosanctum concilium*), since such an understanding of the church

139. UR 3.
140. UR 14, 18, 22.
141. LG 6.
142. The titles of the chapters were: (1) "The Mystery of the Church," (2) "The Hierarchical Constitution of the Church and the Episcopate in Particular," (3) "The People of God and the Laity in Particular," and (4) "The Call to Holiness in the Church."
143. Hahnenberg, *Concise Guide*, 40.

was central to the council's vision of liturgical reform.[144] Full, conscious, and active participation of all the faithful in the liturgy, which the council so ardently desired,[145] would have lacked coherence within the preconciliar ecclesiological framework of the church as a perfect society. One can see the liturgical and ecclesiological renewals at Vatican II as two sides of the same coin. After the council, it has been perhaps in the liturgy where Catholics have experienced the shift in ecclesiology most profoundly.

The description of the church as the people of God in *Lumen gentium* also includes the idea of divine election, present both in the Old and the New Testaments. The church is the people *of God* on the account of God's free initiative, as the council makes clear in *Lumen gentium* 9: "For those who believe in Christ, who are reborn, not from a corruptible seed, but from an incorruptible one through the word of the living God (cf. 1 Pet 1:23), not from flesh, but from water and the Holy Spirit (cf. John 3:5–6), are finally established as 'a chosen race, a royal priesthood, a holy nation . . . who in times past were not a people, but now are the People of God' (1 Pet 2:9–10)."

Lumen gentium uses the framework of the people of God to set forth a number of other topics in ecclesiology, such as the common priesthood of all believers and the ministerial priesthood,[146] the sense of the faith, charisms,[147] and catholicity.[148] The question of the membership of the church was also addressed within the framework of the people of God. *Lumen gentium* spoke of various groups—Catholics, other Christians, non-Christians (theists and non-theists), and non-believers in terms of how fully they are incorporated within the people of God.[149]

The council presents the church as a *pilgrim* people, as an eschatological community.[150] The image of a pilgrim lends itself well to express the transitory nature of the church as is evident in this passage from *Lumen gentium* 48:

> The Church, to which we are all called in Christ Jesus, and in which by the grace of God we acquire holiness, will receive its perfection only in the glory of heaven, when will come the time of the renewal of all things (Acts 3:21). . . . However, until there

---

144. *Sacrosanctum concilium* was promulgated at the end of the council's second session (December 4, 1963), almost a year prior to the promulgation of *Lumen gentium*.

145. See, for instance, SC 14, 21, 30, 41, 47, 50.

146. LG 10–11.

147. LG 12.

148. LG 13.

149. O'Donnell, *Ecclesia*, 357.

150. See LG 48–51; GS 45, 57; DV 8; UR 6.

be realized new heavens and a new earth in which justice dwells (cf. 2 Pet 3:13) the pilgrim Church, in its sacraments and institutions, which belong to the present age, carries the mark of this world which will pass, and she herself takes her place among the creatures which groan and travail yet and await the revelation of the sons of God (cf. Rom 8:19–22).

The image of a pilgrim who has not yet reached his or her destination allowed the council not only to take a posture of humility and curb the triumphalism of the initial schema on the church, but also to acknowledge the possibility and the need of reform in the church.[151] Moreover, the idea of the pilgrim church, a people on the way guided by the Spirit, allowed the council to say that apostolic tradition develops in the church, that the church grows in the understanding of it, and that the church "is always advancing towards the plenitude of divine truth, until eventually the words of God are fulfilled in her."[152]

The designation of the church as pilgrim people of God relates to the idea of the church as sacrament and sheds light on how the latter should be understood. Sacraments are visible signs of the invisible. By describing the church as the people of God, the council makes the point that all the baptized are the primary visible sign that mediates the church's invisible dimension. The structures of the church, which also constitute a visible sign, are supposed to aid God's people to fulfill their mission. Furthermore, the idea of the church as a *pilgrim* people suggests that the church embodies the salvific presence of God incompletely, which should help avoid ecclesiological triumphalism.

Ecumenism

Central to Vatican II's ecclesiology and to the council as a whole is a concern for ecumenism. In its Decree on Ecumenism (*Unitatis redintegratio*), Vatican II re-envisioned the relation of the Catholic Church to the ecumenical movement. While previously church leaders rejected the movement as being a promoter of indifferentism, modernism, and relativism,[153] the coun-

---

151. LG 8, UR 6.

152. DV 8.

153. See Pius XI, "*Mortalium animos*," no. 9, in Carlen, *Papal Encyclicals*, 316–17. A moderate warming up to the ecumenical movement took place already during the pontificate of Pius XII. The pope recognized the movement as being of serious interest to Catholics and encouraged prayer for its success. He asked bishops and priests to keep well-informed on the subject, and also permitted Catholics who received approval from competent church authorities to meet with non-Catholics to discuss matters of faith.

cil recognized it as an inspiration of the Holy Spirit.[154] Furthermore, the council reconceived the purpose of ecumenism; its goal was no longer envisioned in terms of a "return" of non-Catholics to the Catholic Church,[155] but rather as "restoration" of unity that in part still exists in varying degrees. The council adopted the notion of communion to frame its discussion of divisions among Christians. Its starting point was an affirmation that those "who believe in Christ and have been properly baptized are put in some, though imperfect, communion with the Catholic Church."[156] The council conceived the situation of divided Christian churches in terms of degrees of communion that exist among them. The Decree on Ecumenism affirmed that many of the most significant elements that build up the church exist outside the visible boundaries of the Catholic Church,[157] and that the Holy Spirit has not refrained from using the separated churches as a means of salvation for their members.[158]

Recognizing that ecclesial communion exceeds the boundaries of the Catholic Church meant that the standard affirmation of Catholic ecclesiology of an exclusive identification between the church of Christ, the mystical body of Christ, and the Roman Catholic Church became inadequate.[159] Instead of asserting that the church of Christ *is* the Roman Catholic Church, as the initial draft of *De ecclesia* had done,[160] the council taught that the church of Christ *subsists in* (*subsistit in*) the Catholic Church.[161] It is this nuanced formulation that made participation of Catholics in ecumenical dialogues possible. It "brought out the point that the Catholic Church is wholly within the Body of Christ and its life is sustained and enriched by that union, but that there is room for other Christian Churches and ecclesial communities within the same Body of Christ, even if their union with it is not of the same order as the Catholic Church's."[162] While the precise meaning of the expression "subsists in" became a disputed theological point, there should be

---

See Supreme Sacred Congregation, *Ecclesia Catholica*.

154. UR 1.

155. See Pius XI, "*Mortalium animos*," no. 10, in Carlen, *Papal Encyclicals*, 3:317.

156. UR 3.

157. The Decree gave the examples of the written Word of God; the life of grace; faith, hope, and love; and visible elements of the church (UR 3).

158. UR 3.

159. See, for instance, Pius XII, "*Mystici corporis*," no. 13, in Carlen, *Papal Encyclicals*, 4:39–40; "*Humani generis*," no. 27, in Carlen, *Papal Encyclicals*, 4:179.

160. See AS 1.4.15.

161. LG 8.

162. McBrien, *Church*, 177.

no doubt that it does not mean the same thing as "is."¹⁶³ That would make several affirmations in the Decree on Ecumenism and in the Dogmatic Constitution on the Church incoherent. For instance, the affirmations: that the separated churches and ecclesial communities have been by no means deprived of significance and importance in the mystery of salvation since the Spirit of Christ has not refrained from using them as means of salvation¹⁶⁴; that the separated Eastern churches not in full communion with Rome are recognized as "particular churches" in a theological sense¹⁶⁵; and that non-Catholic Christians, in addition to baptism, recognize and receive other sacraments in their churches and ecclesial communities.¹⁶⁶ How could the exclusive identification between the church of Christ and the Roman Catholic Church be reconciled with these affirmations of the council?

The Local Church

Among the major contributions of Vatican II toward the renewal of Catholic ecclesiology was the council's rediscovery of the local church. Catholic ecclesiology in the second millennium, especially after the Reformation, was universalistic. The focus was on the whole or universal church rather than on a local community. Local communities were not considered churches in the full theological sense but parts or branches of the whole church governed by the pope. For the most part, Vatican II's ecclesiology still unfolds within this universalistic paradigm. In several places, however, the council documents broke out of this framework and made advances in the theology of the local church. The most significant of these is the affirmation of the full ecclesial reality of the local church and the subsequent understanding of the universal church as a communion of local churches. A detailed discussion of the council's theology of the local church will be presented in chapter four.

Church and World

Vatican II redefined the relationship of the church to the world. For fifteen hundred years, this relationship reflected the dichotomy that Augustine set

---

163. For various views on this issue, see, for instance, Becker, "Church and Vatican II," 514–22; CDF, "Responses to Certain Aspects," 134–36; Sullivan, "Meaning of *Subsistit in*," 116–24; "Further Thoughts on the Meaning," 133–47; Schelkens, "*Lumen Gentium*'s 'Subsistit In' Revisited," 875–93; Welch and Mansini, "Lumen Gentium no. 8," 602–17.
164. UR 3.
165. UR 14–18.
166. LG 15.

forth in *The City of God* (426) between the heavenly city and the city of Cain. John Markey notes that Augustine's great work "functioned unofficially, and often unconsciously, as a kind of underlying constitution shaping the primary way for viewing the Church's relationship to the world."[167] In light of the dualism that characterizes Augustine's thought, "the Church and world, the spiritual and the temporal, the sacred and the profane, the holy and the ordinary, comprised two fundamentally different, even if related, aspects of history and, hence, of human experience."[168] The Church thus understood itself as distinct and separate from the world and saw its relationship with the civic, secular, and political realms in terms of opposition and conflict. This was particularly visible in the church's response to modernity, which was the backdrop for the council's treatment of the relation between the church and the world.

"Modernity" refers to a mentality or mindset that arose in Western Europe in the seventeenth century following the scientific revolution and Thirty Years War. It was bolstered by the eighteenth-century Enlightenment and continued its influence in the nineteenth and twentieth centuries. Modernity was already anticipated by the Renaissance and the Protestant Reformation, but these were still relatively mild corrective movements in comparison to the scientific revolution and the Enlightenment, which unleashed devastating criticisms of the past understanding of almost everything: the physical sciences, politics, philosophy, economics, and religion. By exalting human reason and personal autonomy, religion, faith, and revelation came to be seen as irrelevant to the progressive enhancement of human life, which was modernity's chief concern.[169]

Some Catholics attempted to reconcile their faith tradition with modernity, but they were often labeled "modernists" by church authorities and marginalized. Their views were condemned and several were even excommunicated.[170] Leaders of the Catholic Church could find hardly anything positive or constructive in the claims of modernity. They opposed it vigorously and positioned the church over against the modern world, its values, and aspirations. As Timothy McCarthy observes, "by choice the church became an isolated fortress surrounded by an alien world made up not only of other Christian churches and other religions but also of atheists, secular scientists, and governments that had overthrown such traditional values as monarchical rule and the union of church and state in the name of lib-

---

167. Markey, *Creating Communion*, 28.

168. Markey, *Creating Communion*, 28–29.

169. McCarthy, *Catholic Tradition*, 23–24.

170. See, for instance, O'Malley, *What Happened at Vatican II*, 53–92; Talar, "'Synthesis of All Heresies,'" 491–514.

eration and democracy."¹⁷¹ This siege mentality, as it has been often called, characterized the official attitude of the Catholic Church to the modern world until the dawn of the Second Vatican Council.

Vatican II's treatment of the church's relation to the world took shape in the context of this long-lasting history of dualistic opposition between the two. The bishops, who became awakened to the historical consciousness, wished to overcome the dichotomy between the church and the world without collapsing one into another. They reevaluated their predecessors' assessment of the modern world and defined the relationship of the church and the world in a new light. This happened primarily in the Pastoral Constitution on the Church in the Modern World (*Gaudium et spes*), but also in other documents, such as the decrees on ecumenism (*Unitatis redintegratio*) and the church's missionary activity (*Ad gentes*), and in the declarations on religious liberty (*Dignitatis humanae*) and on non-Christian religions (*Nostra aetate*). Upon their promulgation, these documents struck many Catholics as a breath of fresh air as they brought to an end the Catholic Church's negative response to modernity represented by the *Syllabus of Errors* of Pius IX (1864) and by the encyclical *Pascendi* of Pius X (1907). The bishops at Vatican II placed the Catholic Church resolutely within the modern world.

It was of particular significance that the council did not frame its discussion in general terms of the church *and* the world, but rather in terms of the church *in* the world, and specifically, in terms of the church in the world *of today* (*huius temporis*) or the *modern* world. The language of the church *and* the world might have been perceived as a continuation of the framework in which the church was understood as a self-contained entity radically different from the world. The bishops, however, wished to set aside the dualistic opposition of the church to the world on the grounds that God dwells within the world through all of creation and particularly through the church. By "world" they meant "humanity in its historical existence with all the social, political, and economic structures which shape that existence."¹⁷² The bishops thus understood the world to be a human creation and an expression of the human spirit¹⁷³ and, as such, autonomous from the church.¹⁷⁴ The council did not see the church and the world to be necessarily "in a competitive or adversarial relationship, except where sin prevails."¹⁷⁵ Instead, the council saw them as mutually related and inter-

---

171. McCarthy, *Catholic Tradition*, 39–40.
172. Lawler et al., *Church in the Modern World*, 1.
173. GS 53–55.
174. GS 34–36.
175. Haight, *Christian Community in History*, 2:397.

twined. The church exists in the world and is impacted by it. Moreover, the church exists for the world; its purpose is to be a leaven or spiritual principle of the world.[176] The bishops intentionally chose the leaven metaphor in order to express that "the church was sent into the world to transform it *from* within."[177] They wanted to distance themselves from portraying the church in terms of an autonomous entity standing over against the world as a perfect society unaffected by the world's joys and hopes (*gaudium et spes*), or sorrows and anxieties, as the opening paragraph of *Gaudium et spes* articulated so movingly.[178]

The pastoral approach of the council is clearly on display in portraying the mission of the church as a servant of humankind. In the view of the council, mission is not merely something that the church *has*; rather, mission enters into the very definition of what the church *is*. The council made it clear that the church is not an end in itself. Its mission and its very *raison d'être* is to give witness to the gospel. For the bishops at Vatican II, this entailed a real engagement with the world. They did not see the mission of the church "as merely a kind of spiritualized mission, but actual, material, and concrete witness to the liberation of humans from various evils that afflict and enslave, including material poverty, intellectual and spiritual ignorance, physical hunger and various hungers of the human heart."[179] For the council, the mission of the church included addressing, reducing, and, where possible, eliminating human suffering insofar as it stands in the way of God's reign manifesting itself in history.

The themes of Vatican II's ecclesiology presented so far apply to the church in its entirety, as both the laity and the clergy. The following two themes will apply specifically to these two groups within the church.

Laity

An earlier discussion of the history of Catholic ecclesiology highlighted that from the time of the Reformation until the twentieth-century Catholic theologians envisioned the church predominantly in institutional, societal, and juridical terms. This view focused on the role of the hierarchy

---

176. GS 40. For additional references to "leaven" in the documents of Vatican II, see LG 31; AA 3; AG 15; GE 8; PC 11.

177. Gaillardetz and Clifford, *Keys to the Council*, 93.

178. "The joys and hopes and the sorrows and anxieties of people today, especially of those who are poor and afflicted, are also the joys and hopes, sorrows and anxieties of the disciples of Christ, and there is nothing truly human which does not also affect them" (GS 1).

179. Lawler et al., *Church in the Modern World*, 59.

in the church, while the laity were considered passive followers of their pastors. Vatican II presented a theology of the laity that is in stark contrast with this conception. As a matter of fact, the official acknowledgement that the laity ought to play a more active role in the church had happened already before Vatican II and was reflected in the approval the Catholic Action movement received from church authorities. Catholic Action, which emerged in Western Europe at the beginning of the twentieth century, referred to associations of lay Catholics who organized in order to further the mission of the church. It was understood as "the participation of the laity in the apostolate of the Church's hierarchy."[180] Church leaders recognized that the laity have an apostolate in the church, or rather, a role to play within the apostolate of the hierarchy. As Edward Hahnenberg notes, "the Catholic Action approach to lay activity never escaped the hierarchical and clericalistic presuppositions of the institutional model of the church.... It was unclear whether or not the laity engaged in activity that belonged to them by virtue of their baptism."[181]

Vatican II provided a rather different understanding of the laity's role in the church. Already the preparatory schema *De ecclesia*, which in other aspects of ecclesiology remained very much within the bounds of *societas perfecta* ecclesiology, was theologically much more up-to-date concerning the laity. It contained a whole chapter on the laity (chapter 6), in which it spoke about not only their duties, but also their rights and exhorted them to active participation in the life of the church.[182] The council treated the laity in several of its documents: the Decree on the Apostolate of the Laity (*Apostolicam actuositatem*), the Dogmatic Constitution on the Church (especially in chapter 4), the Constitution on the Sacred Liturgy, and the Pastoral Constitution on the Church in the Modern World.

Vatican II grounded its teaching on the laity in a theology of the baptismal call. Perhaps the most significant act of the council with regard to a theology of the laity was the decision, made during the drafting of *Lumen gentium*, to treat the church as the whole people of God first before considering the hierarchy and the laity separately.[183] It was a clear signal that the council was distancing itself from the traditional institutional approach to ecclesiology in which clergy were considered to be church in a superior way to the laity. The council taught that the laity share equally with the hierarchy

---

180. Pius XI, "Discourse to Young Women," 14, quoted in Hahnenberg, *Ministries*, 104.

181. Hahnenberg, *Ministries*, 104–5.

182. See AS 1.4:38–44.

183. O'Donnell, *Ecclesia*, 247.

in the threefold office of Christ as priest, prophet, and king.[184] They are called to full, conscious, and active participation in the liturgy.[185] It is their right and responsibility to be actively involved in the church's apostolate[186] and also in the transformation of the temporal order.[187] Like the hierarchy and professed religious, the laity are called to a life of holiness.[188] Over all, Vatican II advanced the theology of the laity considerably, even though its treatment of the subject was not completely consistent.[189]

Collegiality of Bishops

One of the main contributions of Vatican II towards completing the unfinished business of Vatican I concerned the relationship of the pope and the rest of the bishops. After the First Vatican Council, which defined papal primacy and infallibility, many Catholic theologians tended to exaggerate papal prerogatives and gave the impression that bishops were simply vicars of the pope. While Vatican II never retreated from the teachings of Vatican I, it complemented them with the teaching on episcopal collegiality which intended to bring balance to a one-sided emphasis on the ministry of the pope. Collegiality was one of the most controversial matters treated at the council, for many bishops feared that it would violate the primacy of the pope. Drafters of *Lumen gentium* had to go to great pains to reassure those bishops that collegiality would not usurp what belongs properly to the pope.

The council's teaching on episcopal collegiality can be seen as a corollary of its understanding of episcopal ministry and of the church as communion. The council taught that the fullness of the sacrament of holy orders resides in a bishop and that episcopal consecration confers not only the office of sanctifying, but also the offices of teaching and ruling[190]; consequently, bishops could not be considered vicars of the pope.[191] The jurisdiction that bishops exercise over a particular group of the faithful is not delegated to them by the pope, but is proper to them. To articulate how bishops relate to one another and how they as a group relate to the bishop of Rome, the council used the notion of episcopal collegiality. The council taught that

---

184. LG 34–36.
185. SC 14.
186. LG 30, 33.
187. LG 31; GS 43.
188. LG 39–42.
189. See Gaillardetz, *Church in the Making*, 53–55.
190. LG 21.
191. LG 27.

Christ formed the apostles as a college with Peter being its head[192] and that bishops are the successors of the apostles.[193] The college of the apostles thus has continued in history as the college of bishops. The pope, who is the successor of Peter, is a member of the college.[194] In essence, episcopal collegiality means that the college of bishops shares with the pope, never apart from him, supreme authority in governing the whole church.[195] The idea of shared power and authority over the universal church is the core of the teaching on collegiality. By placing the pope *within* the college of bishops as its head, the council intended to overcome a dispute in Catholic ecclesiology, prevailing to a greater or lesser extent since the conciliarist crisis, which tended to see the relationship of the pope and the bishops as a zero-sum game. Vatican II taught that "even when the pope exercises his authority apart from the explicit cooperation of the bishops, his actions must presuppose an enduring communion between the pope and the college within which the pope always stands as head."[196]

The proponents of collegiality saw it as a great promise that would make the church more communal and less centralized. In many ways this promise still awaits a more substantial fulfillment.

Conclusion

The Second Vatican Council was a decisive moment in the twenty centuries of theological reflection on the church. The council can be seen as a culmination of a movement that originated in the early nineteenth century and whose goal was to retrieve and reintroduce insights from the first millennium into Catholic ecclesial consciousness. In many ways the council followed the directions of this renewal movement. As a result, Vatican II introduced a shift into Catholic ecclesiology. After centuries of theological reflection that placed an emphasis primarily on the societal, institutional, and juridical dimensions of the church, the council subordinated these to the church's transcendent, spiritual dimensions. As Patrick Granfield notes, "emphasis has shifted dramatically from the sociological to the biblical; from the jurisdictional to the sacramental; from the sectarian to the ecumenical; from the papal to the episcopal; from the hierarchical to the collegial."[197] With its ecclesiology, Vatican

---

192. LG 19.
193. LG 20.
194. LG 22.
195. LG 22.
196. Gaillardetz, *Church in the Making*, 78.
197. Granfield, "Church as *Societas Perfecta*," 445–46.

II moved away from the one-sided institutional view of the church toward a view grounded in the notion of communion.

Vatican II displaced *societas perfecta* ecclesiology and sought to restore equilibrium in the Catholic approach of thinking about the church by assigning a prominent place to the church's spiritual, liturgical, and communal dimensions. Yet the council did not reject everything in the traditional societal approach to ecclesiology. For instance, the council affirmed the social nature of the church while, for the most part, avoiding the term *societas*.[198] Instead it presented the social dimension of the church through the notion of communion. The council also affirmed that the church has all the means necessary to achieve its end.[199] Lastly, the council insisted that the church ought to be free to carry on its mission without the state's interference.[200] Nevertheless, the shift in Vatican II's approach to ecclesiology made the concept of the church as a perfect society no longer suitable to be an entry point into the reality of the church, and the values of a perfect and unequal society no longer fitting to be dominant values pertaining to the church.[201]

The shift that the council effected is no small matter. First, it brought vindication for several theologians whose scholarship made Vatican II possible but were met with earlier suspicion from church authorities. Prior to the council, some of them were disciplined for doctrinal problems in their writings.[202] Second, the shift meant that one could not continue doing ecclesiology as before. After the council, in reaction to the centuries-long dominance of institutional and juridical ecclesiology and in light of the enthusiasm generated by the renewal brought by Vatican II, many ecclesiologists showed preference for more spiritual approaches and the institutional approach was rejected as an integrating model. The new approaches worked out specifically theological views of the church and accentuated what made the church different from other human communities.

This shift in Catholic ecclesiology forms the context for Joseph Komonchak's ecclesiological project, to the analysis of which this study will now transition. After a short biographical introduction and a discussion of key influences on Komonchak's thinking about the church, the focus will be on three areas of his contribution to ecclesiology: method, theology of the local church, and authority in the church.

---

198. The term is used, for instance, in LG 8, 20; PO 2.

199. See LG 11, 20; UR 3

200. Granfield, "Rise and Fall," 7. See DH 1; GS 42, 44, 76.

201. Congar, "Moving towards a Pilgrim Church," 135.

202. For instance, Henri de Lubac, Marie-Dominique Chenu, Yves Congar, and John Courtney Murray.

2

Life and Major Influences

Life

JOSEPH ANDREW KOMONCHAK WAS born in Nyack, New York on March 13, 1939, to Joseph and Hazel [Meehan] Komonchak, the fifth of twelve children and the first boy.[1] He grew up in Nanuet, a small town about twenty-five miles from New York City. His family's background was Slovak on his father's side, and British and Irish on his mother's side. Komonchak was raised with the cultural heritage of both families, although he admits that when it came to religious traditions and practices, and cuisine in particular, the Slovak heritage played a larger role.

Komonchak attended public elementary school in his hometown. Already by the sixth or seventh grade he began thinking about becoming a priest. At the time, going to a minor seminary was a path many adolescent boys took if they were discerning priesthood or religious life. It prepared them academically and spiritually for a major seminary. After completing his elementary education, Komonchak thus went to Cathedral College in New York—a minor seminary of the New York Archdiocese. It consisted of four years of high school and two years of college. During those years (1952 to 1958), he commuted every day, taking the 6:30 a.m. bus and then a subway to be in school for 8:00 Mass. He remembers those years as a great blessing. He received a very good education in the humanities, particularly in literature, classical languages, and history, but regrettably less so in math and science. In Cathedral College, young Komonchak met David Tracy.[2] They struck up a close friendship that has lasted until the present.

---

1. The biographical information that follows has been gathered from a personal correspondence with Komonchak.

2. David Tracy (born 1939) is a prominent American theologian and professor

After graduating from Cathedral College, Komonchak entered St. Joseph's Seminary in Yonkers, New York, popularly known as Dunwoodie. At the time, education and formation in a major seminary lasted six years. Philosophy was the focus of the first two years; the main goal was to provide philosophical foundations for the study of theology. In the late 1950s, philosophy was taught from textbooks written (supposedly) according to the mind of St. Thomas Aquinas. Some textbooks were in Latin and some in English, but lectures at Dunwoodie were all in English. Like many others of his generation, Komonchak found neoscholastic philosophy quite unexciting, causing him to be put off by Aquinas for several years. His interest was piqued instead by church history and Scripture. He began to read Church Fathers and found them thrilling. Inspired by one of his best teachers, Myles M. Bourke, Komonchak began to read widely in the latest biblical scholarship. For some time, he thought of specializing in Scripture.

At Dunwoodie, Komonchak began teaching himself French to broaden the languages in which he could read and research. He already had some knowledge of Italian, which he studied at the Cathedral College. Later he also taught himself German. His talent for languages and the hard work he put into learning them helped him earn the reputation of a first-rate scholar. The familiarity with theological literature in French, German, and Italian, which his writings exhibit, is worthy of admiration.

In 1960, after finishing his philosophy studies at Dunwoodie and earning a Bachelor of Arts, together with his best friend, David Tracy, and four other classmates, Komonchak was chosen to continue his studies in Rome. The North American College became their new seminary, and Gregorian University was where they studied theology. Courses consisted of lectures in Latin. They were delivered to hundreds of seminarians without any non-seminarians in attendance. The course of studies followed the neoscholastic sequence of one year of fundamental theology followed by three years of dogmatic theology. Courses were taught from theological manuals or notes written by professors. Semesters concluded with oral exams conducted in Latin. While there was little contact with primary sources, and professors depended heavily on Aquinas, Komonchak noticed a difference in the quality of education between the Gregorian and Dunwoodie. He found that his professors in Rome excelled in the depth of their inquiries and their attempts to exploit the achievements of modern Catholic scholarship. He especially appreciated Bernard Lonergan, René Latourelle, Juan Alfaro,

---

emeritus at the University of Chicago. Ordained in 1963, he received his doctorate from the Gregorian University, Rome, in 1965. He has published extensively in the area of foundational theology and hermeneutics.

Zoltan Alszeghy, and Maurizio Flick for making their own efforts at systematic understanding.³

Komonchak's studies at the Gregorian coincided in part with the Second Vatican Council. He had the opportunity to watch at close hand the two years of the council's preparation (1960–1962) and the unfolding of its first two sessions (1962–1963). On the opening day of the council, dressed in a cassock, Komonchak joined an entourage around one bishop and was able to get past the Swiss Guard and make it all the way to the front door of St. Peter's where he watched the bishops and John XXIII enter the Basilica. It was certainly exciting to be in Rome at the time of such a momentous event. Komonchak followed what was happening at the council through the available sources, such as the summaries of the daily discussions at the council provided by the conciliar press office. He was aware of tensions between conservatives and liberals and commented on them in letters he sent home. Several of his professors were involved in the work of the council as theological experts, but in their lectures they commented on it only minimally. Komonchak was ordained in Rome at the Chiesa San Ignazio on December 18, 1963 for the Archdiocese of New York. He graduated with a Licentiate in Theology (STL) in the spring semester of 1964.

The studies in Rome were intellectually revitalizing for him. When he arrived in the fall of 1960, he still saw himself being anti-scholastic and anti-Thomist, preferring to study Scripture and the Fathers. Four years in Rome, however, reconciled him with Aquinas, and encountering the Canadian Jesuit Bernard Lonergan (1904–1984) made the crucial difference. Komonchak took four courses with him: on the Incarnation, the Trinity, theological method, and operative grace in Aquinas. The last two were seminars. In Lonergan, Komonchak encountered a first-rate mind at work, which gave him hope that the Catholic intellectual tradition was still alive. Komonchak credits Lonergan for saving his intellectual soul. During the summer break after his second year in Rome, when the seminarians were not allowed to return home, Komonchak undertook a formidable challenge. He decided to read Lonergan's *Insight* cover-to-cover (almost 800 pages), which he succeeded in doing in just eight days. Reading that dense and complex theory of human understanding, Komonchak realized, that one of the main weaknesses of his philosophical education at Dunwoodie was that it did not even attempt to show that metaphysical concepts referred to events within one's own consciousness and that one might seek to verify their occurrences within oneself. In Lonergan, Komonchak also found a mentor. He and his friend Tracy met with their professor regularly and discussed an array of topics.

3. Komonchak, "Future of Theology," (2004) 19.

Komonchak returned from Rome in the summer of 1964 and was appointed a curate of St. Bartholomew Parish in Yonkers, New York. He also secured a position teaching theology at the College of New Rochelle. In the spring of 1967, he was given permission to do doctoral studies, but those plans were put on hold when he received an appointment to the faculty at St. Joseph's seminary, where he had begun his theological training a decade earlier. At the age of twenty-eight, without a terminal degree, he found himself an assistant professor of systematic theology, teaching students who were just a few years younger than himself. He remained at Dunwoodie for the next ten years, during which he taught mainly ecclesiology, but also Christology, anthropology, and the theology of creation. During most of that time (1970–1977), he also served as chaplain to the Ursuline community at the College of New Rochelle. He did not give up on doctoral studies, however. While on the faculty at St. Joseph's, he enrolled at the Union Theological Seminary in New York, first earning a Master's degree (1969) and then a PhD (1976). He wrote his dissertation on Newman's discovery of the visible church, under the direction of Cyril Richardson.

The completion of his doctorate coincided with a level of dissatisfaction with his position at Dunwoodie. He applied to various Catholic colleges and universities. The Department of Religion and Religious Education at the Catholic University of America offered him a position, and he started there in the fall of 1977. From 1996 until his retirement in 2009, he held the John and Gertrude Hubbard Chair of Religious Studies. During the forty-five years of nearly full-time teaching, Komonchak also taught at Princeton Theological Seminary, the University of Notre Dame, Boston College, and Yale University.

In his teaching and writing Komonchak has concentrated on ecclesiology, the Second Vatican Council, the thought of John Henry Newman and John Courtney Murray, and modern theology in general. He has written prolifically, publishing more than 160 articles, essays and book chapters. Komonchak also published one monograph,[4] one collection of essays,[5] and has edited seven books.[6] A chronological glance through his bibliography reveals that different issues and topics have occupied his interest during his nearly fifty years of research and writing.[7] In the 1970s, Komonchak addressed various topics, such as the authority of the ecclesial magisterium,

---

4. Komonchak, *Who Are the Church?* (2008).

5. Komonchak, *Foundations in Ecclesiology* (1995).

6. Komonchak et al., *New Dictionary of Theology* (1987); Komonchak et al., *Reception of Vatican II* (1987); Alberigo and Komonchak, *History of Vatican II* (1995–2006).

7. For Komonchak's bibliography, see pp. 167–78.

the theology of liberation, ministry in the church, and the relationship of the church and world. During the 1980s, he focused on foundational issues in ecclesiology and on the theology of the local church. The core of his vision in these areas comes from this period.

In 1980, Komonchak attended a seminar on the reception of Vatican II, held in Bologna. This entrée into the European theological and historical milieu led to his membership on the international team directed by Giuseppe Alberigo that was to produce the five-volume *History of Vatican II*. This project became Komonchak's scholarly focus throughout the 1990s and the first part of the 2000s. He became the project's English-language editor and contributed two chapters.[8]

Since his retirement from full-time teaching, Komonchak has devoted himself to continued research, writing, and lecturing. He has been working on several projects, one of which is an English translation of the preparatory documents for Vatican II.

Major Influences

Komonchak belongs to a generation of theologians who witnessed a shift in Catholic theology. While they were trained entirely or in part in the neoscholastic tradition and its manuals, their theological careers as teachers and scholars began to unfold in a different context, one ushered in by the Second Vatican Council. Neoscholasticism was in many ways challenged at Vatican II, which on a number of topics bypassed that approach and followed instead the insights of the *ressourcement* theologians. Komonchak's generation was given the task of joining forces with the theologians whose work made Vatican II possible—a good number of whom were his generation's teachers—to be the pioneers of the council's reception and the renewal it called for.

In the summer of 1964, when Komonchak returned from his four years of studies at the Gregorian University, he did not aspire to be an ecclesiologist. In fact, teaching ecclesiology ranked rather low among the things Komonchak wanted to do. The only course in ecclesiology he took in Rome was a course in apologetics taught by Francis Sullivan, S.J. In the spring of 1961, the course was presented in a typical neoscholastic fashion. It was designed to demonstrate that Jesus founded the church, gave it a hierarchical and monarchical structure, and that this church was to be found in the Roman Catholic Church. The course also contained a treatment of

---

8. See note 12 below.

the theology of the teaching office.[9] Komonchak never took a course that treated the dogmatic elements of the church. Needless to say, when in the late summer of 1967 he was asked to teach ecclesiology at Dunwoodie, he felt underprepared for the task. He began to fill in the gaps in his ecclesiological training, and the sources to which he turned at the time became the most significant influences on his own thinking about the church.

Vatican II

It will come as no surprise that Komonchak's thinking about the church has been shaped by the teachings of the Second Vatican Council. Komonchak immersed himself in the study of the council and over time became one of the foremost authorities on the council's history, theology, and interpretation. He has published numerous articles and book chapters that explore the topic of the hermeneutics of the council.[10] During the 1990s and 2000s, he took part in a massive international project dedicated to the history of Vatican II. The project was overseen by Giuseppe Alberigo and sponsored by the John XXIII Foundation for Religious Sciences, which is an Italian research institution in Bologna (Fondazione per le scienze religiose Giovanni XXIII).[11] Komonchak was the editor of the English-language edition of the work and a contributor to two volumes.[12]

Several of the affirmations made at Vatican II strongly influenced Komonchak's ecclesiology. First, the council brought the inner, spiritual dimension of the church into the center of ecclesiology. Second, the council approached the question of who belongs to the church not through the category of the church's membership, but through the notion of degrees of incorporation. The advantage of the latter approach was that it could account for the council's affirmations that many elements of the church exist in other Christian churches and communities and that the communion characteristic of the church of Christ exceeds the boundaries of the Catholic

---

9. Typically, professors published their courses in the form of a theological manual. See Sullivan, *De ecclesia*.

10. Komonchak, "Enlightenment and the Construction," (1985) 31–59; "Interpreting the Second Vatican Council," (1987) 81–90; "Vatican II and the Encounter," (1994) 76–99; "Interpreting the Council," (1995) 17–36; "Modernity and the Construction," (1997) 353–85; "Vatican II as an 'Event,'" (1999) 337–52; "40 Years after Vatican II," (2002) 11–14; "Benedict XVI and the Interpretation," (2007) 323–37; "Novelty in Continuity," (2009) 5–6; "Interpreting the Council," (2012) 164–72.

11. See Alberigo and Komonchak, *History of Vatican II*.

12. Komonchak, "Struggle for the Council," 167–356; "Toward an Ecclesiology of Communion," 1–93.

Church. The broadening of ecclesial belonging led the council to nuance the simple identification of the Roman Catholic Church with the church of Christ hitherto operative in Catholic ecclesiology. Third, Vatican II made an important attempt at recovery of the theology of the local church. Fourth, the council rehabilitated the place and the role of the laity in the church. Lastly, the council rethought the relation of the church and the world. The council entered into *dialogue with* the modern world, rather than undertaking a generic discussion *of* the world.[13] In all these areas, Vatican II and its ecclesiology influenced Komonchak's thinking about the church and functioned as a springboard for his ecclesiological investigations.

Bernard Lonergan

The single theologian who has exerted the most influence on Komonchak's thinking about the church is Bernard Lonergan. The Canadian Jesuit was known mostly for his work on the theory of human understanding[14] and on method in theology,[15] although he also wrote extensively in Latin in the area of Christology and Trinitarian theology.[16] Studying Lonergan's work, Komonchak learned a great deal about theology and the dynamics of human knowing; he found particularly compelling Lonergan's anthropology and his analysis of the structure and dynamism of human consciousness. He also learned intellectual courage, that is, that he should read as widely and in as many areas as he could.

Lonergan was not an ecclesiologist and never produced a theological study specifically on the church. Yet in his *Insight* and *Method in Theology* Komonchak found categories of heuristic value pertinent to ecclesiology. They helped Komonchak envision how one could lay foundations for ecclesiology as a systematic understanding of the church. From Lonergan, Komonchak appropriated the distinction between common sense and theory and applied it to his conception of ecclesiology as a critical, systematic theological discipline. Lonergan's theology of conversion inspired Komonchak's conception of a methodological shift in ecclesiology, that is, of re-envisioning the church in terms of a human community marked by transformed intersubjectivity. Komonchak's understanding of the church as a community of common meaning and value, and as a process of self-communication,

13. See Komonchak, "Ecclesiology of Vatican II," (1999) 763–68; "Significance of Vatican Council II," (2000) 69–92.
14. Lonergan, *Insight*.
15. Lonergan, *Method in Theology*.
16. Lonergan, *De Verbo Incarnato*; *De Deo Trino*.

and his insistence that ecclesiologists engage social sciences have roots in Lonergan too.[17]

Lastly, Lonergan influenced Komonchak in developing a connection between the church and redemption. At the beginning of one of his articles, Komonchak reveals how this came about.[18] He explains that as students in Rome, David Tracy and he used to visit Lonergan and "pester him with questions."[19] On one occasion they inquired about redemption and the four Aristotelian causes. Lonergan's answer surprised them. He explained that those categories were not adequate to articulate the reality of redemption and suggested that a theory of history and historical categories were needed instead. At the time, Komonchak did not understand what Lonergan had in mind. A few years later, when Komonchak was already teaching ecclesiology, he reread the epilogue to Lonergan's *Insight*, and one section stood out in particular:

> It may be asked in what department of theology the historical aspect of development might be treated, and I would like to suggest that it may possess peculiar relevance to a treatise on the Mystical Body of Christ. For in any theological treatise a distinction may be drawn between a material and a formal element: the material element is supplied by Scriptural and patristic texts and by dogmatic pronouncements; the formal element, that makes a treatise a treatise, consists in the pattern of terms and relations through which the materials may be embraced in a single, coherent view. Thus the formal element in the treatise on grace consists in theorems on the supernatural, and the formal element in the treatise on the Blessed Trinity consists in theorems on the notions of procession, relation, and person. Now while the Scriptural, patristic, and dogmatic materials for a treatise on the Mystical Body have been assembled, I would incline to the opinion that its formal element remains incomplete as long as it fails to draw upon a theory of history.... It may be that the contemporary crisis of human living and human values demands of the theologian, in addition to treatises on the unique and to treatises on the universal common to many instances, a treatise on the concrete universal that is mankind in the concrete and cumulative consequences of the acceptance or rejection of the message of the Gospel. And as the remote possibility of thought on the concrete universal lies in the insight that grasps the

---

17. These points will be discussed in detail in the next chapter.
18. See Komonchak, "Lonergan and the Church," 77–78.
19. Komonchak, "Lonergan and the Church," 77.

intelligible in the sensible, so its proximate possibility resides in a theory of development that can envisage not only natural and intelligent progress but also sinful decline, and not only progress and decline but also supernatural recovery.[20]

This text became for Komonchak one of the most important statements of Lonergan on the church. Komonchak began to see the connection between Lonergan's remarks back in Rome about redemption and the church—that redemption had to be treated from the perspective of historical causality, as the effect of Christ on history. The formal element, which according to Lonergan was still incomplete in ecclesiology, had to be a theory of history. Redemption then had to be approached as a historical phenomenon in the treatise on the church, where the church had to be conceived as a community "through which Christ continues to have a redemptive impact on history."[21]

Unexpected Influences

Besides Lonergan, the most significant influence on Komonchak's thinking about the church came—perhaps surprisingly—from several US Protestant theologians: Claude Welch, James Gustafson, John Knox, and Langdon Gilkey.[22] Their writings helped Komonchak think through the changes in Catholic ecclesiology brought about by Vatican II; in particular, they helped him articulate the key questions that pertain to ecclesiology. Most importantly, their reflections on the church showed Komonchak how to express the human and social realities of the church while avoiding the pitfalls of sociological and theological reductionism.

Welch, Gustafson, Knox, and Gilkey helped Komonchak identify the central challenge that ecclesiology faces and offered important insight to

20. Lonergan, *Insight*, 742–43.

21. Komonchak, *Foundations in Ecclesiology*, viii. See also Komonchak, "Lonergan and the Church," (1988) 88.

22. Claude Welch (1922–2009) was a historical theologian and an ordained Methodist minister specializing in Karl Barth and nineteenth-century theology. Welch taught at Princeton, Yale, and the Graduate Theological Union in Berkeley, California. James M. Gustafson (born 1925) is a prominent theologian mostly known for his work in theological ethics. Now retired, he held teaching posts at Yale, the University of Chicago, and Emory University. John Knox (1900–1990) was a Methodist and Episcopalian theologian. His teaching career included Emory University, the University of Chicago Divinity School, and Union Theological Seminary (New York) among others. His scholarship focused on the New Testament and early Christianity. He was the editor of *Christian Century* and the *Journal of Religion*. Langdon B. Gilkey (1919–2004) was an ecumenical theologian. A student of Reinhold Niebuhr and Paul Tillich, his teaching career included Vanderbilt and Chicago Divinity Schools. Gilkey was a prolific author

address it. Komonchak saw their work as a reaction to an overemphasis on the invisible dimension of the church in Protestant ecclesiologies and as an attempt to recover the sense of the church as a created reality and a human community. In the latter part of 1960s when Komonchak began teaching ecclesiology and became acquainted with the work of these theologians, it seemed to him that Catholic ecclesiology was moving in the opposite direction, that is, of emphasizing the church's transcendent and spiritual dimensions while leaving the connection between these dimensions and the concrete communities of believers unarticulated.[23] These Protestant theologians captured Komonchak's attention by making "serious attempts to explore theologically the human and sociological aspects of the Church."[24] Conceiving the church as a human and social reality became an important part of Komonchak's ecclesiology as well.

In the work of Welch and Knox, Komonchak found a compelling account of the human reality of the church.[25] Welch was critical of ecclesiological one-sidedness, by which he meant the treatment of the church as wholly discontinuous from other social groups, communities, and institutions. The latter could be subjected to sociological scrutiny while the church was considered exempt from it. To Welch, however, the church appeared very much like other human communities and could even be mistaken as being nothing more than that.[26] He argued that the church must be seen as a created reality that "stands unequivocally on our side of the Creator/creature distinction."[27] Welch articulated his understanding of the human reality of the church most clearly in the following statement, which relates the church to the kingdom of God:

> The church is not itself the objective rule of God. Though one might affirm that the kingdom is apprehended only in the church, that to apprehend the Kingdom is to be in the church, or even that God's realm is coextensive with the church . . . he [sic] must still say that the church stands over against God's rule as a "subjective pole," as the community which acknowledges and lives in response to God's rule. The church may be fully dependent on God's act, but it is not simply God acting. It is a people believing, worshipping, obeying, witnessing. Thus we can and must make fast at the outset our understanding of the

---

23. Komonchak, *Foundations in Ecclesiology*, viii.
24. Komonchak, "History and Social Theory," (1981) 4–7.
25. See Welch, *Reality of the Church*; Knox, *Early Church*.
26. Welch, *Reality of the Church*, 19.
27. Welch, *Reality of the Church*, 43.

church as a body or community of human beings, albeit existing in response to the activity of God. In this sense, the ontology of the church means in the first instance the humanly subjective pole of the relationship.[28]

Komonchak found a similar emphasis on the human reality of the church in the work of John Knox. Knox argued that the church should to be seen as a human response to God's action in Christ, in fact, as the "the sole residuum" of the event of Christ. Knox explains:

> The only difference between the world as it had been just after the event [of Christ] and the world as it had been just before is that the church was now in existence. A new kind of human community had emerged; a new society had come into being. There was absolutely nothing besides. This new community held and prized vivid memories of the event in which it had begun. It had a new faith; that is, it saw the nature of the world and of God in a new light. It found in its own life the grounds—indeed, anticipatory fulfillments—of a magnificent hope. But the memory, the faith, and the hope were all its own; they had neither existence nor ground outside the community. Only the church really existed. Except for the church the event had not occurred.[29]

These accounts of the human reality of the church by Welch and Knox had a strong impact on Komonchak. Thinking about the church in terms of a human reality became a trademark of his own ecclesiological vision.

Welch also warned against a simple parallelism between the nature of the church and the human nature of Christ. The classical Christological doctrine states that the subject of the human nature of Christ is the second person of the Trinity. This, however, cannot be asserted about the church. The key point for Welch is that while fully dependent on God, the church is not God but a human community responding to God's call.[30] Komonchak found this point of critical importance and made it central to his thinking about the church.

The work of James Gustafson provided Komonchak with an additional conceptual tool to articulate what the central problem in ecclesiology is. In his *Treasure in Earthen Vessels*, Gustafson integrated social and theological approaches to ecclesiology.[31] Like Welch, he constructed an interpretation of the church as a human and social reality. Komonchak found particularly

28. Welch, *Reality of the Church*, 48.
29. Knox, *Early Church*, 45.
30. Knox, *Early Church*, 45.
31. See Gustafson, *Treasure in Earthen Vessels*.

relevant Gustafson's discussion of theological reductionism: an "exclusive use of Biblical and doctrinal language in the interpretation of the Church."[32] Gustafson thinks that theological reductionism is methodologically flawed, resting on an assumption that the church "is so absolutely unique in character that it can be understood only in its own private language,"[33] implying thus that there is no commonality between the laws that govern the life of the church and those that govern human communities in history. Gustafson wonders whether such interpretations of the church refer to anything "historical and social in character."[34] Because it fails to account for the human elements in the life of the church, Gustafson deems theological reductionism inadequate to the full reality of the church. He considers the task of an ecclesiologist in part "to make theologically intelligible the human forms and processes that can be understood and interpreted from a social perspective."[35] Komonchak found Gustafson's criticism of theological reductionism compelling and appropriated it to express his reservation about some methodological choices Catholic ecclesiologists made in the twentieth century.

In Langdon Gilkey's *How the Church Can Minister to the World without Losing Itself*, Komonchak found an intellectually stimulating discussion of the semantic problems involved in a discourse on the church.[36] Gilkey argued that ecclesiology is marked by disjointedness between theological language about the church and the way the church is experienced by both believers and outsiders. With regard to some highly theological statements about the church, Gilkey remarked:

> One cannot help wondering what possible entity on land or sea is the referent for these flattering words. Is this the church as it *is*, and if so what does the present tense mean here—for even ecumenical theologians have never found a church in actual practice remotely resembling these descriptions. Does it represent a present Aristotelean "essence" of the church lying within the actual churches; a Platonic idea of the church in heaven in the divine mind; a Kantian law or imperative for the church to realize in future history; or finally, an eschatological church to come at the end of time? And what sort of existence do these "faithful congregations" enjoy, for surely they are not the people who, with ourselves, make up the church on the corner? What angelic congregations hear the "purely preached Word" and

32. Gustafson, *Treasure in Earthen Vessels*, 100.
33. Gustafson, *Treasure in Earthen Vessels*, 100.
34. Gustafson, *Treasure in Earthen Vessels*, 105.
35. Gustafson, *Treasure in Earthen Vessels*, 105.
36. See Gilkey, *How the Church Can Minister*.

celebrate the "duly enacted Sacraments" that characterize this true church? For little of our preaching and few services can be so defined. Such descriptions of the nature of the church make good theological reading, but one closes the book... wondering what community in what galaxy has just been described.[37]

Gilkey diagnosed the problem as a "category mistake," by which he meant that "symbols expressing the *relation* of God to the life of the existing churches have been mistaken for the substantial *elements* out of which the church is itself composed."[38] In other words, the church is described not as if it existed out of concrete human beings attempting to live out their Gospel commitments, but rather as if it was made up by biblical symbols themselves. Like Welch and Gustafson, Gilkey was critical of ecclesiologists who failed to account sufficiently for the human and social elements of the church. Consequently, such interpretations of the church tended to be abstractions in the sense that their referent is purely conceptual. Gilkey argued that ecclesiologists ought to speak of the church on the one hand as a human and social reality, but on the other as "one with a peculiar vertical or religious relation with which God works quite uniquely for the salvation of the total human community."[39] Otherwise, Gilkey believed, theological language about the church will refer to some other church than the one actually existing and will therefore be incapable to guide the life of the church.[40]

As will be clear from the next chapter, Welch, Gustafson, Knox, and Gilkey exerted influence on Komonchak in several ways. First, he came to conceive the central challenge of ecclesiology as understanding "how the quite human could be the locus of the quite transcendent."[41] Second, he came to think of theological reductionism as one of the main problems that has prevented a more successful integration of Vatican II's vision of the church. Third, the importance these theologians placed on conceiving of the church as a human and social reality helped Komonchak see why ecclesiologists should incorporate the social sciences into their interpretations of the church.

Influences from the Social Sciences

Lastly, in addition to theologians, social theorists also influenced Komonchak's thinking about the church, especially Peter Berger, Thomas Luckman,

37. Gilkey, *How the Church Can Minister*, 133–34.
38. Gilkey, *How the Church Can Minister*, 134.
39. Gilkey, *How the Church Can Minister*, 138.
40. See Gilkey, *How the Church Can Minister*, 140.
41. Komonchak, *Foundations in Ecclesiology*, viii.

Anthony Giddens, Richard Bernstein, and John Searle. For instance, from their work Komonchak appropriated the notions of "intersubjectivity" and "reification," which became crucial for his understanding of the church's genesis and ontology. He also drew a parallel between Berger's and Luckman's view of society as a human and social product and between the church as a human, social and ecclesial product. As the next chapter will show, once Komonchak came to appreciate the human and social reality of the church, the work of social scientists became of obvious interest. He came to the conclusion that one cannot construct a theology of the church adequately without an engagement with the social sciences.

Komonchak numbers among those theologians who were the first to appreciate the importance of the social sciences for their work. They embraced the idea that theology is not the full science of human existence.[42] The foundations for ecclesiology Komonchak constructed urge his fellow ecclesiologists to incorporate insights from the social sciences in their interpretations of the church.

---

42. See Lonergan, *Method in Theology*, 364.

3

Method in Ecclesiology

IN THE SUMMER OF 1966, those who were preparing to teach a course in ecclesiology faced a considerable challenge. They knew that they needed to bring the course up-to-date with the teachings of the Second Vatican Council, which had concluded just a few months earlier on December 8, 1965. Yet they could not simply take their previous syllabus and make room for the ecclesiology of Vatican II. Pouring new wine into old wineskins did not seem a viable option.

The shift in ecclesiology that Vatican II effected was different from the one produced by Pius XII's encyclical *Mystici corporis* two decades earlier.[1] There, the pope officially sanctioned the view of the church as the mystical body of Christ, which had recently gained in prominence. This was an important step, because it signaled an openness to something different than merely a juridical approach to understanding the church. Still, the encyclical presented the theology of the mystical body within the dominant ecclesiological framework of *societas perfecta*. The status quo had not changed. Therefore, in the summer of 1943, professors could simply add a section on the mystical body of Christ to their courses, and they were up-to-date. They did not need to rethink thoroughly how to structure their course in ecclesiology.

The Second Vatican Council, however, was different; it rendered the neoscholastic approach to understanding the church no longer feasible. Whereas the neoscholastic manuals of ecclesiology presented the church as a static, juridical institution, Vatican II presented the church as a historical, dynamic community. After the council, most theologians responded to this situation by focusing their attention primarily on the newly recovered

---

1. The encyclical was issued on June 29, 1943.

biblical and theological dimensions of the church, which had previously been in the shadow of its institutional dimensions. Only a few made a sustained effort to rethink *how* to theologize about the church in the ecclesiological climate produced by Vatican II. Joseph Komonchak was one of these theologians. This chapter discusses and critically evaluates Komonchak's contribution to method in ecclesiology, especially as it concerns his vision of ecclesiology as a critical, systematic theological discipline.

Why Method?

Komonchak's most distinctive and substantive contribution to ecclesiology concerns its foundations or method. No theologian writing in English has thought through the foundational questions in ecclesiology as thoroughly as he has. Even a cursory reading of Komonchak's articles reveals that methodological issues are never absent from his thinking about the church.[2] Essentially, the great service Komonchak has done for contemporary ecclesiology consists in laying out the foundations for a theology of the church that surpasses the level of images and models to reach the level of theory. Taking up Bernard Lonergan's challenge from the epilogue of his *Insight*,[3] Komonchak worked out several formal categories, which—compared to other systematic disciplines such as Trinitarian theology, Christology, or anthropology—ecclesiology was lacking. Komonchak's vision of the foundations in ecclesiology is comprehensive, interconnecting multiple issues that together form the building blocks for ecclesiology's critical, systematic character.

Method refers to the means used to arrive at an interpretation; it refers to the way theologians go about making their claims. Method thus belongs to the very foundations of the discipline of theology. As Roger Haight explains:

---

2. The most important of Komonchak's writings in which he engages methodological issues are: *Foundations in Ecclesiology*, (1995); *Who Are the Church?* (2008); "History and Social Theory," (1981) 1–53, [reprinted in *Foundations*, 3–46]; "Lonergan and the Task," (1981) 265–73 [reprinted in *Foundations*, 47–56]; "Ecclesiology and Social Theory," (1981) 262–83 [reprinted in *Foundations*, 57–76]; "Ministry and the Local Church," (1981) 56–82; "Towards a Theology," (1986) 1–41; "Church: God's Gift," (1987) 735–41; "Church," (1988) 222–36 [reprinted as "Lonergan and the Church," in *Foundations*, 77–94]; "Epistemology of Reception," (1997) 180–203; "People of God," (1998) 91–102; "Lonergan and Post-Conciliar Ecclesiology," (2008) 165–83. For the articles reprinted in *Foundations in Ecclesiology*, my references will be to *Foundations*.

3. See chapter 2, pp. 58–59.

Method involves the premises and presuppositions of a theologian's position. Method concerns the starting point and the elementary data the theologian appeals to in taking a position. Method includes the logic, the kind of argument and its coherence, through which the theologian understands experience. In other words, a theologian's method generates the position he or she takes, so that beneath every position taken lies the method that generated the position.[4]

Theological method, however, is not something mechanical that by itself predetermines a theologian's position on a particular topic. Two theologians who employ similar methods can arrive at different conclusions. A survey of various theologians over time would reveal that, in spite of its centrality and importance, there is no one method that theologians agree on and follow. A non-specialist might find it surprising that theologians do not share a set of common presuppositions and working principles. Theology is a discipline of many methods.[5]

Komonchak's writings on the church attend to the topic of method or foundations in ecclesiology for several reasons. First, historically method has been a neglected topic in ecclesiology in part because of the ideological role ecclesiology has played, especially since the time of the Reformation. Second, an extraordinary interest in the subject of the local church after Vatican II, in contrast to its wide neglect prior to the council, needed both an explanation and a validation.[6] Third, method in ecclesiology has been a prominent subject in Komonchak's writings on the church because he has needed to ground one of his key claims, namely, that ecclesiology should begin and center upon the local church. It should also be noted that Komonchak's attention to method in ecclesiology intersected with a general interest in questions of theological method in the 1970s and 1980s, as reflected in such authors as Bernard Lonergan, David Tracy, Francis Schüssler Fiorenza, Wolfhart Pannenberg, and George Lindbeck.[7]

---

4. Haight, "Critical Witness," 187.

5. Haight, *Dynamics of Theology*, 189. For a comprehensive introduction to method in theology see, for instance, Schüssler Fiorenza, "Systematic Theology," 1–78.

6. Komonchak, "Toward a Theology," 1.

7. See Lonergan, *Method in Theology*; Tracy, *Blessed Rage for Order*; Schüssler Fiorenza, *Foundational Theology*; Pannenberg, *Theology and Philosophy of Science*; Lindbeck, *Nature of Doctrine*.

Diagnosis of Deficiencies in Catholic Ecclesiology after Vatican II

Komonchak's engagement with method in ecclesiology stemmed from reservations he had about certain developments that took place in Catholic ecclesiology after the Second Vatican Council.[8] As I showed in chapter one, the period from the nineteenth century until the eve of Vatican II saw a gradual retrieval and reintroduction of theological insights from the first millennium into Catholic ecclesial consciousness. The council endorsed this movement of theological renewal, which brought about a shift in Catholic ecclesiology. Fundamentally, the shift consisted in a recovery of the spiritual, liturgical, and communal dimensions of the church, which had been long neglected, and in giving them priority over the previously dominant ecclesiology, which focused on the church's institutional and juridical elements. After the council, most theologians showed a preference for the newly recovered approaches, and the institutional approach lost its place of prominence. This was an understandable reaction against the almost exclusive attention of the neoscholastic manuals to the church as a perfect society. While Komonchak considers the recovery of these neglected dimensions of the church to be a significant gain, he has also argued that it has not been without problems. He has identified three issues in post-Vatican II ecclesiology that he sees as key counter-forces that have prevented a more successful integration of the council's vision of the church.

Models Dot Not Go Far Enough

One of the issues has been a lack of consensus on the kind of understanding ecclesiology should pursue. Komonchak's view has been that it ought to be "a unifying systematic understanding."[9] He observes, however, that for several reasons, both in Catholic theology in general and ecclesiology in particular, there has been a decline of interest in systematics. First, this is due to an insufficient acknowledgement of systematic exigence, namely, that while common sense categories of understanding suffice for everyday living, they do not suffice in all circumstances, and in some of these more theoretical categories are necessary. Second, there is a lack of agreement pertaining to the methods and categories of theology. Third, in the climate of theological pluralism which replaced the dominance of neoscholasticism, attempts to

---

8. See Komonchak, "History and Social Theory," 3–12; "Ministry and the Local Church," 65; "Towards a Theology," 2–4; "Church: God's Gift," 737.

9. Komonchak, "Ecclesiology and Social Theory," 65.

construct a theology that aims at unifying claims is often perceived as unduly impositional and thus theologically suspect.[10]

For Komonchak, the models approach of Avery Dulles exemplifies an ecclesiological method that does not pursue sufficiently a systematic understanding of the church.[11] In his *Models of the Church*, Dulles attempted to bring some order into Catholic ecclesiology, which after Vatican II was marked by a plurality unparalleled in history.[12] He presented several theologies of the church, which after the council displaced the previously dominant institutional approach. Inspired by H. R. Niebuhr's *Christ and Culture*, Dulles attempted a version of comparative ecclesiology. He constructed five "approaches," "types," or—as he preferred to call them—"models" of the church and thought that a balanced ecclesiology would incorporate the major affirmations of each model. He examined Scripture, early Christian tradition, and *Lumen gentium*, which provided a variety of images or symbols for the church. Initially, Dulles examined them as first-order expressions and then subjected them to a second-order reflection, which yielded five models of the church: institution, mystical communion, sacrament, herald, and servant. In the second edition of his book (1987), Dulles added "community of disciples" as a sixth model. His understanding was that the models function in a synthetic and heuristic way; namely, they express a variety of aspects of the church and provide questions for further exploration. Dulles proceeded from an assumption that since the church is a mystery, it is not possible to speak about it directly, but only analogically. Methodologically, this ruled out the possibility that an ecclesiology would start with clear concepts or definitions.[13] Furthermore, this assumption led Dulles to conclude that it was not possible to integrate models into one synthetic vision, but rather that an ecclesiologist had to work simultaneously with different models.[14]

Dulles's models approach has had a great impact on contemporary ecclesiology. Many still find it to be a helpful introduction into the ecclesiological landscape created by Vatican II and use it in ecclesiology courses. The key strength of Dulles's models approach lays in deactivating the dominance of the institutional model on Catholic ecclesiology and in opening one's imagination to other ways of thinking about the church.

10. Komonchak, "Ecclesiology and Social Theory," 65.

11. See, for instance, Komonchak, "History and Social Theory," 4–12; "Synod of 1985," 342–43; "Church: God's Gift," 737–38; "People of God," 91–95; *Who Are the Church?*, 23–34

12. See Dulles, *Models of the Church*.

13. Dulles followed Yves Congar and Michael Schmaus on this point. See Congar, "Peut-on définir l'Église?," 21–44; Schmaus, *Dogma*, 4:6–9.

14. Dulles, *Models of the Church*, 9–33.

Without dismissing it, Komonchak has argued that the models approach is methodologically inadequate because it sets the goal of systematic ecclesiology too low. Komonchak considers Dulles's distinction between first-order images and concepts and second-order models to be valid. He also agrees that no single model could capture adequately the mystery of the church. Komonchak argues, however, that Dulles is not always consistent in distinguishing between those two orders of language. More importantly, Komonchak does not agree with Dulles that because the images of the church are plural and at times incompatible with one another, their insights cannot be synthesized, and that one is consequently "condemned,"[15] as Dulles put it, to work with several models all at once.[16] For Komonchak, the task of an ecclesiologist is precisely,

> to attempt a critical and systematic integration of all the insights generated by the first-order images. For this, it is possible to use one or another of those images as the integrating principle either because of its prominence at the first-order level or because it offers particularly powerful integrative possibilities. "People of God" and "Body of Christ" are notable examples. But whether a governing image is used or a notion is employed that is not itself an image, the very task of systematic understanding is precisely to sublate the variety of first-order languages into a synthetic vision. For that reason, pluralism of first-order images is not itself an argument for pluralism in second-order syntheses, just as incompatibility at the level of images cannot itself justify the conclusion that second-order synthesis is impossible.[17]

With regard to method or foundations in ecclesiology, Komonchak thus differs from Dulles in two significant ways. The first concerns the kind of goal(s) systematic ecclesiology ought to pursue. Komonchak puts a stronger emphasis than Dulles on ecclesiology's task of integration. The second difference concerns the implications of the notion of mystery for theologizing. Komonchak seems to be more confident than Dulles about what second-order language can achieve.

Herwi Rikhof and Neil Ormerod expressed similar reservations about the models approach to ecclesiology. Like Komonchak, they have been critical of the thesis that because the church is a mystery, one cannot define it, but can only describe it by employing images, metaphors, and/or models.[18]

---

15. Dulles, *Models of the Church*, 196.
16. Komonchak, "People of God," 91–96; *Who Are the Church?*, 23–28.
17. Komonchak, "Synod of 1985," 343.
18. See Rikhof, *Concept of the Church*, 1–7, 193–236; Ormerod, *Re-Visioning the*

For Rikhof, the impossibility of defining it would mean not only that the church would become "a meaningless and vacuous term,"[19] but also that a systematic ecclesiology would be difficult to imagine. Rikhof contends that only if one made the church part of the Trinity or called it a mystery in an incoherent way could a case against the possibility of defining it be made. For Rikhof, understanding the church as mystery does not mean that what the church is cannot be expressed. Rikhof does not believe that appealing to the church's uniqueness can decide the question of whether or not the church can be defined, for the notion of uniqueness does not exclude classification. As he explains, "complete uniqueness, like complete newness, can neither be noticed nor conceived."[20] In a similar vein, Ormerod has argued that appeals to mystery "can never be used as an excuse for a flight from understanding."[21] For him, the models approach is not a proper method for ecclesiology. Like Komonchak, Rikhof and Ormerod do not believe that arguments from its mystery preclude the possibility of a real definition of the church.[22]

False Dichotomy between the Church as God's Gift and as Our Task

In Komonchak's view, another issue that hindered a more successful integration of the council's ecclesiology was a dichotomy between two conceptions of the church that became widespread among theologians. On the one hand, there was an understanding of the church as "something that we receive from God" and, on the other hand, the notion of the church as "something that we make."[23] For Komonchak, this either/or approach to thinking about the church is a false choice. Perhaps the most prominent advocate of this view has been Joseph Ratzinger.[24] He argues that implementation of Vatican II has been flawed in a number of ways and blames it on several mistaken ideas about the church. His famous book of interviews, provides an insight into his thinking.[25] In the context of discussing the notion of *com-*

Church, 14–17.

19. Rikhof, *Concept of the Church*, 216.
20. Rikhof, *Concept of the Church*, 220.
21. Ormerod, *Re-Visioning the Church*, 17n57.
22. Another criticism of the models approach is Healy, *Church, World*, 25–51.
23. Komonchak, "Church: God's Gift," 738–39.
24. A close examination of Komonchak's writings reveals that Ratzinger has been among his most important interlocutors.
25. See Ratzinger and Messori, *Ratzinger Report*, 45–53.

munio sanctorum, Ratzinger explains that the bond between Christ and the members of the church (both living and dead) "is the real reason why the Church is not *our* Church, which we could dispose of as we please. She is, rather *his* Church. All that which is only *our* Church is not Church in the deep sense; it belongs to her human—hence secondary, transitory—aspect."[26] In another context, Ratzinger asserts:

> We must always bear in mind that the Church is not ours but his. Hence the "reform," the "renewals"—necessary as they may be—cannot exhaust themselves in a zealous activity on our part to erect new, sophisticated structures. The most that can come from a work of this kind is a Church that is "ours," to our measure, which might indeed be interesting but which, by itself, is nevertheless not the true Church, that which sustains us with the faith and gives us life with the sacrament.[27]

A similar either/or interpretation of the church also marked deliberations of the 1985 Extraordinary Synod of Bishops. The report of the German-language group, of which Ratzinger was a prominent member, states that when applied to the church, the widespread ideology of universal and technical feasibility (*machbarkeit*) "has created the tendency to want to make the church *ourselves*, instead of receiving it as a gift. The correct statement that 'We *are* the church' has often become the false statement that 'We *make* the church.'"[28]

Pope John Paul II convoked the synod to review, evaluate, and celebrate the achievement of the Second Vatican Council two decades after its close. Perhaps the key impact the synod has had on Catholic ecclesiology concerns the way its Final Report presented the council's vision of the church. The section of the report summarizing the council's teaching on the church focused on the notions of mystery and communion, but conspicuously left out the notion of the church as the People of God. Despite its prominent role in the documents of Vatican II, it appears that one reason the synod avoided this notion was its alleged association with a purely sociological conception of the church. This likely underlies the assertion in the synod's Final Report that "we cannot replace a false unilateral vision of the church as purely hierarchical with a new sociological conception which is also unilateral."[29]

---

26. Ratzinger and Messori, *Ratzinger Report*, 48.

27. Ratzinger and Messori, *Ratzinger Report*, 53. See also Ratzinger, "Ecclesiology of the Second Vatican Council," 244.

28. Quoted in Komonchak, "Church: God's Gift," 736.

29. Extraordinary Synod of Bishops, "Final Report," 446–47.

Komonchak considers the dichotomy between "the church we receive from God" and "the church we make" to be false. He argues that Catholic ecclesiology ought to affirm that the church is at once the *ecclesia de Trinitate* (the church that has its origin in the Triune God's plan of salvation), the church from above, and the *ecclesia ex hominibus* (the church made of people), the church we make. While the former requires that ecclesiologists not reduce the church merely to another human community, the latter demands that they keep in mind that God's church exists in history only insofar as women and men freely respond to the Gospel. Komonchak believes that interpreting the church in opposing terms as either God's gift or our task is not a genuine option for Catholic ecclesiology. He rejects the idea of one-sided sociological interpretations of the church as well as one-sided mystical views. Komonchak's position is that believers do make the church and that sociological approaches to understanding the church should not be rejected outright.[30]

Komonchak appeals to *Lumen gentium* 8 as an example of a more balanced vision of what the church is.[31] The relevant section of the article states:

> The one mediator, Christ, established and ever sustains here on earth his holy Church, the community of faith, hope and charity, as a visible organization through which he communicates truth and grace to all men [sic]. But, the society structured with hierarchical organs and the mystical body of Christ, the visible society and the spiritual community, the earthly Church and the Church endowed with heavenly riches, are not to be thought of as two realities. On the contrary, they form one complex reality which comes together from a human and a divine element. For this reason the Church is compared, in a powerful analogy, to the mystery of the incarnate Word. As the assumed nature, inseparably united to him, serves the divine Word as a living organ of salvation, so, in a somewhat similar way, does the social structure of the Church serve the Spirit of Christ who vivifies it, in the building up of the body (cf. Eph. 4:15).

The central point is that the church is one reality and that one ought not think about its divine and human dimensions as being separate from one another. Komonchak finds it regrettable, however, that except for a brief comparison to the Incarnation, the council did not attempt to explain how

---

30. Komonchak, "Church: God's Gift," 738-39; "Theological Debate," (1986) 56; "Synod of 1985," 335-36; Introduction to *Synode Extraordinaire*, 22.

31. See Komonchak, "Towards a Theology," 2; "Theological Debate," 56; "Synod of 1985," 335-36; "Church: God's Gift," 73; "People of God," 94; "Preparing for the New Millennium," 50; *Who Are the Church?*, 20-21.

the two sets of descriptions about the church refer to one and the same reality. One could interpret Komonchak's own ecclesiological project as an attempt to offer such an explanation.

Theological Reductionism

A third issue that Komonchak believes prevented a more successful integration of Vatican II's vision of the church is theological reductionism. Komonchak appropriated the concept from James Gustafson, who used it to disapprove of ecclesiologies that employed almost exclusively biblical and doctrinal language in their interpretation of the church.[32] Gustafson raised his criticism shortly before Vatican II and directed it at Protestant theologians. His main point was that ecclesiologies that constructed an understanding of the church almost entirely in biblical and doctrinal language failed to do justice to the church's human dimension.

Komonchak has found the notion of theological reductionism pertinent to the situation of Catholic ecclesiology after Vatican II. He argues that because of a heavy reliance on the newly recovered biblical and liturgical language, some recent ecclesiologies leave underdeveloped the relationship between the transcendent dimensions of the church and the concrete communities of believers. They do not communicate clearly, in Komonchak's view, that the remarkable theological language about the church, which Vatican II restored to the center of Catholic ecclesiology, has as its referent the concrete men and women who gather as the church. Komonchak does not fault the recent ecclesiologies for denying the human and societal dimensions of the church, but for perceiving them to be secondary in importance. Nevertheless, he argues that the failure to explore seriously the human and sociological aspects of the church makes these ecclesiologies susceptible to the charge of theological reductionism.[33] Komonchak suggests that the key question ecclesiologists should consider is whether there are any predications of the church that "do not require to be verified in some concrete created community."[34]

---

32. See Gustafson, *Treasure in Earthen Vessels*, 100–5.

33. Komonchak, *Foundations in Ecclesiology*, viii; "History and Social Theory," 5–6; "Toward a Theology," 4–6; "Church: God's Gift," 738.

34. Komonchak, "Epistemology of Reception," 187.

The Central Challenge for Ecclesiology

In light of these reservations concerning the state of Catholic ecclesiology after Vatican II, Komonchak came to realize that the central challenge of ecclesiology is to bridge the gap between the grand theological claims about the church found in Scripture and tradition, and the way the church exists concretely as communities of believers.[35] He began to conceive the central challenge or task of ecclesiology as an attempt "to understand how the quite human could be the locus of the quite transcendent,"[36] or, in other words, how to understand the church as one reality comprised of two dimensions: human and divine.

This challenge has never been absent from ecclesiology, but it became particularly noticeable in the course of efforts aimed at the renewal of Catholic ecclesiology in the nineteenth and the first half of the twentieth centuries. From the inception of formal ecclesiological treatises in the fourteenth century, the focus was primarily on the church as a society and a hierarchical institution. This approach to ecclesiology privileged the church's visible dimension, and its invisible interior dimension was neglected. When the latter became of serious interest to ecclesiologists, expressing adequately how the two dimensions relate, and especially how they are two aspects of just one reality, became a considerable challenge. For instance, inspired by the work of Möhler and Scheeben, various theologians in the first half of the twentieth century recovered the spiritual dimension of the church by reviving the idea of the church as the mystical body of Christ. While this was welcomed as a needed corrective to a one-sided institutional and juridical approach to ecclesiology, criticisms were also raised that the theology of the mystical body left unclear the relationship between the visible and the invisible aspects of the church.

The challenge that ecclesiologists face is similar to the challenge that lay beneath the Christological disputes of the first millennium. While Christians by and large agreed that both divinity and humanity ought to be predicated of Jesus, it took some time to reach conceptual clarity about how Jesus' two natures form just one reality, one subject. After several controversies, the formula of the Council of Chalcedon (451) became the Christological standard for most Christian understanding of who Jesus is. The council taught that the union of the two natures takes place in the person of the eternal Son of God, the second person of the Trinity. Divinity and humanity are predicated of him. The similarities between Christ and the church

---

35. Komonchak, *Foundations in Ecclesiology*, vii.
36. Komonchak, *Foundations in Ecclesiology*, viii.

notwithstanding, theologians cannot simply adopt the notion of hypostatic (personal) union from Christology and apply it to the church because, unlike Christ, the church is not an incarnation of one of the persons of the Trinity. Ecclesiologists need to develop a different understanding of how the visible and the invisible aspects of the church mutually relate, and how they make the church one reality.

What the Church Is

At the outset of his *Church, World and the Christian Life*, Nicholas Healy makes an important observation. He states:

> Beliefs about the nature and function of the church on the one hand, and the question of how we should go about doing ecclesiology on the other, bear upon one another so as to determine the kinds of things we can and cannot say about the church. Thus any argument for a methodological proposal about ecclesiology will necessarily involve making some constructive proposals as to what sort of thing the church is and what sorts of things it can and should do.[37]

The interrelatedness between *what* one understands the church to be and *how* one ought to pursue ecclesiology is on full display in Komonchak's writings and is a major asset of his ecclesiological project.

At the outset of his 2008 Père Marquette lecture, Komonchak notes that in forty years of thinking about the church he has pursued a single question, which concerns "the relationship between the glorious things that are said in the Bible and in the tradition about the Church . . . and the concrete community of limited and sinful men and women who gather as the Church at any time or place all around the world."[38] He explains that he has developed a hypothesis that for every statement one makes about the church, one should be prepared to answer the following questions: "Of whom is one speaking when one speaks of the Church? To whom does the word refer? Of whom is it true? *In* whom is it true?"[39] Unless these questions are asked, Komonchak thinks ecclesiology will become "a study of abstractions."[40]

---

37. Healy, *Church, World*, 1.
38. Komonchak, *Who Are the Church?*, 10–11.
39. Komonchak, *Who Are the Church?*, 9.
40. Komonchak, "Lonergan and Post-Conciliar Ecclesiology," 172.

Congregatio fidelium

Conceiving the church as a *congregatio* or *convocatio fidelium*, an assembly or community of believers, is key to Komonchak's foundations in ecclesiology. As noted above, he adopts a different stance than Avery Dulles on the question of whether a single definition of the church is possible or whether one must use a variety of models to describe the church. Komonchak affirms the former and considers *congregatio fidelium* not only the referent of the word "church," but also an approximation of a real definition of the church. In his view, *congregatio fidelium* expresses both what constitutes the church and what makes it different from other human gatherings.[41]

Komonchak thinks that Dulles's exposition of different models of the church presupposes that one is operating with some preliminary or heuristic understanding of what the church is—otherwise one would not be able to determine that various images, symbols, concepts, and models indeed refer to the same reality, the church.[42] Komonchak believes that *congregatio fidelium* is such a preliminary understanding and an unstated assumption that Dulles makes. Komonchak argues that the notion of the church as a community of disciples, which Dulles presented as the sixth model in the second edition of his *Models of the Church*,[43] is not an additional model of the church at all; instead it is a designation of the church. Komonchak explains that referring to the church as a community of disciples,

> tells us who it is that the first-order images are describing, who it is to whom the second-order models refer. It identifies, in other words, the subject of ecclesiology: the Church is the community of disciples of Jesus Christ. "Community of disciples" serves to designate what it is that is said to be, say, People of God, the Body of Christ, the Temple of the Holy Spirit, what it is that is proposed for critical and systematic understanding when it is set forth as an institution, *communio*, sacrament, herald, servant.[44]

"Community of disciples" is for Komonchak tantamount to one of the oldest and most common terms for the church—*congregatio* (or *convocatio*) *fidelium*. As such, it is the referent of the word "church" and of any other designation of the church on earth, such as mystical body of Christ, bride of

---

41. Komonchak, *Who Are the Church?*, 31.
42. Komonchak, *Who Are the Church?*, 23–28.
43. Dulles, *Models of the Church?*, 204–26.
44. Komonchak, *Who Are the Church?*, 30.

Christ, sacrament, temple of the Holy Spirit, or communion. It is what the church always and everywhere is in history.[45]

Komonchak believes that conceiving the church as *congregatio fidelium* carries both sociological and theological precision. Sociologically, it explains that what is being referred to is not merely an aggregate of people who find themselves together by accident. They are a community and the social sciences can provide rich reflection on what that means. Theologically, *congregatio fidelium* makes clear that faith is constitutive of what it means to be church. There is nothing prior to faith except for God's offer of self.[46]

In Komonchak's view *congregatio fidelium* is not an image, metaphor, model or paradigm of the church.[47] As John Dadosky explains, *congregatio fidelium* is for Komonchak "a third order definition of the Church, one that reflects what Lonergan calls a critical exigence."[48] This third order definition relates images and models to one another as first and second order definitions of the church respectively. The significance of conceiving the church as *congregatio fidelium* is at least two-fold: (1) it brings to mind what the first-order images and the second-order models are the images and models of, and (2) it points to the concrete reality of the church, which helps clarify that the object of ecclesiology is a concrete community of believers.

Community Constituted by Meaning and Mediated by Value

Komonchak understands the church to be a community constituted by meaning and mediated by value.[49] He explains that the church exists as one of many worlds constituted by meaning and value and differs from them in that it "defines itself by reference to Jesus Christ and lives by the grace of the Spirit."[50] This heuristic and purely formal understanding of community, which he adopted from Lonergan, provides Komonchak with sets of questions one can ask of various groups in order to determine whether

---

45. Komonchak, *Who Are the Church?*, 31–32. See also Komonchak, "Epistemology of Reception," 193; "Lonergan and Post-Conciliar Ecclesiology," 171.

46. Komonchak, "People of God," 96; *Who Are the Church?*, 31–32.

47. Paradigm is a dominant model. See Dulles, *Models of the Church*, 29.

48. Dadosky, "Who/What Is/Are," 787. The notion of critical exigence refers to the need to relate the world of commonsense to the world of theory. For more, see Lonergan, *Method in Theology*, 83.

49. Komonchak, "History and Social Theory," 39; "Lonergan and the Church," 87; "Church and the Mediation," 153; "Church Universal as the Communion," 31; "Toward a Theology," 11, 12; "Epistemology of Reception," 189.

50. Komonchak, "Lonergan and the Church," 87.

they are communities. Such questions would ask, for instance, "what is the common experience that provides the potential for the self-realization of the Church, what are the common understandings and judgments that give form and act to the potentiality for community given in the experience, what are the commitments and decisions, values and goals, that render the community effectively present?"[51] Komonchak believes that it is legitimate to ask such questions also of the church if one considers it a community. He believes that identifying answers to such questions is one possible way of understanding how the church is a human community of meaning and value, and also a way of discovering what it means to call this human community the people of God, the body of Christ, and the temple of the Holy Spirit. He doubts that the question of the relationship between the divine and human aspects of the church can even be posed without this or some other similar effort, since the element pertaining to the human reality of the church would be absent.[52]

Human and Social Reality

Komonchak unambiguously affirms that the church is a human and social reality. While aware that such affirmation can be a point of contention, he argues that the affirmation is theologically valid and that it does not compromise the church's grounding in God's call, just as it is theologically correct to say that faith is a human act, though only possible through grace.[53] Paraphrasing Claude Welch, Komonchak articulates the church's human reality as follows:

> Whatever Christian faith may say about the divine origin, center, and goal of the Church, it never pretends that the Church does not stand on this side of the distinction between Creator and creature. The Church is not God; it is not Jesus Christ; it is not the Holy Spirit. If the Church is the People of God, the Body of Christ, the Temple of the Holy Spirit, it is all of these as a human reality, that is, because certain events occur within the mutually related consciousnesses of a group of human beings.[54]

---

51. Komonchak, "Ministry and the Local Church," 68; "Toward a Theology," 11–12.
52. Komonchak, "Ministry and the Local Church," 68; "Toward a Theology," 11–12.
53. Komonchak, "Ecclesiology and Social Theory," 63.
54. Komonchak, "Ecclesiology and Social Theory," 63.

I concur with Roger Haight that this description definitively lays to rest the objection that the unequivocal statement that the church is a human reality undermines or compromises the transcendent and divine character of the church.[55]

Komonchak's affirmation of the social reality of the church includes a clear distinction between social and merely natural realities. Komonchak illustrates the difference between these by explaining how an arrowhead and a piece of flint, a wink and a facial tic, or a city and a beehive differ from one another. He explains that "physically and chemically, the arrowhead is not distinct from another piece of flint; but an arrowhead is much more than mere flint—human hands have worked on it and meant something by it."[56] This distinction between social and merely natural realities applies to how one conceives of the church. The church is not something that happens by chance; it is not simply a group of people. Rather, it is a group of people that share a commitment to the Gospel and this commitment constitutes them as church—the church of God has a human face.

Komonchak argues that since the church is a social reality, one should expect to observe in it the processes, operations, and acts which are characteristic of social relations in other social realities. He advocates that ecclesiologists utilize social theory to learn how social realities are constituted and then apply what they learn to their interpretation of the church. He argues that some social theory—even if implicit—is indispensable for the work of an ecclesiologist, just as some implicit philosophy is indispensable for a theologian in general. For him, the truly critical character of ecclesiology consists in part of making the implicit explicit.[57]

Historical Subject of Its Self-realization

Komonchak conceives the church as a historical subject of its self-realization.[58] This portrayal of the church exposes the event character of the church's existence and is required, in his view, once one recognizes that transcendent language about the church refers to a concrete group of men and women who gather as church. The notion of the church as a historical

---

55. Haight, "Historical Ecclesiology," 29; *Christian Community in History*, 1:36.

56. Komonchak, "Towards a Theology," 10. See also Komonchak, "Epistemology of Reception," 189.

57. Komonchak, "Ecclesiology and Social Theory," 64.

58. Komonchak appropriated the notion of self-realization (*selbstvollzug*) from Karl Rahner and Bernard Lonergan. See Rahner, *Theology of Pastoral Action*; Lonergan, *Method in Theology*, 363.

subject of its self-realization also logically follows from Komonchak's conception of the church's coming-to-be or its genesis.[59]

Genesis of the Church

Komonchak's view of the church's genesis acts as the lynchpin for his ecclesiology in general, and for his theology of the local church in particular. His account of how the church comes-to-be underlies not only his description of the church as the historical subject of its self-realization, but also explains why ecclesiology should start with and focus on the local church. Furthermore, it shows the significance of the notion of "reception" for ecclesiology and functions as a key building block for his view of the church's ontology. Komonchak's account of the church's genesis is an elaboration on the dictum of Venerable Bede (672/673-735) that "every day the Church gives birth to the Church"[60]; it also roughly corresponds to the traditional idea of the two inseparable aspects of the church as mother (*ecclesia congregans*) and as children (*ecclesia congregata*).[61]

Komonchak distinguishes two inseparable moments or principles in the church's genesis: one objective and the other subjective. The former pertains to God's initiative in Christ and the Spirit. Since it is given, he has called this first moment or principle "objective." God's initiative stands vis-à-vis every new generation of potential believers as something already realized by the previous generation. It also stands as a challenge—as one of the many worlds the new generation may choose to realize. The objective principle makes the church a reality distinct from other human communities and, were it lacking, a particular community would be something other than the church. This objective moment is the principle of the church's unity across generations and cultures.[62]

More specifically, the objective moment of the church's genesis refers to one generation's communication of the Christian meaning and value to another generation. Komonchak describes it as "the objectification of the previous generation's subjectivity."[63] In other words, the objective moment in the church's genesis is one generation's handing down to another what it

---

59. Komonchak, "Ministry and the Local Church," 64-69. See also Komonchak, "Lonergan and Post-Conciliar Ecclesiology," 169.

60. Bede, *Explanatio Apocalypsis*, 2.7, in *Patrologia Latina*, 93:166. For a comparative study of this concept see Tan, "Every Day the Church."

61. See, for instance, de Lubac, *Splendor of the Church*, 55-86; Congar, "Mother Church," 37-44.

62. Komonchak, "Lonergan and the Church," 89; "Towards a Theology," 23-24.

63. Komonchak, "Towards a Theology," 24.

itself had received and appropriated from the generation that preceded it. Every new generation is thus invited to enter the world constructed by the previous generation. Komonchak's description of this process has been, for me personally, one of the most moving lines in his writings. He says: "We are asked to believe what they have believed, to love what they have loved, to hope for what they hoped for. We are asked to recreate the world they have created, to continue in the world the social body that carries on the word of Christ and embodies in its fellowship and in its service the grace of the Spirit."[64] Most people probably do not expect that writings in ecclesiology will occasion an experience of transcendence but, for me, these few lines have brought to mind the amazing women and men in my life who handed down the Gospel to me and whose lives of faith, hope, and love have often raised the question: *Si isti et istae, cur non ego?*[65]

Komonchak argues, however, that the objective moment is only a potential principle of the church's genesis, which in and of itself does not yet generate the church. The church does not come to be solely on the basis of divine initiative, but is realized only when God's offer is "received and appropriated by each successive generation of Christians."[66] The church's coming-to-be requires a free human response to God's initiative. This act of personal and communal appropriation of the Gospel constitutes the subjective principle in the genesis of the church.[67]

Komonchak's account of *ecclesiogenesis* illumines what he means by calling the church a historical subject of its self-realization, namely, that the church is an event in progress, that it is a process, and that in a real sense it is an achievement of its members. The church does not simply receive its existence from God; it is not just God's gift. Rather, as other human and social realities, the church comes-to-be "by the conscious operation of its members,"[68] who are its historical subject. They make the church, quite literally. The church exists because they respond to God's self-communication and because, by God's grace, they believe, hope, and love. If there ceased to be a group of people who did that, the church would cease to be.[69]

Conceiving the church unambiguously as an achievement of its members is a trademark of Komonchak's ecclesiology, clearly distinguishing

---

64. Komonchak, "Towards a Theology," 24.

65. "If these ones and those ones have done it, why can't I?" The saying is attributed to Augustine of Hippo, who has a similar statement in his *Confessions* 8, 27.

66. Komonchak, "Lonergan and the Church," 89

67. Komonchak, "Lonergan and the Church," 89–90; "Towards a Theology," 24–27.

68. Komonchak, "Lonergan and the Church," 89.

69. Komonchak, "Ministry and the Local Church," 68.

him from Joseph Ratzinger, for whom "one cannot *make* the Church but only receive it, that is, receive it from where it already is and where it really is: from the sacramental community of Christ's body passing through history."[70] It appears that Ratzinger wants to defend the view of the church as a supernatural mystery and cautions against reducing the church to merely a sociological reality, which could end up collapsing the faith and its content to merely human and historical arbitrariness.[71] While his concern is understandable, drawing a sharp wedge between the church as a reality that is received by its members and the church as a reality that they make does not do justice to the church's historical coming-to-be. The reception that takes place in the process of ecclesiogenesis is certainly more complex than Ratzinger acknowledges. For him, the faithful receive the church passively as one receives an object that is external to the receiver. For Komonchak, however, the faithful receive the church actively as subjects of the church, that is, as those who make the church what it is. The difference between Komonchak and Ratzinger thus lies in the way they understand the faithful's involvement in the church's coming-to-be. This is a very important point. One can hardly imagine that the church could respond to the signs of the times if its members simply received what the church used to be in the previous generation(s). Similarly, one could hardly develop an idea of a living tradition if the faithful could not make the church but only receive it from the past.

Reflecting further on the idea of the church as the historical subject of its self-realization and appropriating the definition of a society from the social theorists Peter Berger and Thomas Luckman,[72] Komonchak describes the church as a human and ecclesial product. In this sense the church is a community of language, belief, and freedom.[73] In Komonchak's view, asserting that the church is a human reality and a human product the way he does is not a violation of the church's transcendence. The point of such an affirmation is that,

> what God's word and grace have produced in the world is the human community whose historical subject is the group of men and women who are its members. These men and women gather around common meanings and values which they consider to

70. Ratzinger, "Ecclesiology of the Second Vatican Council," 244 (italics mine). See also above, pp. 71–74.

71. See Ratzinger and Messori, *Ratzinger Report*, 46.

72. Berger and Luckman say, "Society is a human product. Society is an objective reality. Man is a social product" (Berger and Luckman, *Social Construction of Reality*, 61, quoted in Komonchak, "Church and the Mediation," 165).

73. See Komonchak, "Church and the Mediation," 153–64.

be God's own self-communication, and even their very gathering in this faith they attribute to the grace of the Spirit. Still it is they who gather, and, under grace, in ways so similar to the ways in which other communities assemble that it can be said that the Church is a human product.[74]

This is a masterful account of the reality of the church that not only accounts for its transcendent and human/social dimensions, but also explains cogently how these two are predicated of one and the same reality.

The subjective principle of the church's genesis grounds the logic of Komonchak's insistence that ecclesiological reflection ought to start and center on the local church. This is because the appropriation of God's gift, which constitutes the subjective moment of the church's coming-to-be, takes place in and is mediated by the existential and historic questions of a particular generation of men and women. The logic of the subjective principle leads Komonchak to conclude that "the genesis of the Church is always and foremost the genesis of the local Church."[75] In other words, the genesis of the church does not take place in the abstract but is, rather, a concrete achievement of a particular group of people who respond to the Gospel.

Ontology of the Church

Komonchak's conception of the church's ontology is of particular significance for his overall account of what the church is.[76] It stems from his understanding of the church's genesis and complements it. Traditionally, ecclesiologists discussed ontology of the church using the four Aristotelian causes or Aristotle's categories of form and matter. Neoscholastic manuals, generally speaking, identified the hierarchy as the formal cause of the church, the laity as the material cause, the Trinity as the remote efficient cause, Christ as the immediate efficient cause, and the beatific vision as the final cause.[77] Even theologians who attempted to break out of neoscholastic patterns of thinking about the church continued to rely on these categories.[78] Komonchak has concluded, however, that the traditional categories cannot articulate adequately the human and social reality of the church. In

---

74. Komonchak, "Church and the Mediation," 153–64, 165.

75. Komonchak, "Toward a Theology," 25.

76. "Ontology" is a philosophical term that—in this context—refers to the idea of what sort of being the church is.

77. Doyle, *Communion Ecclesiology*, 41.

78. See, for instance, Journet, *Church of the Word Incarnate*, 45–49; Congar, *True and False Reform*, 88–90.

particular, they cannot account adequately for the role that believers play in the church's coming-to-be.

Komonchak constructs his view of the church's ontology by drawing a contrast with the view of Yves Congar. Congar remained wedded to the classical metaphysical terms of form and matter and distinguished two moments in the church's genesis.[79] The form of the church encompasses all that comes from God and is God's gift. The people who respond to God's initiative and receive it are the matter of the church. Komonchak argues that this conception of the church's ontology is inadequate because, in classical metaphysics, form is pure activity and matter is pure passivity and receptivity. The problem is, however, that with regard to the church, not only the form but the matter too plays an active role in its coming-to-be. God's initiative on its own does not yet make the church unless some human beings respond to it in freedom. The Gospel cannot be simply imposed on them like the form of King David can be imposed on a slab of marble when a sculptor makes a statue of the king. As for the church, matter is not passive but is formally constitutive of the church as it exists in history.[80]

Komonchak argues that the subjective principle of the church's genesis underscores the significance of *reception* for ecclesiology. In the decades since Vatican II, theologians have explored this notion at some length. It has been a subject of intense reflection in connection with the reception of the church teaching, the reception of Vatican II, and/or in general as a foundational theological category.[81] Komonchak's central insight about the relation of reception and the church is that "the whole ontology of the Church—the real 'objective' existence of the Church—consists in the reception by faith of the Gospel. Reception is constitutive of the Church."[82] Without the continual reception of the Gospel by believers, the church would cease to be.

Komonchak defines the church's ontology in terms of *intersubjectivity*, as an "event of intersubjectivity."[83] He adopts this notion from social theorists.[84] Komonchak has found the idea of intersubjectivity to cohere well with several elements of his ecclesiology, such as his understanding of how the

---

79. See Congar, *True and False Reform*, 88–90.

80. Komonchak, "Culture and History," 50–53.

81. See, for instance, Gaillardetz, *Teaching with Authority*, 227–73; Alberigo et al., *Reception of Vatican II*; Routhier, "Reception in the Current Theological Debate," 17–52.

82. Komonchak, "Epistemology of Reception," 193.

83. Komonchak, "History and Social Theory," 39.

84. See Berger and Luckman, *Social Construction of Reality*; Searle, *Construction of Social Reality*. See also Welch, *Reality of the Church*. For the influence of Welch on Komonchak, see chapter 2, pp. 60–61.

church comes-to-be, his view of the church as a human and social reality, and his conception of the church as a historical subject of its own self-realization. During a course on method in ecclesiology that I had the pleasure to attend, Komonchak explained that when he presents his view of the church's ontology to a class of seminarians, it usually meets with some resistance. Some say that his view does not sound like the church that Jesus promised to build on a rock. It is clear that the students do not think of the church as being different from merely physical realities. Komonchak's account of the church's ontology makes clear, however, that unlike mere physical realities such as Mount Everest, the church is a reality that does not exist apart from human acts of meaning and value. Like friendship, marriage, university, government, or economy, the church does not exist apart from acts of shared intentionality. The church's ontological reality consists of the common intentional acts of meaning and value of its members. Their subjectivity—that is, their active believing participation—co-constitutes the church.[85]

Komonchak argues that subjectivity and intersubjectivity define the church's ontology both vertically and horizontally, that is, with regard to the church's transcendent and human dimensions. At one and the same time, the free and initiating subjectivity of God constitutes the church's transcendent dimension, and the free and receptive subjectivity of the believers constitutes the church's human dimension.[86]

In addition to Aristotelian metaphysics, Komonchak considers reification of the church as a key obstacle to constructing an adequate ontology of the church. Appropriating the concept from Berger and Luckman, Komonchak understands reification as a misrepresentation of the ontology of social realities such as church or society.[87] It takes place when they are thought to exist independently of human activity.[88] The church gets reified when it is portrayed as a supra-personal reality existing somewhere above and apart from the communities of believers as, for example, when it is asserted that the members of the church are all sinners but the church itself is without sin.[89]

---

85. Komonchak, *Who Are the Church?*, 34. See also Komonchak, "Epistemology of Reception," 181–87.

86. Komonchak, "Epistemology of Reception," 193–94.

87. See Berger and Luckman, *Social Construction of Reality*, 88–92.

88. Komonchak, "Epistemology of Reception," 188.

89. See, for instance, Journet, *L'église*; Maritain, *De L'Eglise du Christ*.

Redemptive Community

Komonchak envisions a close connection between the church and redemption. Appropriating Lonergan's theory of human history, Komonchak thinks of Christianity as addressing the problem of the human inability for sustained development, which is rooted in existential, social, and cultural bias. Komonchak sees the church as being part of a solution to the problem. The solution lies in experiencing community as an event of redemption.[90]

Influenced by a suggestion in the *epilogue* of Lonergan's *Insight*, Komonchak thinks of redemption in terms of historical causality, namely, as an effect of Christ on history. He envisions the church as a redemptive community, as a group of people who have accepted the Gospel and who, by living it out, manifest the historic significance of Jesus. Christ's redemptive impact on history is thus realized in this mode of historical causality.[91] Komonchak suggests that redemption should be treated in ecclesiology, since the church's mission in history is to be a sign of God's redemptive purpose.[92] The role of the church, as Komonchak sees it, is to make a difference.[93]

God's Gift and Our Task

To sum up this section, Komonchak conceives the church at once as God's gift and as our task. He rejects the idea that one ought to choose between these two views of what the church is. For Komonchak, ecclesiologists must avoid making such a choice because, for Catholic theologians, those two views ought not to be seen as genuine alternatives.[94] He rejects both sociological and theological reductionisms as incapable of generating an adequate theory and practice of the church. Komonchak insists that two sets of statements must be made about the church: that the church is a human community subject to everything that human communities are subject to in history, and that as such it is the people of God, the body of Christ, and the temple of the Holy Spirit.[95]

---

90. Komonchak, "Church and Redemptive Community," 167–68.

91. Komonchak, *Foundations in Ecclesiology*, viii. See also Komonchak, "Lonergan and the Church," 88.

92. Komonchak, "Lonergan and the Church," 82.

93. See Komonchak, "Christians Must Make a Difference," 4–5.

94. Komonchak, "Church: God's Gift," 741.

95. Komonchak, "Church: God's Gift, 739.

Solution of the Central Challenge for Ecclesiology

The key issue that propelled Komonchak's pursuit of ecclesiology is the relation between the exalted language about the church in Scripture and tradition and the concrete communities of believers. The former expresses the church's invisible, graced reality, and the latter pertains to its visible, human dimension. Explaining how they make the church one reality, Komonchak considers the central challenge that ecclesiologists face.

Komonchak argues that conceiving of the church as "the human community which is the effect in the world of God's self-communication in Christ and the Spirit"[96] resolves the challenge. The key lies in affirming several propositions at once: that God's self-communication defines the church as a distinctive reality, that God's self-communication must be met with a human response, that the church is the subject of its self-realization as a human and social reality, and that the transcendent language about the church is predicated about concrete communities of believers.

The way Komonchak conceives of how the church's visible and invisible dimensions form just one reality offers an alternative to understanding the issue through an analogy with the Incarnation. Comparing the church to the Incarnation has been common in Catholic ecclesiology since the early nineteenth century. It was promoted by Möhler and became a key component of the mystical body of Christ theologies. *Lumen gentium* followed this line of thinking. In article 8 one reads: "just as the assumed nature serves the divine Word as a living instrument of salvation, inseparably joined with him, in a similar way the social structure of the church serves the Spirit of Christ who vivifies the church towards the growth of the body."

Employing the concept of the hypostatic union, even analogically, to explain how the visible and the invisible dimensions of the church form one reality is theologically problematic, however. Unlike in the case of Jesus, where the divine and human natures comprise one reality on the account of the second person of the Trinity, who assumed human nature, there is no such personal union between the church and one of the persons of the Trinity. Likening the church to the Incarnation has had a tendency to exaggerate the divine aspect of the church, as critics of Möhler and mystical body of Christ theologies have pointed out. The analogy runs the risk of what Congar called "ecclesiological monophysitism," that is, "a construal of the unity of the divine aspect and the human aspect of the church that jeopardize[s] its human character."[97]

---

96. Komonchak, "Ministry and the Local Church," 66.
97. Hinze, "Releasing the Power," 354.

Komonchak's view of the unity between the invisible interior dimension of the church and its visible expression is modeled on the understanding of the unity between the sign and its referent in the notion of a sacrament. As it is with sacraments, where visible signs make present the invisible, so it is with the church, where its visible dimension reflects the invisible, graced dimension. These two dimensions of the church comprise just one reality on account of concrete communities of believers which mediate God's saving love before the world. Insofar as they do that, they—the believers, the church—can be seen as the body of Christ, the sacrament or communion of salvation, the New Jerusalem, the temple of the Holy Spirit, etc. *Lumen gentium* compares the human nature of Jesus and the social structure of the church. While Komonchak does not downplay the role of the church's social structure, he makes clear that what makes the church visible in the first place are the believers.

Conceiving the unity of the human and divine aspects of the church as Komonchak does is superior to likening the church to the Incarnation. It avoids ecclesiological monophysitism by maintaining both a unity and a distinction between the human and the divine without collapsing one into the other. It expresses clearly that the "who" of the church—its subject—is not a preexistent divine person, as it is with Jesus, but communities of believers. As Komonchak argues in *Who Are the Church?*, it is the men and women who believe, hope, and love on the account of the Gospel who are the church. The locus of the unity of the human and divine dimensions of the church is in them.

Vision of Systematic Ecclesiology

When Komonchak began to publish on the theology of the church in the early 1980s, he thought that, in ecclesiology and in church practice, Catholics had not yet integrated well the vision of Vatican II.[98] The shift that the council effected meant that one could not continue doing ecclesiology as before. Vatican II disrupted the status quo, rendering the method of the neoscholastic manuals no longer suitable to communicate the council's vision of the church. How theologians should proceed in this new situation, however, was not evident. The manuals were replaced in various ways: by historical accounts of the church's development,[99] by narrative ecclesiologies,[100] and

---

98. See Komonchak, "Church: God's Gift," 738.

99. For example, Cooke, *Ministry to Word and Sacraments*; Jay, *Church*; Schillebeeckx, *Church with a Human Face*.

100. For example, Küng, *Church*; Sanks, *Salt, Leaven, and Light*.

by the models approach.¹⁰¹ These new approaches recovered the church's spiritual, graced dimension, which the manuals neglected, but unlike the manuals, they showed little interest in pursuing a unifying, systematic understanding of the church.¹⁰² Whether such an ecclesiology was still possible and desirable became a question.

Komonchak's ecclesiological project is rooted in the conviction that the weakening of systematic endeavor in ecclesiology was a deficiency, and that new ecclesiologies needed to be complemented with foundations capable of accounting for ecclesiology's systematic character. This is what Komonchak has provided: a robust vision capable of raising ecclesiology again to the position of a systematic theological discipline. The foundations in ecclesiology he worked out are inspired primarily by Bernard Lonergan, through whose influence Komonchak has conceived of the foundations in terms of discovering the general and special categories for a theology of the church. By articulating a vision of ecclesiology as a critical, systematic theological discipline, Komonchak has rendered an indispensable service to contemporary Catholic theology.

Theory as the Goal of a Critical, Systematic Ecclesiology

An investigation into the renewal of Catholic ecclesiology in the twentieth century would reveal that two methodological approaches played prominent roles.¹⁰³ Both of these interpreted the church on the basis of key images or metaphors. The first approach, which theologians used both before and after Vatican II, constructed an ecclesiology around one central metaphor, such as body of Christ, people of God, or communion. The second approach, which became popular after the council, examined various images and metaphors of the church present in the tradition and organized them into models of the church. Specific to this second approach is the use of multiple models at once and balancing out their strengths and weaknesses. The renewal that these approaches brought about was a significant gain that Catholic ecclesiology badly needed. Yet some questioned whether either of these methodological strategies were adequate for ecclesiology as a systematic theological discipline; Komonchak was among them. He developed his vision of systematic ecclesiology in critical engagement with these dominant methodological strategies. He did not object in principle to employ-

---

101. For example, Dulles, *Models of the Church*; Mondin, *Le nuove ecclesiologie*.

102. Cf. Haight, "On Systematic Ecclesiology," 220; "Systematic Ecclesiology," 253–54.

103. See Flanagan, *Communion, Diversity, and Salvation*, 1–7.

ing metaphors in ecclesiology since, as symbolic language is in general, metaphors are a means of expressing the theological, graced dimension of the church. Komonchak has maintained that constructing a more systematic theology of the church, one which moves beyond the enumeration of ecclesial metaphors or models and has theory as its goal, is not only possible, but also necessary.

Komonchak has argued that ecclesiology ought to be a systematic theological discipline based on the distinction that Lonergan worked out between common sense and theory.[104] Both of these treat the same realities but from different perspectives. The realm of common sense characterizes everyday living. Lonergan defines common sense as,

> the realm of persons and things in their relation to us. It is the visible universe peopled by relatives, friends, acquaintances, fellow citizens, and the rest of humanity. We come to know it, not by applying some scientific method, but by a self-correcting process of learning, in which insights gradually accumulate, coalesce, qualify and correct one another, until a point is reached where we are able to meet situations as they arise, size them up by adding a few more insights to the acquired store, and so deal with them in an appropriate fashion. Of the objects in this realm we speak in everyday language, in which words have the function, not of naming the intrinsic properties of things, but of completing the focusing of our conscious intentionality on the things, of crystallizing our attitudes, expectations, intentions, of guiding all our actions.[105]

There exists a realm of meaning, however, for which common sense is inadequate. The need for this realm reveals itself when one begins to inquire into what everyday living takes for granted. At that point one recognizes the need for precise definitions and contexts for the realities treated in common sense fashion; one recognizes the need for theory. The realm of theory asks questions that common sense takes for granted. Theory "develops technical terms, assigns them their interrelations, constructs models, and adjusts them until there is reached some well-ordered and explanatory view of this or that realm of experience."[106] The realm of theory forms the context for questions that are raised by systematic exigence and that common sense is not able to answer.[107] Common sense and theory are thus two different

---

104. Lonergan, *Method in Theology*, 81–85; see also 276–79, 304–5.
105. Lonergan, *Method in Theology*, 81–82.
106. Lonergan, *Method in Theology*, 304.
107. Lonergan, *Method in Theology*, 82.

worlds of meaning employing two different languages and attempting to answer different questions.

Komonchak argues that contemporary ecclesiology would benefit from appropriating this distinction between common sense and theory. He proposes that ecclesiologists aim at theory in their interpretation of the church. Komonchak defines the theoretical understanding that is at the basis of systematic inquiry as an understanding that "asks questions about what is taken for granted in the understanding that suffices or appears to suffice for everyday living."[108] He believes that ecclesiology ought to be systematic because there are questions about the church that common sense cannot address adequately. Komonchak observes, however, that in ecclesiology, theory became taken for granted. He describes contemporary ecclesiology as post-systematic, by which he means that theologians use the language of theory outside of its theoretical context and content. Komonchak believes that ecclesiology would benefit from examining the taken-for-granted and that this would help differentiate between common sense and theory as well as among theories themselves. He urges ecclesiologists to work out a theoretical rather than common sense understanding of such commonly used terms in ecclesiology as individual, community, authority, meaning, and history.[109]

As discussed earlier, Komonchak does not think that conceiving of the church as mystery rules out the possibility of systematic ecclesiology.[110] He understands mystery as a surplus of intelligibility, not its lack. He considers the surplus to be the reason why theologians should not abandon, but rather pursue, the effort to construct a systematic understanding of the church.[111] As he explains, "not all efforts to speak of Mystery are equally inadequate and that Mystery is not legitimately invoked as a reason for not exploring fundamental differences in the efforts or for not criticizing and evaluating them."[112]

Komonchak's proposal that ecclesiology ought to aim at theory recovers the insight of Johann Sebastian Drey (1777–1853), the founder of the Catholic Tübingen School, teacher and mentor of Möhler. As Michael Himes explains, Drey reconceived why the church was fundamental for theology. He envisioned the relation between the church and a theologian to be the same as between the state and a political scientist or the animal

---

108. Komonchak, "Ecclesiology and Social Theory," 58.
109. Komonchak, "Lonergan and the Task," 50–53.
110. Komonchak, "Ecclesiology and Social Theory," 65.
111. Komonchak, "People of God," 95–96.
112. Komonchak, "People of God," 66.

organism and a veterinarian. Drey understood the task of theology as expressing theoretically and systematically the life of the church.[113]

Methodological Shift in Ecclesiology

Komonchak has argued that arriving at a systematic understanding of the church will require a methodological shift in ecclesiology. He has conceived of this shift as analogous to the one that Lonergan proposed with respect to the theology of grace. Lonergan showed that Aquinas reinterpreted Augustine's theology of conversion by transposing the psychological categories of Augustine's theology of grace into the metaphysical categories of Aristotle.[114] Lonergan believed, however, that those metaphysical categories were not suited well today to theologize about grace and proposed a shift to a phenomenological approach. Lonergan argued that his analysis of intentionality and conversion, which conceives of grace as a state of being in love without qualification, renders accurately the scholastics' view of grace as the created effect in persons of the uncreated self-gift of God.[115] As Komonchak explains, Lonergan's analysis of intentionality and conversion reinterprets Aquinas's metaphysical categories and results in a theology of grace as transformed subjectivity.[116]

Komonchak has suggested that a similar transposition was needed in ecclesiology. Without denying the newly recovered spiritual and transcendent dimension of the church, theologians should turn their attention to the church as a human community. He explains:

> As an adequate theology of grace must speak of the created effect of uncreated grace and do so, in Aquinas's terms, as an entitative habit or, in modern terms, as a transformation of subjectivity, so an adequate theology of the Church must speak of it as the human community or transformed intersubjectivity which results from the word of Christ and the grace of the Spirit.[117]

Komonchak thinks that the shift in ecclesiology he envisions might overcome the gap between the lofty theological language that became the mainstream in Catholic ecclesiology after Vatican II and the concrete

---

113. Himes, "Development of Ecclesiology," 55.
114. See Lonergan, *Grace and Freedom*.
115. See Lonergan, *Method in Theology*, 120–24, 281–93.
116. Komonchak, *Foundations in Ecclesiology*, ix. See also "Towards a Theology," 6–7; "Lonergan and the Task," 54–55.
117. Komonchak, "Towards a Theology," 7.

communities of the faithful, which realize such notions of the church as the mystical body, *una persona mystica*, or *Ursakrament*.[118] The bottom line for Komonchak is that as Lonergan transformed the theology of grace, so must critical systematic ecclesiology be rooted "in an analysis of the social and historical conditions and consequences of conversion."[119]

The Object of Ecclesiology

The object of ecclesiology is what ecclesiology seeks to understand, namely, the church. As discussed earlier, Komonchak has worked out a multifaceted understanding of what the church is. It is a human community that exists as an effect of God's self-communication. It is at once God's gift and a human achievement. It is always a gathering of believers. Komonchak understands this concrete, historical reality of the church to be the object of ecclesiology.[120] He argues that ecclesiologists should not see their task merely as interpreting what Scripture and tradition say about the church, but that the object of their investigations should incorporate the self-realization of the community of believers. While statements about the church are an important part of the church's self-realization throughout history, the church's coming-to-be involves more.[121] That "more" Komonchak describes as "the set (or sets) of experiences, understandings, symbols, words, judgments, decisions, actions, relationships, and institutions which distinguish the group of people called 'the Church.'"[122] The goal of ecclesiology, for Komonchak, is to understand how and why these related elements constitute the group of people who are by faith recognized as the Church.[123]

Ecclesiology as Theory about Practice

Komonchak considers ecclesiology to be an area of theology where theory and practice cannot be kept separate. He conceives of ecclesiology as a theory about a practice because the object of ecclesiology is not the church

---

118. Komonchak, "Lonergan and the Task," 55.
119. Komonchak, *Foundations in Ecclesiology*, ix.
120. Komonchak, "People of God," 96.
121. Komonchak, "Lonergan and the Task," 49; "Ecclesiology and Social Theory," 67.
122. Komonchak, "Ecclesiology and Social Theory," 57. See also Komonchak, "Lonergan and the Task," 51–52.
123. Komonchak, "Ecclesiology and Social Theory," 57. See also Komonchak, "Lonergan and the Task," 51–52.

in the abstract, but the concrete historical reality of the church. He envisions the work of an ecclesiologist as both interpreting the self-realization of the church as a redemptive community and serving that self-realization.[124]

Social Sciences and Ecclesiology

One of the most distinctive features of Komonchak's vision of systematic ecclesiology concerns the critical role that the social sciences ought to play in interpreting the church. Komonchak does not consider ecclesiology to offer full understanding of the church, just as he does not think that theology in general provides full understanding of human existence.[125] His understanding of the church as a human and social reality, subject to the same dynamics as other human and social realities, led him quite naturally to the human and social sciences. Komonchak envisions that a systematic understanding of the church will resemble the systematic understanding of other social realities, and that the work of an ecclesiologist will be similar to that of a social theorist.[126] This will also have an impact on how ecclesiologists approach their discipline; it will require that they think of ecclesiology primarily as an interpretation of social existence, rather than of texts about the church.[127]

Komonchak has observed that contemporary ecclesiologies are weak in engaging seriously with social theory, which has not always been the case. He has noted that early ecclesiological treatises employed the social and political theory of their time and attended to the reality of the church as a human society. This was true especially of conciliarist ecclesiology, which understood the church on the basis of corporation theory. Perfect society ecclesiology was in conversation with modern juristic thought, although it was used in a limited fashion, primarily to defend and vindicate the freedom of the church. Insofar as pre-Vatican II ecclesiologies engaged some social and political theories, they were much less susceptible to theological reductionism.[128]

Komonchak argues that without some effort to work out social and historical categories, contemporary ecclesiology will remain pre-systematic.[129]

---

124. Komonchak, "Church and Redemptive Community," 168–77; "Church: God's Gift," 735.
125. Cf. Lonergan, *Method in Theology*, 364.
126. Komonchak, "Ecclesiology and Social Theory," 67–73.
127. Komonchak, "Lonergan and the Task," 53.
128. Komonchak, "History and Social Theory," 6–12; "Toward a Theology," 4–5.
129. Komonchak, "History and Social Theory," 12.

He proposes that ecclesiologists become familiar with methods used in the human and social sciences and with what they say about such commonly used terms in ecclesiology as community, society, structure, or institution. Such terms overlap in the work of ecclesiologists and social theorists. They are what Komonchak calls "general categories" as distinct from "special categories," which are proper to theology.[130] Komonchak does not think that an ecclesiologist can address critically what it means to call the church an institution, a community, or a society without learning what social theorists say about those concepts. He explains:

> Can an ecclesiologist hope to understand what authority in the Church is without examining first what a social relationship is and then exploring what social theorists have to say about "authority," "power," "legitimation," and so on and about the types of relationships in which they are found? Could not social theory help ecclesiologists to escape from such blind alleys as the dichotomies between "institution" and "event," "charism" and "office," "essence" and "forms," and *Wesen* and *Unwesen*?[131]

Komonchak thinks that in all these areas ecclesiologists could learn from social theorists how to pose their questions more critically as well as how to derive general categories through which they would articulate a systematic understanding of the church.

Komonchak's proposal that ecclesiologists look into the social sciences to work out definitions of the general categories they employ has been a trademark of his ecclesiological project. This proposal envisions a new dialogical partner for ecclesiology. Traditionally, philosophy has been the dialogical partner *par excellence* of theology.[132] It has been commonly assumed that one could not do serious theological work without an engagement with some philosophical system. This has been true for such theological disciplines as the theology of God, Christology, theological anthropology, sacramental theology, and others, including ecclesiology.[133] While not disinviting philosophy from ecclesiological conversations, with his proposals that social sciences become integrated in the work of ecclesiologists, Komonchak has suggested enlarging the circle of conversation partners in ecclesiology.

---

130. Komonchak, "Lonergan and the Church," 83.

131. Komonchak, "Ecclesiology and Social Theory," 70.

132. For a historical survey of the influence of philosophy on theology, see Shakespeare, "Ecclesiology and Philosophy," 655–73.

133. For the role philosophy has played in ecclesiology, see O'Meara, "Philosophical Models in Ecclesiology," 3–21.

The application of the social sciences to the study of religion has been accepted in religious studies since the pioneering work of Émile Durkheim in the beginning of the twentieth century.[134] In theology, however, a dialogue with social sciences is more an exception than a rule. Theologians have been somewhat hesitant in this matter, though not completely mute. Their hesitancy is understandable since incorporating social sciences into their work would require theologians to become familiar with another field of discourse. Another difficulty faced by theologians is that sociology is a methodologically divided discipline.[135] Both of these reasons create a significant challenge for ecclesiologists.

Incorporating the human and social sciences in ecclesiology might help avoid reifying the church. Reification misrepresents the ontology of the church by treating it as a natural, not social reality. Theoretical understanding of natural and of social realities, however, differs greatly. Unlike natural scientists, those who study human and social realities must take into consideration that their data are produced by conscious operations and acts; they must take into account the intelligence and freedom of the objects they study.[136] Active engagement with the human and social sciences would condition ecclesiologists to perceive the church as a reality that does not exist apart from human acts, as happens when the church is reified.

Although some calls to incorporate the social sciences into theology in general and ecclesiology in particular were made prior to Komonchak,[137] his articulation of the role of the social sciences in ecclesiology has been one of the most comprehensive, especially among theologians who write in English. Unfortunately, ecclesiologists have not yet developed ways to engage the social sciences fruitfully in their reflections on the church. In spite of some recent encouraging attempts in this direction by Roger Haight and Neil Ormerod,[138] Komonchak's call to incorporate social sciences into ecclesiology remains largely unheeded as "a voice crying out in the wilderness."[139]

---

134. See Durkheim, *Formes* élémentaires.

135. For this point, see, for instance, Baum, "Sociology and Theology," 22–31; Ormerod, "Ecclesiology and the Social Sciences," 640–41.

136. For Komonchak's treatment of systematic understanding of human and social realities, see Komonchak, "Ecclesiology and Social Theory," 59–62.

137. For the status of sociology in ecclesiology around the time when Komonchak began publishing his articles on foundations in ecclesiology, see, for instance, Wackenheim, "Ecclesiology and Sociology," 32–41. For the impact of sociology on Catholic theology in general, see Baum, "Impact of Sociology," 1–29.

138. See Haight, *Christian Community in History*; Ormerod, *Re-Visioning the Church*.

139. Ormerod, "Voice Cries in the Wilderness," 203.

Conclusion

The significance and distinctiveness of Komonchak's contribution to method in ecclesiology can be seen best by situating his ecclesiological project within the dynamics of the transition that Catholic ecclesiology has been undergoing as a result of the Second Vatican Council. The council disrupted the way ecclesiology had been done for centuries and, after its close, it became evident that theologians needed to rethink how to theologize about the church. Yet thinking through the methodological issues of ecclesiology as a systematic theological discipline has been the domain of only a small minority—Komonchak among them.[140] Most ecclesiologists have sidestepped this task and focused rather on expounding further the neglected aspects of ecclesiology, which the council restored to the mainstream of Catholic ecclesiology. Typically, their approach was to treat the church in its historical development or focus on selected topics pertaining to ecclesiology.

Komonchak's work on method in ecclesiology is a major contribution to the discipline, and it also carries implications for church practice. His work can be seen as an attempt to fine tune post-Vatican II ecclesiology in order to articulate a critical, systematic understanding of the church. His writings offer an alternative to the two main approaches to theologizing about the church that dominated ecclesiological renewal prior to and following Vatican II. Both of them interpreted the church on the basis of key images and metaphors: the first constructed an ecclesiology around one central image or metaphor, and the second organized the images and metaphors of the church into the category of models or ideal types of the church. Komonchak's thinking about the church embodies a different imagination. It attempts to define the church—to say what the church always is in history. He identifies the traditional notion of *congregatio fidelium* (assembly of the faithful) as such a definition. This definition does not exhaust the church's reality; it does not pretend to capture the fullness of how the church is experienced in faith. It simply identifies the referent of the word "church," and in this way it attempts to bring order into discourse about the church. It functions as a criterion of theologically rightful speech. Whatever assertion one makes about the church in history, it ought to be a statement about some assembly of believers. In the absence of this or a similar definition, ecclesiology would lack a criterion of normativity and would fail to be theology. It would be merely a descriptive discipline.[141] One can thus appreciate the conceptual clarity imbedded in the definition of the church as *congregatio*

---

140. Others include Severino Dianich, Avery Dulles, Herwi Rikhof, Roger Haight, Gerard Mannion, Nicholas M. Healy, and Neil Ormerod.

141. Cf. Haight, "Systematic Ecclesiology," 254n7.

fidelium, for it can ground a theological discourse about the church that moves beyond an array of images, metaphors, or models of the church, on the basis of which everything might be possible and permissible.[142]

Defining the church as *congregatio fidelium* is for Komonchak a hermeneutical lens that cracks open the ecclesiological imagination and functions as an organizing principle for further insights about the church: it contains the elements that are needed to do justice to the church's human and transcendent dimensions (*congregatio* accounts for the human side and *fidelium* for the transcendent side); it provides the logic for Komonchak's unequivocal affirmation of the human and social reality of the church and calls naturally for the incorporation of human and social sciences in the work of ecclesiologists; it explains why the church cannot be understood properly apart from its members' act of faith, thus relating the church to God; and it is key to avoiding theological and sociological reductionisms in ecclesiology.

Komonchak's writings offer the most coherent and cogent solution of a central issue in ecclesiology, which is to explain how the visible (human and societal) and invisible (transcendent, graced) dimensions of the church comprise a single reality. The solution lies essentially in conceiving of the visible, human dimension of the church as being simultaneously a response to God's offer of self and a mediation of God's saving love before the world. This is an alternative to the traditional way of thinking about the issue, which has been to compare the church to the Incarnation and understand the Holy Spirit to function similarly in relation to the church as the Word of God functioned in relation to Jesus' humanity. There are several problems with this traditional approach, however: it lacks needed precision since the church is not actually an incarnation of one of the persons of the Trinity, it tends to exaggerate the transcendent and downplay the human dimension of the church, and it often fosters theological reductionism. The solution that Komonchak offers invokes the sacramental imagination and identifies the human aspect of the church as the locus of the unity of the visible and the invisible dimensions. Komonchak's conception of how the visible and invisible dimensions comprise the single reality of the church thus avoids the problems of the incarnational approach.

This is a major contribution to the discipline of ecclesiology and might be seen as a key piece of the mosaic that depicts the renewal of Catholic ecclesiology before and after Vatican II. Since the inception of formal theological treatments of the church, ecclesiologists emphasized the church's societal and juridical dimensions, almost to the exclusion of its transcendent,

---

142. Cf. Rikhof, *Concept of the Church*, 1.

graced dimension. The latter was recovered in part during the nineteenth and especially during the first part of the twentieth centuries, and it was given an official stamp of approval at Vatican II. The desired balance in treating the church's societal and the transcendent aspects, however, did not ensue. The pendulum swung in the opposite direction: reflections on the church showed strong preference toward the church's transcendent dimension. While Vatican II asserted that the visible and the invisible aspects of the church form one single reality, the explanation of how this is the case simply compared the church to the Incarnation.[143] The council did not break new ground. How one should think more clearly of the church as one reality remained an unresolved issue. Komonchak's writings engage it at length, and the resolution they offer is theologically more adequate than likening the church to the Incarnation.

Concreteness is another distinctive feature of the imagination that marks Komonchak's foundations in ecclesiology. He achieves it not only by defining the church as an assembly of believers, but also by considering the human response to God's initiative to be constitutive of the church's actual existence, and by understanding the church's ontology in terms of intersubjectivity. The concreteness that characterizes Komonchak's thinking about the church addresses aptly the issue of idealization of the church. This has been pointed out as a weakness of various communion ecclesiologies that gained prominence in recent decades. As Neil Ormerod observes,

> if one were to read many current books on ecclesiology the word [church] would probably evoke a highly idealized vision of church, one which relates not to any particular historical period or even denominational community but to a sort of timeless "universal" church to which we would all like to belong if we could find it, but which sadly does not exist in this earthly realm.[144]

Communion ecclesiologies would benefit from incorporating the imagination that permeates Komonchak's foundations in ecclesiology. Working out interpretations of the church as he has proposed would help articulate that the church is not some supra-historical reality, but rather concrete people committed to living the Gospel. They are the communion that the church is said to be—both vertically and horizontally.

143. See LG 8.

144. Ormerod, "Ecclesiology and the Social Sciences," 639. See also Ormerod "Structure of a Systematic Ecclesiology," 27–28; *Re-Visioning the Church*, 29. Similar criticisms have been raised by Healy, "Communion Ecclesiology," 448, 452; "Ecclesiology and Communion," 274; Looney, "*Koinonia* Ecclesiology," 145–66; McLoughlin, "*Communio* Models of Church" 181–90; Watkins, "Objecting to *Koinonia*," 326–43; Comblin, *People of God*, 56–61.

The concreteness of Komonchak's thinking about the church may hold a promise for church practice. For Christians in the early centuries, the church was what they had in mind when they used the first-person plural. In our days, it is often not clear what Christians mean when they say "church." Instead of the first-person plural, they commonly speak of the church in the third-person. For example, before the start of Sunday liturgies, one often hears a greeting that says, "Good morning and welcome to . . . Today the church celebrates . . . Sunday in ordinary time." Welcoming an assembly of believers in this way gives the impression that the church is separate from them, that it is somewhere "out there." The third-person language about the church is commonplace. Sometimes it is undetected even by trained theologians. For instance, consider this statement by the International Theological Commission: "As she awaits the return of the Lord, the church and her members are constantly confronted with new circumstances."[145] What is meant by a church that exists in addition to her members? Or consider the following statements in the preparatory document of the 15th ordinary general assembly of the Synod of Bishops: "By listening to young people, the Church will once again hear the Lord speaking in today's world,"[146] and "The Church must involve young people in its decision-making processes and offer them more leadership roles."[147] The "young people" in both statements are members of the church. Whom does the word church designate, only the bishops?

The critique that these examples attempt to raise is that portraying the church as something "out there" separate from the believers, or equating the church with the clergy, misconceives and miscommunicates what the church is. It can hardly result in communities of faith that foster discipleship, inspire participation, and promote accountability. Engendering in all believers that they are the church, that the church should be a first-person word for them, does not guarantee a vibrant church, but it certainly seems to be a condition of the possibility for such a church. Komonchak's writings provide theological foundations out of which such a church could emerge.

This exposition and critical analysis of Komonchak's contribution to method in ecclesiology will be followed by an investigation of Komonchak's theology of the local church and authority in the church. In these two areas, Komonchak's method in ecclesiology comes on full display.

---

145. International Theological Commission, "'Sensus Fidei,'" 70.

146. Synod of Bishops, "Young People." The statement is in the third paragraph of the introduction.

147. Synod of Bishops, "Young People," 12.

4

The Local Church

THE LOCAL CHURCH HAS been a subject of immense interest for Catholic theologians since the close of Vatican II. There are many reasons for this: the council's re-evaluation of episcopal ministry, a desire on the part of many for a less centralized church, and the involvement of episcopal conferences in implementation of the liturgical reform.[1] Heightened interest in the local church persisted until the 1990s when it was disrupted first by a 1992 letter from the Congregation for the Doctrine of the Faith on some aspects of the church as communion (*Communionis notio*) and then by the 1998 apostolic letter of Pope John Paul II on the theological and juridical nature of episcopal conferences (*Apostolos suos*). The current pontificate of Pope Francis, which has attempted to revive synodality within the church, may invigorate interest in the local church again.

The New Testament speaks of "the church" and of "the churches" without the qualifying adjectives such as "local," "particular," "whole," or "universal," which later became key categories in ecclesiology.[2] Once these terms entered theological discourse, it became possible to distinguish two basic conceptions of the church.[3] The first, documented since the second century and prevalent in the first millennium in both east and west, envisions the church as a communion of local churches. The second, characteristic of Roman Catholic ecclesiology in the second millennium, envisions

---

1. The council envisioned that some elements of the liturgical reform would be regulated by the competent territorial ecclesiastical authority. See SC 22, 39, 44.

2. See, for instance, Brown, "New Testament Background," 1–14; Antón, "Iglesia Universal," 409–24.

3. For the historical development of the theology of the local church, see, for instance, Alberigo, "Local Church in the West," 125–43; Prusak, "Theology of the Local Church," 287–308; González de Cardenal, "Development of a Theology," 11–43.

the church as a universal entity governed by the pope; this church is like a single diocese encompassing the whole world. In this latter view, dioceses are not considered churches the same way as the universal church; they are deficient in their ecclesial character. Essentially, they are seen as administrative units of the whole church and to some extent as extensions of the local Church of Rome. This latter view had its origin in the Gregorian Reforms in the eleventh century but became dominant only after the Council of Trent (1545–1563) and especially after the First Vatican Council (1869–1870). During this period, concepts such as *societas inequalium, hierarchica*, and *perfecta* began to be used by ecclesiologists and canonists to refer to the church. In these ecclesiological perspectives, the local church was not considered fully church because it lacked the totality of jurisdictional power, even though it did not lack anything in terms of sacramental life. Following Vatican I, local churches were often treated in effect as "branch offices" of the universal church. Vatican II recognized that such understanding of the (local) church was discontinuous from the larger tradition and attempted to articulate the tradition's breadth by counterbalancing one-sided universalistic ecclesiology with the ecclesiology prevalent during the first millennium.[4] The council succeeded only partially.

The discussion of Joseph Komonchak's contribution to ecclesiology will now shift to his theology of the local church. Besides method in ecclesiology, it is the most important ecclesiological subject that Komonchak explored. Several features of his foundations in ecclesiology come on full display addressing this topic. As I explained in the previous chapter, Komonchak's engagement with foundational questions in ecclesiology stemmed from a desire to understand the extraordinary interest in the subject of the local church that took place after the closing of the Second Vatican Council. For Komonchak, interest in the local church raised various methodological questions pertaining to ecclesiology, and the insights these questions produced he then applied to a theology of the local church.[5]

---

4. For a concise overview of the official Roman Catholic teaching with regard to the local church prior to Vatican II, see Lanne, "Local Church," 288–97.

5. Komonchak's key publications related to the local church are "Church Universal," (1981) 30–35; "Ministry and the Local Church," (1981) 56–82; "Towards a Theology," (1986) 1–43; "Local Realization of the Church," (1987) 77–90; "Local Church," (1989) 320–35; "Local Church and the Church Catholic," (1992) 416–47; "Theology of the Local Church," (1996) 35–49; "Catholicity and the Redemption of History," (1997) 602–13; "Culture and History," (2000) 48–65; "À propos de la priorité," (2006) 245–68. Although this last essay was published in French, its original is in English of which I am in possession. When I cite this essay, I will not be translating from the French but will use the English original.

Before considering Komonchak's contribution, I will set the context by presenting the council's recovery of the local church. This section will build on the material from chapter one, but take it in a more specific direction.

The Local Church at Vatican II

The Second Vatican Council retrieved several ecclesiological themes which, in the course of history, had become deemphasized if not forgotten. Although not systematic in its treatment of the local church, one teaching of the council is clear; no one has expressed it better than Jean-Jacques von Allmen: "A local church is wholly church, but it is not the whole church."[6] The council restored the local church to its full ecclesial reality and reinserted into Catholic ecclesiology the concept that the universal church is the church of churches. After the council, this rediscovery of the local church became a catalyst for several creative developments, which were not without controversy: it grounded the implementation of the liturgical renewal mandated by the council, led to the emergence of so-called local theologies, resulted in a greater appreciation of the various cultures in which local churches exist and was the catalyst for inculturation, and was also a source of hope that the church would become less centralized and more collegial. In more than one way then, the theology of the local church could be seen as a hallmark of the council's ecclesiological vision.

The restored appreciation of the local church at Vatican II was not accidental but the fruit of a retrieval of ancient ecclesial consciousness by theologians in the first half of the twentieth century.[7] The groundwork for this, however, was laid a century earlier in the work of the Tübingen theologian Johann Adam Möhler (1796-1838) who articulated the first modern Catholic ecclesiology. The influence of so-called eucharistic ecclesiology developed by Orthodox theologians, especially those associated with the Russian diaspora, also played an important role. Essentially, the retrieval of the patristic understanding of the ministry of the bishop, of catholicity, and of the connection between the Eucharist and the church made a re-entry of the local church into the ecclesiological discourse possible.[8]

There is no doubt that the rediscovery of the local church at Vatican II is of vast importance for Catholic ecclesiology. Yet there are compelling reasons for remaining modest in one's claims about how much the council

---

6. von Allmen, "L'Église locale parmi," 512.

7. For instance, Emile Mersch, Yves Congar, Henri de Lubac, and Jérôme Hamer.

8. For an excellent survey of this development, see Ruddy, *Local Church*, 9-53. See also González de Cardenal, "Development of a Theology," 11-43.

actually accomplished in this regard. One cannot say, for instance, that the local church structures the conciliar documents. Vatican II's theology of the local church is provisional and consists of just a few statements that stand in contrast to the council's prevailing universalistic ecclesiology. These statements establish some basic principles for a more systematic reflection. As Christopher Ruddy aptly stated, "if one speaks of Vatican II's theology of the local church, then, it must be admitted that it has more of the seed than of the fruit, more of the sketch than of the formal portrait."[9]

This lack of focus is mainly methodological since the council's ecclesiology for the most part unfolds within a universalistic framework. Its starting point is the whole or universal church rather than a local community centered on the bishop and the Eucharist. In this framework, bishops are first of all members of the episcopal college whose head is the pope and with whom they exercise supreme authority over the whole church. Within this framework, the local church can play only a minor role, if any at all. Another methodological drawback of Vatican II's ecclesiology is that the theology of the local church did not play a major role in the genesis of the conciliar documents. As González de Cardenal observes, the key conciliar teachings about the local church "developed at the margins of the general redaction of *Lumen gentium*."[10] For instance, one key assertion about the local church is that, according to the New Testament, legitimately organized local groups of the faithful united to their pastors are considered churches.[11] This statement is an interpolation prompted by a speech of the Auxiliary Bishop of Fulda, Edward Schick.[12] Hans Küng, who prepared the speech, explained why this statement appears so late in the Dogmatic Constitution on the Church. According to Küng, Charles Moeller, a council *peritus* from the University of Louvain and an advisor to the council's Theological Commission involved in the drafting of *Lumen gentium*, asked Küng where the passage about the local church should be inserted. Küng allegedly suggested that it should appear as soon as possible in the document since in the New Testament the church is originally a local church. Moeller replied, however, that this was not possible since chapters one and two of *Lumen gentium* were already finalized. Thus this statement on the local church appears in chapter three.[13]

9. Ruddy, *Local Church*, 49.
10. González de Cardenal, "Development of a Theology," 42.
11. LG 26.
12. The English text of the speech can be found in Küng et al., *Council Speeches of Vatican II*, 35–38.
13. See Küng, *My Struggle for Freedom*, 369.

The council developed its ecclesiology in stages. Its foundations were initially articulated in the "Constitution on the Sacred Liturgy," *Sacrosanctum concilium* (1963). The doctrine of the church was then laid out most thoroughly in the "Dogmatic Constitution on the Church," *Lumen gentium* (1964), and in the "Pastoral Constitution on the Church in the Modern World," *Gaudium et spes* (1965). Some themes from *Lumen gentium* such as episcopacy, ecumenism, and catholicity received additional, and in some respects more refined, treatment in other council documents such as the "Decree on the Pastoral Office of the Bishops in the Church," *Christus Dominus* (1964), the "Decree on Ecumenism," *Unitatis redintegratio* (1965), and the "Decree on the Church's Missionary Activity," *Ad gentes divinitus* (1965).

The Issue of Terminology

Before embarking on a more detailed treatment of the local church at Vatican II, it ought to be noted that the council's documents are not consistent in the way they employ the terms "particular" and "local" church.[14] Generally, the term "particular church" refers to a diocese.[15] Several times, however, it designates a grouping of dioceses such as patriarchates, which are in union with the pope, but have their own discipline, liturgical customs, and theological and spiritual heritage.[16] The term "local church" is used less frequently. In a few passages it too designates a diocese.[17] On one occasion it refers to patriarchates,[18] but on two occasions "local congregations" gathered for the Eucharist are also called "churches."[19] Lastly, in one passage the terms "particular" and "local" are used at the same time, without distinction, referring to Eastern-rite churches.[20] After the council, theologians tried to clarify this terminological inconsistency, but they did not reach consensus. As a result, many ecclesiologists use "local church" and "particular church" interchangeably.

---

14. The use of these terms is reviewed in, for instance, de Lubac, *Motherhood of the Church*, 171–213; Killian, "Meaning and Nature," 251–53; Granfield, "Local Church," 256–58; Legrand, "La réalisation," 145–59; Ghirlanda, "Universal Church, Particular Church," 240–45; Routhier, "'Église locale,'" 283–87.

15. See SC 13b, 111b; LG 23a (3x), 27a, 45b; CD 3b, 11a, b, 23e, 28a, 36a; AG 6c, d, 20a, g.

16. See LG 13b; OE 2, 3, 4 (2x), 10, 16, 17, 19 (2x); AG 22b.

17. See AG 19d, 27a, 32d.

18. See LG 23d.

19. See LG 26a, 28d.

20. See UR 14a.

Three Key *Loci* of Vatican II's Treatment of the Local Church

Even someone not trained in theology can easily recognize that the notions of renewal and reform play a key role in the council's constitution on the liturgy. The topic of the local church is different, however; it does not stand out so conspicuously in the council's teaching on the church. Rather, it appears implicitly in the council's treatment of the relationship of the Eucharist and the church, of catholicity, and of the relationship of the bishop and the local church. These three themes will serve as anchors for discussion of the central points of Vatican II's theology of the local church.

Bishop, Eucharist, and the Church

The topic of the local church initially emerges in the course of a reflection on the relationship among the bishop, the Eucharist, and the church. This takes place in *Sacrosanctum concilium*, the very first document promulgated by the council.[21] Most aptly this relationship is expressed in article 41 which states:

> The bishop is to be considered as the High Priest of his flock from whom the life in Christ of his faithful is in some way derived and upon whom it in some way depends. Therefore all should hold in the greatest esteem the liturgical life of the diocese centered around the bishop, especially in his cathedral church. They must be convinced that the principal manifestation of the Church consists in the full, active participation of all God's holy people in the same liturgical celebrations, especially in the same Eucharist, in one prayer, at one altar, at which the bishop presides, surrounded by his college of priests and by his ministers.[22]

Lumen gentium, which chronologically follows *Sacrosanctum Concilium*, also makes a connection between the Eucharist and the church. In article 7, it says:

> Really sharing in the body of the Lord in the breaking of the Eucharistic bread, we are taken up into communion with him and with one another. "Because the bread is one, we, though many, are one body, all of us who partake of the one bread" (1 Cor. 10:17). In this way all of us are made members of his body (cf. 1 Cor. 12:27), "but severally members one of another" (Rom. 12:4).

---

21. For a study of the significance of *Sacrosanctum concilium* for Vatican II's ecclesiology, see Faggioli, *True Reform*.

22. For other examples, see SC 2, 7, 10, 42.

The strongest articulation of the connection among the bishop, the Eucharist, and the church is in *Lumen gentium* 26, which amounts to nothing less than a *magna carta* of the theology of the local church. It states:

> The bishop, invested with the fullness of the sacrament of Orders, is "the steward of the grace of the supreme priesthood," above all in the Eucharist, which he himself offers, or ensures that it is offered, from which the Church ever derives its life and on which it thrives. This Church of Christ is really present in all legitimately organized local groups of the faithful, which, insofar as they are united to their pastors, are also quite appropriately called Churches in the New Testament.

As I mentioned above, this statement is an interpolation prompted by a speech delivered by one of the bishops. Two important claims are made here: (a) that the local church is a real presence of the universal church, and (b) that the word "church" refers to a concrete community of Christians. The former assertion is then further explained:

> In [the local groups] the faithful are gathered together through the preaching of the Gospel of Christ, and the mystery of the Lord's Supper is celebrated. . . . In each altar community, under the sacred ministry of the bishop, a manifest symbol is to be seen of the charity and "unity of the mystical body, without which there can be no salvation." In these communities, though they may often be small and poor, or existing in the diaspora, Christ is present through whose power and influence the One, Holy, Catholic and Apostolic Church is constituted.

Further significance of *Lumen gentium* 26 lies in allowing one to identify congregations of the faithful on the intra-diocesan level as local/particular churches. A *relatio* of the council's Doctrinal Commission supports this interpretation when with regard to article 26 it says, "It is understood . . . that a particular church, especially within a diocese, whether it is a parish or it has been assembled for another reason, is nevertheless always subject to the bishop."[23]

The texts considered so far show that the council retrieved the integrity of the local church by recovering the ancient patristic notion that "the Eucharist makes the church." As Richard Gaillardetz explains, the import of such statements for the theology of the local church is in affirming that a gathering of a local community for the celebration of the Eucharist,

---

23. "Consideratur . . . Ecclesia particularis praesertim infra diocesim, sive sit paroecialis, sive alia ratione convocetur, semper tamen sub dependentia ab Episcopo" (AS 3.1:253).

especially when presided over by the bishop, is not just a matter of Christ's sacramental presence in the eucharistic species, or, as one could say, a matter of the church making the Eucharist. Rather, it is equally a matter of Christ's ecclesial presence in those who are gathered, who become the Body of Christ in that place.[24] The key theological insight is that since Christ gives himself fully, each local eucharistic community must be fully church. It ought not to be seen as a mere subdivision of the church universal, but its local realization. This is one of the central points of Vatican II's theology of the local church, namely, that each local church contains the full theological reality of the one, holy, catholic, and apostolic church, though it is not the whole church.[25]

Article 11 of the "Decree on the Pastoral Office of Bishops," *Christus Dominus*, is also counted among the pillars of Vatican II's theology of the local church. It reflects the same understanding of the local church as *Lumen gentium* 26. The article states:

> A diocese is a section of the People of God entrusted to a bishop to be guided by him with the assistance of his clergy so that, loyal to its pastor and formed by him into one community in the Holy Spirit through the Gospel and the Eucharist, it constitutes one particular church in which the one, holy, catholic and apostolic Church of Christ is truly present and active.

By asserting that a diocese constitutes one particular church in which the one, holy, catholic, and apostolic church of Christ is truly present and active, this article reaffirms that the local church is not merely an administrative district of the universal church. In addition, it is theologically significant that the designation "one, holy, catholic, and apostolic church" is here applied to a particular church, rather than being reserved exclusively for the church universal.

Yet the opening statement that a diocese is a section or a portion of the people of God (*populi Dei portio*) may be seen as in tension with the recognition of the full ecclesial reality of the local church since it is not clear in what sense the diocese is "*populi Dei portio.*" If this "portion" is understood as a part of a larger whole, then as a particular church, the diocese would not be the full realization of the universal church. Emmanuel Lanne has shown, however, that the intention of the opening statement in *Christus Dominus* 11 was to define the diocese in canonical terms. Thus the expression "*populi Dei portio*" should be understood as defining the limits of the bishop's jurisdiction in the sense that the bishop's direct jurisdiction is limited to

---

24. Gaillardetz, *Church in the Making*, 46.
25. Cf. von Allmen, "L'Église locale parmi," 512–37.

that portion of God's people entrusted to him. This expression should be understood as referring to the canonical aspect of the bishop's jurisdiction over the diocese and should not be seen as contradicting an affirmation of the full ecclesial reality of the local church.[26]

Catholicity of the Church

Vatican II's theology of the local church is further implicit within the council's treatment of the church's catholicity. The pre-Vatican II theological manuals treated catholicity in terms of universality, that is, as the church's geographical extension throughout the whole world.[27] As Gaillardetz notes, with some exceptions such as the nineteenth-century Tübingen School, "catholicity was practically collapsed into the marks of unity and apostolicity, that is, visible union with and obedience to the apostolic see of Rome."[28] Catholicity meant uniformity, which left little room for diversity at the level of the local churches.

Vatican II expanded this understanding of the church's catholicity by retrieving its qualitative dimension, which was part of the theological consciousness in the first millennium. This qualitative dimension of catholicity combines unity and diversity and refers to unity-in-diversity or to fullness-in-unity. Although the universalistic or quantitative notion of catholicity is still present in the conciliar documents,[29] in several places there is a shift toward a catholicity that is qualitative in character. This is the case in the "Constitution of the Sacred Liturgy" when the council speaks with approval about particularity and diversity. For instance, article 37 says:

> Even in liturgy the Church does not wish to impose a rigid uniformity in matters which do not involve the faith or the good of the whole community. Rather does she respect and foster the qualities and talents of the various races and nations. Anything in these people's way of life which is not indissolubly bound up with superstition and error she studies with sympathy, and if, possible, preserves intact. She sometimes even admits such

---

26. Lanne, "Local Church," 301–2.

27. See, for instance, Tanquerey, *Synopsis theologiae dogmaticae fundamentalis*, 418–30; Van Noort, *Dogmatic Theology*, 2:143–49; Salaverri, "On the Church of Christ," 499–501; Ott, *Fundamentals of Catholic Dogma*, 306–8.

28. Gaillardetz, *Church in the Making*, 61.

29. It is present, for instance, in *Lumen Gentium* 13, which states: "All men [sic] are called to belong to the new People of God. This People, therefore, whilst remaining one and only one, is to be spread throughout the whole world and to all ages in order that the design of God's will may be fulfilled."

things into the liturgy itself, provided they harmonize with its true and authentic spirit.[30]

As Josef Jungmann explains, the council here rejects a rigid uniformity manifested in the Europeanization of Catholicism and welcomes the values of other cultures.[31]

Perhaps the most paradigmatic statement that celebrates the qualitative notion of catholicity as unity-in-diversity is in *Lumen gentium* 13:

> This character of universality which adorns the People of God is a gift from the Lord himself whereby the Catholic Church ceaselessly and efficaciously seeks to recapitulate the whole of humanity and all its goods under Christ the Head in the unity of his Spirit. In virtue of this catholicity each part contributes its own gifts to other parts and to the whole Church, so that the whole and each of the parts are strengthened by the common sharing of all things and by the common effort to attain to fullness in unity.

Catholicity here refers to the transformation and recapitulation of everything in Christ.

This qualitative notion of catholicity as unity-in-diversity is present also in the "Decree on Ecumenism." Article 4 states:

> While preserving unity in essentials, let everyone in the Church, according to the office entrusted to him [sic], preserve a proper freedom in the various forms of spiritual life and discipline, in the variety of liturgical rites, and even in the theological elaborations of revealed truth. In all things let charity prevail. If they are true to this course of action, they will be giving ever richer expression to the authentic catholicity and apostolicity of the Church.

This text, which reads like an elaboration on the famous dictum attributed to Augustine,[32] rejects the understanding of catholicity as uniformity and presents it rather as multiplicity or diversity within unity.

Respect for particularity and diversity, especially that of culture, is nowhere better developed than in the "Decree on the Church's Missionary Activity," *Ad gentes*, which is the only document of Vatican II that has a chapter dedicated specifically to particular/local churches.[33] In article 22 it says:

---

30. See also SC 38–40, 123.

31. Jungmann, "Constitution on the Sacred Liturgy," 27.

32. "In necessariis unitas, in dubiis libertas, in omnibus caritas [In necessary things, unity; in uncertain things, freedom; in everything, charity]."

33. See AG 19–21.

> Just as happened in the economy of incarnation, the young churches, which are rooted in Christ and built on the foundations of the apostles, take over all the riches of the nations which have been given to Christ as an inheritance. They borrow from the customs, traditions, wisdom, teaching, arts and sciences of their people everything which could be used to praise the glory of the Creator. . . . [Without syncretism and false exclusiveness], the Christian life will be adapted to the mentality and character of each culture, and local traditions together with the special qualities of each national family, illumined by the light of the Gospel, will be taken up into a Catholic unity. So new particular churches, each with its own traditions, have their place in the community of the Church.[34]

What does the qualitative understanding of catholicity with its affirmation of diversity and particularity have to do with the theology of the local church? The positive treatment of the diversity and particularity of church life, which is most evident in various local churches, means that the diverse local churches *qua* diverse contribute to the catholicity of the church as a whole. As *Lumen gentium* 23 states: "This multiplicity of local Churches, united in a common effort, shows all the more resplendently the catholicity of the undivided Church." Vatican II thus presented locality and diversity as not being at odds with catholicity, but as building it up. What is at odds with catholicity is uniformity. In this insight lies the significance of the council's expanded view of catholicity as unity-in-diversity or fullness-in-unity.

The Bishop and the Local Church

The acknowledgement of the full ecclesial reality of the local church has implications for the conception of the relationship between the local and the universal church. If prior to the council, within the ecclesiology of *societas perfecta*, local churches were conceived as *parts* of the whole/universal church, after the council's recognition of the full ecclesial reality of the local church, this was no longer adequate. The local church that is wholly the church cannot relate to the universal church as a part to a whole.

The relationship between the local and the universal church is treated by Vatican II explicitly, albeit very briefly and not in sufficient depth, in article 23 of *Lumen gentium* in the context of reflecting on the relationship between the bishop and the local church. This article is part of the third chapter, which deals with the hierarchical structure of the church, and is the last in a

---

34. For more examples, see AG 8–11, 16, 23, 26; OE 2, 5; UR 14, 16–18; GS 53–55, 58, 61, 91.

series of several articles (18–23) in which the council treats collegiality—the notion that the college of bishops (including the pope) rules the church—and teaches among other things that episcopal consecration confers the fullness of the sacrament of Orders.[35] Article 23 marks a shift in the conceptualization of the college of bishops. The preceding articles (20–22) treat the collegiality of bishops within the universalistic ecclesiological framework. The starting point is the college as a whole and the focus is on the bishop's membership in the college, which together with the pope as its head and never apart from him, shares in the supreme authority in the church as a whole. In article 23, the starting point shifts from the college and from the bishop's membership in it to the bishop's relationship to his local church. The college of bishops is thus conceptualized in relation to the communion of local churches. The pertinent section of the article says:

> Collegiate unity is also apparent in the mutual relations of each bishop to individual dioceses and with the universal church. . . . The individual bishops are the visible source and foundation of unity in their own particular Churches, which are constituted after the model of the universal Church; it is in these and formed out of them [*in quibus et ex quibus*] that the one and unique Catholic Church exists. And for that reason precisely each bishop represents his own Church, whereas all, together with the pope, represent the whole Church in a bond of peace, love and unity.

It appears that this statement wants to assert the mutual interrelationship, in the sense of inclusion and interiority, between the local churches and the universal church. The phrase *in quibus et ex quibus* excludes an understanding of particular churches as parts of the church, which exists by assembling those parts together as if the universal church is a federation of particular churches.

Nevertheless, the formulation of the mutual relationship between the local and the universal church is ambiguous. The difficulty is that *Lumen gentium* 23 simply juxtaposes seemingly contradictory assertions. On the one hand, it states that particular churches are constituted after the image of the universal church, and thus implies a priority of the universal church. On the other hand, it asserts that the one and unique catholic church is formed in and out of the particular churches, which implies the priority of the particular church. How both of these assertions can be true at the same time, within the same conceptual framework, is not clear. The

---

35. LG 21.

council thus left the issue of the relationship between the local and the universal church ultimately unresolved.

These are the basic contours of the council's treatment of the local church. One can conclude that even though Vatican II did not develop a robust and a fully coherent theology of the local church, it can nevertheless be credited with significant advances in this area. After a rather long neglect of this topic in Catholic ecclesiology, the council provided some core insights that can serve as spring-boards for ecclesiologists to construct a more comprehensive and systematic theology of the local church. By assigning full ecclesial reality to local eucharistic gatherings of the faithful, especially those presided over by their bishop, Vatican II implicitly said that local churches could not be viewed as mere administrative divisions of the universal church, and that the universal church was not like a multi-national corporation with local churches as its branch offices. The council recovered the experience of the church from the first millennium, according to which the whole or universal church is a communion of local churches.

The council's expanded notion of catholicity is also significant for the theology of the local church. Vatican II recovered the qualitative dimension of catholicity and in several places presented it in terms of unity-in-diversity or fullness-in-unity. Central to this understanding of catholicity is the positive appreciation of diversity and particularity. In this understanding, catholicity is not in tension with locality and diversity, but with uniformity. Locality and diversity actually build up catholicity. Related to this view of catholicity is the notion that local churches not only receive from, but also offer to, the universal church their gifts and insights. This exchange of gifts, whether cultural or social, points to the fact that church is not only a noun, but also a verb. It is an event which happens in particular social and cultural contexts. By broadening the understanding of the church's catholicity as unity-in-diversity, Vatican II raised a question concerning the relationship between the local and the universal church. Without resolving this issue, it seems that the council wanted to assert that there exists a relationship of mutual interdependence between the local church and the universal church.

Overall Vatican II achieved several key advances with regard to the theology of the local church: the notion of the local church as fully church though not the whole church, the understanding of the universal church as a *communio ecclesiarum*, the notion of the mutual relationship between the local churches and the church universal, and the attribution of the church's catholicity not only to the universal church but also to local churches.

Komonchak on the Local Church

Almost everything the council said on the subject of the local church was said implicitly in the course of treating other topics. Nevertheless, what the council said about the local church, whether implicitly or explicitly, deserves to be seen as a major achievement since, with a few exceptions in the second half of the nineteenth and the first half of the twentieth century, the entire second millennium of Roman Catholicism could be characterized as an eclipse of the theology of the local church.[36] The council's retrieval of the full theological reality of the local church made it clear that local churches ought not to be considered mere administrative units or parts of the universal church. Everything else about Vatican II's treatment of the local church is less clear and was left to theologians to be worked out with more precision after the council's close. For instance, the conciliar documents lack clarity on such questions as: (1) what counts as a local church? What should enter into the theological definition of a local/particular church, and consequently what should be considered an individual instance of a local/particular church? (2) what is the import of the enlarged understanding of the church's catholicity for the notion of the church's unity? and (3) what is the relationship between the local and the universal church? Komonchak has addressed these three issues and provided both his interpretation of the conciliar texts and insights that go beyond them. The insight he offered has considerably furthered the theology of the local church.

Komonchak has called the shift initiated by Vatican II from a universalistic ecclesiology to an ecclesiology of communion a "Copernican revolution."[37] He considers *Lumen gentium* 23, 26, 28 and *Christus Dominus* 11 to be the principal texts pertaining to Vatican II's theology of the local church. They are important instances of a shift in the conciliar documents from universalistic ecclesiology to an ecclesiology focused on the local church. They offer a theological vision of the church's coming-to-be in and out of the local churches and spell out what Komonchak has called the spiritual, theological, or generative principles of the church. These principles constitute the church as a reality distinct from other human communities and, where they exist as formal principles of a community, there one finds the church. These principles are: the call of God, the grace of the Holy Spirit, the preaching of the Gospel, the celebration of the Eucharist, the fellowship

---

36. See Lanne, "Local Church," 288–99.

37. For instance, Komonchak, "Ministry and the Local Church," 58; "Toward a Theology," 17; "Local Realization of the Church," 78; "Local Church," 321; "Local Church and the Church Catholic," 432; "Culture and History," 49.

of love, and the apostolic ministry.³⁸ In giving attention to these spiritual principles of the church, Komonchak sees the council's repudiation of an ecclesiology that focuses mainly on the institutional dimensions of the church in terms of the identification and distribution of authority.³⁹

Theological Significance of Locality

Komonchak's most distinctive contribution to the theology of the local church concerns the theological significance of locality. He has argued that locality—socio-political and cultural factors—should enter into the theological definition of the local church.

Descending Approach

After the council adjourned, theologians began to construct a more comprehensive and systematic theology of the local church. Sorting through the terminological inconsistency in the conciliar documents with regard to the terms "local" and "particular" sparked a discussion about which of these terms should be used to designate the churches on the infra-universal level. The question of the criteria for a theological definition of a local church became central in the discussion.

One of the most important attempts in developing such criteria came from Henri de Lubac. He argued that based on the Vatican II documents, the term "particular church" should be used when one wants to define the church theologically, and that this designation should be reserved for a diocese.⁴⁰ For de Lubac, only spiritual and hierarchical considerations enter into the definition of the particular church. While not denying that the church is always bound to a given place and gathers people of various interests together, de Lubac argued that the particular church is not determined "by topography or by any other factor whether of the natural order or of the human order. She is determined by 'the mystery of faith.' We would say, in a word, that her criterion is of an essentially *theological order*."⁴¹ De Lubac agrees that the term "local church" can also be used to define a church,

---

38. Komonchak, "Ministry and the Local Church," 58; "Toward a Theology," 17; "Local Church," 323, 326, 332; "Local Church and the Church Catholic," 417, 420; "Theology of the Local Church," 37, 39, 44; "Epistemology of Reception," 198; "Culture and History," 50.

39. Komonchak, "Theology of the Local Church," 37.

40. See de Lubac, *Motherhood of the Church*, 171–213.

41. de Lubac, *Motherhood of the Church*, 193–94.

not theologically but in terms of various socio-cultural factors. Essentially, his position is that only the particular church "belongs to the fundamental structure of the universal church (the latter being realized only in the former); but the local church, with her singular traits, is nonetheless something useful, or even indispensable *ad bonum Ecclesiae*."[42]

Giuseppe Colombo also argued that the generative principles of the church, rather than the sociological differences among the churches, provided for both the unity and plurality of the local churches. This plurality arises through the varying interplay of these principles and through differences in Christian experience. For Colombo, cultures cannot make the church, only the generative principles can. Thus, cultures cannot be the constitutive element that characterizes local churches. Cultural characterization of local churches can only be conventional and therefore superficial, even misleading.[43] Colombo's view resembles that of de Lubac. In both cases, geographical and socio-cultural designations are secondary at best; in the case of Colombo, they appear to be theologically insignificant categories. The positions of de Lubac and Colombo have not acquired a broad acceptance among ecclesiologists, many of whom use "local church" and "particular church" interchangeably.

Komonchak's position on the question of whether the churches on the infra-universal level should be called local or particular underwent development. In his 1980 article "Ministry and the Local Church," he said that "the inconsistency in the conciliar vocabulary makes the choice of regular vocabulary somewhat arbitrary and the choice of one or another of these terms by commentators does not by itself seem to imply any major theological differences."[44] In his 1986 paper "Toward a Theology of the Local Church," he first rearticulated the earlier position, but then he contended that the choice of terminology nevertheless often "reflects certain important theological options,"[45] such as how one understands what should enter into the theological definition of the local church. Not convinced by de Lubac's or Colombo's reasoning, Komonchak has argued that the designation "local church" should be understood in theological terms.

In arguing his position, Komonchak distinguishes between two approaches to the theology of the local church. The first approach, which he calls *classic* and which is characteristic of de Lubac's view, concentrates on

42. de Lubac, *Motherhood of the Church*, 210.

43. See Giuseppe Colombo, "La teologia della Chiesa locale," 17–38, esp. 32–38; "Il 'Popolo di Dio' e il 'misterio,'" 97–169, referenced in Komonchak, "Local Church and the Church Catholic," 436–37.

44. Komonchak, "Ministry and the Local Church," 56.

45. Komonchak, "Toward a Theology," 15.

identifying the meaning of the noun "church" and of the adjectives "particular/local" and "universal." It first identifies the elements or principles that constitute the church and distinguish it from all other human communities. The full reality of the church, not just a part of it, exists wherever such principles are the formal principles of a community. The classic approach then determines where a normative instance of an individual church can be found. The answer to this has ranged among different theologians from two or three gathered in Jesus' name, to small communities of the faithful, or to parishes, dioceses, and even regional, national, and international groups of dioceses. The most common answer, however, has been a diocese—that is, a community of the faithful presided over by a bishop—and it has most often been designated as a particular church. In the classic approach, all other communities of Christians are then related to this normative instance of an individual church. The third movement in the classic approach is to identify the one church which exists in the individual churches. Since the individual churches are fully churches, not just parts of the one church, this one church is understood as more than the mere sum-total of all the individual churches. It is referred to as "universal" because it is defined by the generative principles which are found in all individual churches, and by abstracting from what distinguishes them from one another. Komonchak notes that because of the role the Bishop of Rome and the college of bishops play in this view, the universal church could be described as the church governed by the pope and the college of bishops. A theology of the local church in this approach thus often becomes a reflection on the relationship between a diocese and the universal church, or between the authority of an individual bishop and that of the pope. The terms *universal* and *catholic* often carry the same meaning in the classic approach.[46]

Komonchak does not think that the use of the term "particular" for a diocese as the normative instance of an individual church is very illuminating because it adds little to what is already known from identifying the church with the constitutive principles that generate it. The only thing that is added is the identification of apostolic ministry with the bishop. The term "particular" does not say anything about the individuating principles of a specific church. For these principles the classic approach uses the term "local," which refers to the socio-cultural and historical factors. While the generative principles are understood as theological or divine, the individuating principles are understood as *just* socio-cultural or human.[47] Even though Komonchak considers de Lubac's position nuanced, he questions some of

---

46. Komonchak, "Local Church and the Church Catholic," 417–18.
47. Komonchak, "Local Church and the Church Catholic," 418.

his presuppositions. Analyzing de Lubac's descriptions of particular church and local church, Komonchak concludes that the result of de Lubac's strict distinction between particularity and locality is that the particular church "appears to float in mid-air, constituted solely by theological, divine, supernatural elements."[48] Furthermore, Komonchak notes that while the focus in the classic approach is on the noun "church," it leaves the dimensions referred to by the adjectives "local," "particular," and "universal underdeveloped." He explains:

> About the only thing particular about the adjective "particular" is the presence of a single bishop, while "universal" is defined by abstraction. The socio-cultural and historical elements that may enter into the definition of "local" are not regarded as ecclesiologically significant except at best in some secondary sense. They are not among the constitutive principles even of the "particular" church, and they are precisely what is abstracted from in the derivation of the abstract and formal universality of the one Church that exists in all the particular churches.[49]

Komonchak argues that the classic approach fails to account for the elements that diversify individual churches and conceives of them as something accidental—as not pertaining to the substance of the church.[50] Komonchak thus considers it central to the theology of the local church to ascertain which elements should enter into the theological definition of a local church. Ultimately it comes down to the ecclesiological significance that should be assigned to the elements of locality, by which Komonchak means political, social, and cultural particularity.[51]

Ascending Approach

The approach to the theology of the local church that Komonchak advocates has as its starting point the recognition of the dimensions of local particularity. He shows preference for the adjectives "local" and "catholic" over "particular" and "universal," and he explains that this preference is not arbitrary but reflects "a different answer to the question whether local individuating elements enter into the very constitution of a local church

---

48. Komonchak, "Local Church and the Church Catholic," 436.
49. Komonchak, "Local Church and the Church Catholic," 419.
50. Komonchak, "Local Church and the Church Catholic," 419.
51. Komonchak, "Local Church," 322–23.

and whether the Church's catholicity is adequately expressed as merely abstract universality."[52]

Komonchak's conception of the church's genesis underpins his theology of the local church. As discussed in the previous chapter, he distinguishes two principles or moments in the genesis of the church: objective and subjective. The former refers to one generation's communication of what it means to be church to another generation, and the latter refers to the reception and appropriation of this communication. The church happens at the intersection of these two moments. It happens when God's gift is received and appropriated as a response to the challenges, problems, and resources of specific persons, times, and places. These challenges, problems, and resources are similar but they also vary according to different social, political, and cultural contexts.[53]

Komonchak argues that when one conceives of the church's genesis in these terms, especially if the emphasis is on the human acts by which the church comes to be, one's focus necessarily shifts from the universal church to the local church.[54] This is so because the human acts that make the church are the acts of concrete men and women living in concrete cultural, social, and political milieu. The universal church does not arise in the abstract but concretely. As he explains:

> It is not the word of God in general that gathers the Church in faith, but the word as preached in specific interpretative contexts and received as a response to concrete threats to authentic human meaning. The Church's hope overcomes quite concrete experiences of the demonic power of evil in persons and structures. The Church does not celebrate the Eucharist in general; it celebrates it in quite concrete human groups, and the communion effected in and through such a Eucharist overcomes quite concrete experiences of alienation.[55]

This is at the center of Komonchak's argument why it is not legitimate to make *locality*—by which he means the social and cultural differences among the churches—a secondary theological principle in the process of the church's self-realization. In contrast to de Lubac, Komonchak considers locality an

---

52. Komonchak, "Local Church and the Church Catholic," 419.
53. Komonchak, "Local Church," 327.
54. Komonchak, "Ministry and the Local Church," 69.
55. Komonchak, "Towards a Theology," 25. See also Komonchak, "Ministry and the Local Church," 69.

intrinsic dimension of the actualization of local churches and finds that it should therefore enter into the theological definition of the church.[56]

Komonchak explains that the existential priority of the local churches can be obscured if the church's unity is considered in abstract terms, that is, when it is argued that the church is one because the same Word of God, or the same Christ, or the same authority of the Scriptures and tradition is present in all the churches. While all this is true, Komonchak insists that it needs to be true concretely. He considers the objective principles to be effective principles of unity in and among the churches "only when and insofar as they mediate the gathering of individuals into local communities and of the local communities into a catholic unity."[57] He does not view the objective principles as effecting the unity among the churches "in virtue of some prior, supposedly universal meaning, ascertainable and interpretable without reference to concrete situations and problems."[58] Instead, they function in this way "in virtue of their capacity to illumine and to transform a nearly infinite variety of situations and problems."[59] The church's unity is thus realized "'from below' in the unity realized in and among the various and different communities."[60]

Komonchak considers Colombo's understanding of the place of locality in the theology of the local church inadequate because it envisions the human element in the church's coming-to-be as merely passive and receptive.[61] Komonchak also notes that Colombo's view illustrates the role anthropology plays in one's ecclesiology. He explains: "If the encounter between the gospel and culture is simply the *contestazione* between grace and sin, then Colombo's view can stand. But if the gospel finds in the various cultures not only what needs to be 'purified' and 'elevated,' but also what can be 'promoted' and 'taken up' (see *LG* 13), then the encounter is far more complex."[62] Komonchak agrees with both Colombo and de Lubac that the gospel and not culture primarily generates a church,[63] but he explains that while "the local factors . . . do not constitute the local Church *qua* Church, they do enter into the constitution of the local Church *qua* local. Without

---

56. Komonchak, "Towards a Theology," 25. See also Komonchak, "Local Church," 327.
57. Komonchak, "Ministry and the Local Church," 70.
58. Komonchak, "Ministry and the Local Church," 70.
59. Komonchak, "Ministry and the Local Church," 70.
60. Komonchak, "Ministry and the Local Church," 70.
61. Komonchak, "Local Church and the Church Catholic," 437.
62. Komonchak, "Local Church and the Church Catholic," 439.
63. See Komonchak, "Local Church and the Church Catholic," 439.

them there is in fact nothing local about the local Church, nothing particular about the particular Church."[64] Komonchak maintains that a local church comes to be in an encounter between the gospel and a particular culture, and he concludes that "this encounter, as it differs from other encounters of gospel and culture, must also generate a constitutively different local church."[65]

There have been other theologians who have argued for the theological significance of locality in a way similar to that of Komonchak. Hervé Legrand has criticized the decision in the 1983 revised Code of Canon Law to reserve the term "particular church" for a diocese[66]—a decision that seems to have followed de Lubac's rationale. Legrand has pointed out that the terms "particular" and "universal" are lexicographical contraries, and that this can lead to the conclusion that universality is a reality extrinsic to particular churches, which he would consider false universality. Legrand believes that Vatican II assigned greater theological significance to sociocultural particularity than de Lubac has acknowledged. Legrand thus prefers to use the term "local church" all the time and to qualify it with such terms as "diocesan" or "parochial" when necessary.[67] Gilles Routhier has also argued that the term "local church" should be used when referring to the church on the infra-universal level. For him this term better expresses the church's mission and catholicity while avoiding the shortcomings of "particular church." Key to Routhier's position is his evaluation of locality as not merely a sociocultural, but rather a theological category.[68]

Given Komonchak's conception of the church's genesis, his point that locality should enter into the theological definition of a local church is well taken. What one should also recognize here is that Komonchak makes a connection between anthropology and ecclesiology, a connection not so common for ecclesiologists to make. Locality, for Komonchak, is not just a geographical category. It is a theological category because it is anthropologically grounded insofar as locality refers to the people who respond to the gospel. It refers to the concreteness of their socio-political and cultural milieu. It also refers to their being subject to sin and open to God's offer of salvation.

Komonchak pushes his reflections on locality and its role in the theology of the local church to their limits. One cannot assign more significance

64. Komonchak, "Response to Gilles Routhier," (2007) 16. See also Komonchak, "Culture and History," 53.

65. Komonchak, "Local Church and the Church Catholic," 439.

66. See Legrand, "La réalisation," 145–59.

67. For Legrand's influence on Komonchak, see Komonchak "Toward a Theology," 15; "Local Church," 322.

68. Routhier, "'Église locale,'" 277–334.

to locality than to argue that it should enter into the theological definition of the local church. Komonchak is effectively saying that different localities will generate different local churches, where differences among the churches will not be accidental, but will enter into their constitution.[69] This view is the direct opposite of universalistic ecclesiology and the uniformity among the churches it fosters. An ecclesiology like that of Komonchak's, which starts with the local church and assigns locality a theologically constitutive place in the church's genesis, reconfigures both the notion of the whole or universal church and of the church's unity.

Perhaps the best analogy for Komonchak's view of locality and its significance for ecclesiology is the human species itself. On the one hand there are certain characteristics that apply to all of us such as that we all share human DNA and a basic human appearance; we all must have certain physical organs to be alive (i.e., heart, brain, lungs); unless severely handicapped, we are self-conscious creatures with the capacity to think, choose, and relate to others. These are analogical to the generative principles of the church in the sense that they are found in all of us. Each one of us, however, possesses a certain uniqueness. This uniqueness pertains both to our physicality and to our interiority (i.e., our personality, character, and other traits of our individuality that are particularly ours). They are not accidental to who we are but constitute us. What pertains to human uniqueness is analogical to what Komonchak means by locality. My uniqueness makes me into a person different from my sister or any other individual, though we are all human beings. Locality makes one church different from another church, though they are all churches. This coheres well with one of the key points of Komonchak's ecclesiological foundations: that churches are people. If churches are made of people, what applies to people should also apply to churches.

Komonchak's conception of locality and its significance for the theology of the local church is of importance for the notion of inculturation. Inculturation could be described as, "the incarnation of Christian life and of the Christian message in a particular cultural context, in such a way that this experience not only finds expression through elements proper to the culture in question, but becomes a principle that animates, directs and unifies the culture, transforming and remaking it so as to bring about 'a new creation.'"[70] As such, inculturation concerns not only the church's missionary activity to non-Christians who have not yet received the gospel, but because of the nature of the church's genesis, its coming-to-be in every gen-

---

69. See Komonchak, "Local Church and the Church Catholic," 439.

70. Arrupe, "Letter to the Whole Society," 9, cited in Schineller, *Handbook on Inculturation*, 6.

eration as elucidated by Komonchak, it concerns every local church.[71] As cultures develop and change, those who want to transmit the Gospel to the next generation must take into account that the reception of the Gospel is a dynamic process, not a simple handing on of ideas, moral codes, and rituals. The interaction between the Gospel and culture is the interaction between one generation's incarnation of Christian life and message, which took place in a particular cultural context, and another generation's locality—its sociopolitical and cultural milieu. Since the questions the new generation asks may be in some respects different from those of the previous generation, the church that will be generated may be in some respects a different church from the one which announced the Gospel. The same applies to announcing the Gospel to new cultures. The interaction between the Gospel and these cultures will produce a church that is different from the one that announced the Gospel. Komonchak's view of the church's genesis and his understanding of locality are illuminating for the process of inculturation. In fact, they may be seen as describing the same reality.

Komonchak's conception of the church's genesis also carries implications for how one thinks about the "nature" and "mission" of the church and how one relates "the church" and "world." First, Komonchak does not think it is possible to separate the "nature" and the "mission" of the church, "as if there were first a moment in which the Church becomes what it is and a second in which it looks around at the world to see what it might bring to it."[72] Rather, quoting Italian ecclesiologist Severino Dianich, Komonchak contends that "the Church's nature essentially consists in its historical mission."[73] Thus, in a text of ecclesiology it is incorrect to treat the church's mission in a later chapter after the church's nature had been treated from the beginning.[74] Second, Komonchak explains that in discussions about the church's mission to the world, the "world" does not refer primarily to the physical place, but rather to what Komonchak refers to as the human self-project. Consequently, to relate the church and the world is to correlate two projects which take place simultaneously: the Christian self-project and the collective human self-project. The Christian self-project is an occasion for the self-realization of the world and is distinct from the world in that it centers on Jesus Christ.[75]

71. For an introduction to the topic of inculturation in the context of the United States, see Phan, "Contemporary Theology and Inculturation," 109–30.

72. Komonchak, "Towards a Theology," 25–26.

73. Dianich, "Soggettività e Chiesa," 118, quoted in Komonchak, "Towards a Theology," 26.

74. Komonchak, "Local Church and the Church Catholic," 444.

75. Komonchak, "Toward a Theology," 26.

Meaning of Catholicity

Another area of the theology of the local church to which Komonchak made a distinct contribution is that of catholicity. In both the Apostles' and the Niceno-Constantinopolitan Creeds, the character of catholicity is attributed to the church. Theological reflection on the church's catholicity has varied over the centuries with an emphasis on either qualitative or extensive catholicity. The former emphasis was prominent in the patristic and medieval period, and the latter in the post-Reformation period. A qualitative notion of catholicity was retrieved in the nineteenth and twentieth centuries and made its way into the Vatican II documents.

Komonchak understands Vatican II as having enlarged the meaning of the church's catholicity. The council departed from the interpretation of catholicity as simple geographical extension or as worldwide uniformity and operated instead with the notion of catholicity as fullness-in-unity. This conception of catholicity sees value in diversity and particularity, especially in terms of culture. Komonchak sees the most pertinent expression of this vision in *Lumen gentium* 23 which says:

> This character of universality which adorns the People of God is a gift from the Lord himself whereby the Catholic Church ceaselessly and efficaciously seeks for the return of all humanity and all its goods under Christ the Head in the unity of his Spirit. In virtue of this catholicity each part contributes its own gifts to other parts and to the whole Church, so that the whole and each of the parts are strengthened by the common sharing of all things and by the common effort to attain fullness in unity.

In this and in several other statements,[76] Komonchak sees the council describing the concrete catholicity of the church according to which the church is a concrete universal, one that exists not despite, but on account of, the variety of the local churches.[77]

The conclusion Komonchak draws is that "if catholicity is considered to be part of the fundamental structure of the Church and if it is taken to mean something more than geographical universality, then diversity is among the fundamental, theologically essential elements of the concretely catholic Church."[78] Komonchak explains that this understanding of catholicity has repercussions for understanding the unity of the church. He writes,

---

76. See, for example, AG 4, 8, 10, 15, 22.

77. Komonchak, "Ministry and the Local Church," 59–60; "Toward a Theology," 18–20; "Local Realization of the Church," 78.

78. Komonchak, "Local Church," 324.

when unity and catholicity are practically identified, locality can only be considered as the ecclesiological equivalent of individuating matter in scholastic philosophy, that is, it is left without intelligible content. When catholicity is understood to add to unity dimensions of plurality and integration, locality (that is, cultural and historical particularity) is seen to be an inner dimension and requirement of catholicity, which is now understood as "fullness of unity" and, so far from a denial of the unity of the Church, as the most splendid illustration of its concretely universal character.[79]

For Komonchak then, locality is by no means an antithesis of catholicity, but rather its very realization. The church's catholicity is realized in and out of the local churches.[80] The unity of the church, then, cannot be conceived as a one-way dependency of some churches on other churches, but it must be achieved through an active common sharing among all the local churches presided over by the bishop of Rome.[81] Based on this understanding of catholicity, Komonchak contends that "the role of the Bishop of Rome is not best conceived as one of mediating between a local church and the universal Church, imagined as something above all the local churches, but between one local church and the other local churches."[82]

For Komonchak, catholicity is not something given but a task that is always to be achieved anew. This follows from his conception of the church's genesis. Since the church comes to be through an interaction of the objective and the subjective principles, and since the reception of the gospel is a continual task on the part of believers, the realization of the church's catholicity cannot be something given once and for all. It must be an ongoing process, something to be achieved again and again by every generation of believers.[83]

Komonchak considers this dynamic understanding of catholicity to be a challenge for the church. On the one hand, it is a challenge for many in positions of leadership because of a tendency toward uniformity and top-down leadership. On the other hand, it is also a challenge for the rest of the faithful, because local churches often tend to consider their particularity so normative that the particularity of other local churches is considered to be at best tolerable. Against these two tendencies, Komonchak has argued that catholicity

---

79. Komonchak, "Local Church and the Church Catholic," 445.
80. Komonchak, "Local Church and the Church Catholic," 445.
81. Komonchak, "Local Realization of the Church," 88.
82. Komonchak, "Local Church and the Church Catholic," 442.
83. Komonchak, "Local Church and the Church Catholic," 446. See also Komonchak, "Culture and History," 63.

does not mean merely allowing variety or diversity to exist, but rather, in interrelating and integrating that diversity into a whole.[84]

Komonchak is aware that the theology of the local church he envisions, with the significance it assigns to local particularity and diversity, has its potential downsides. It runs the danger of local churches closing in on themselves to the point that they lose the sense of belonging to the catholic fullness. In addition, Komonchak thinks it is easily conceivable that when the expressions of beliefs, worship, and practices become more localized, it will be more difficult for the churches to recognize each other as belonging to the same communion, and they may become isolated from one another. Furthermore, there are also temptations to ethnic, racial, political, or nationalistic exclusivism.[85] Komonchak gives examples of ethnic cleansings in Burundi, Rwanda, and in the former Yugoslavia, which took place toward the end of the second millennium. Komonchak considers these atrocities, which were in part religiously motivated and had heavy Christian involvement, a failure of genuine catholicity.[86]

To counteract such dangers, which seem to be real possibilities for a theology of the local church that emphasizes socio-cultural particularities in the self-realization of local churches, Komonchak proposes to conceive catholicity as redemptive integration. He thinks that the shift in understanding catholicity from geographical universality to qualitative wholeness will remain incomplete as long as ecclesiologists continue to emphasize catholicity in its formal and universal elements and see it almost exclusively in theological and ecclesiocentric terms as a dimension of the church's mystery. Komonchak is dissatisfied with the state of reflection on catholicity because, "the focus tends to remain on the inner inclusiveness and variety of the Church, and there is strikingly little discussion of the implications of catholicity for the redemption of history and society, for the role the Church must play as the sacrament not only of intimate union with God but also of the unity of the whole human race."[87]

Komonchak's view of catholicity as redemptive integration is synonymous with the notion of the church as sacrament. Catholicity is in this sense perceived as "a characteristic that, as a 'sign,' displays what the world of God's creation is supposed to be like and that, as an instrument, serves

---

84. Komonchak, "Culture and History," 53. See also Komonchak, "Theology of the Local Church," 49.

85. Komonchak, "Catholicity and the Redemption of History," 603; "Local Realization of the Church," 88. See also Komonchak, "Toward a Theology," 41.

86. See Komonchak, "Culture and History," 54.

87. Komonchak, "Catholicity and the Redemption of History," 605.

the realization of that purpose."[88] With the notion of catholicity as redemptive integration, Komonchak wants to communicate that the church should make a difference in the world. He cautions that the emphasis in the church's genesis upon racial, ethnic, or cultural distinctiveness can be an obstacle to such a vision of catholicity. For him, in order to achieve genuine catholicity conceived in terms of a reconciled and integrated communion, cultural distinctiveness needs to be relativized.[89]

Komonchak's point that diversity belongs to the essential elements of the church's catholicity is well taken. If catholicity is one of the marks of the church professed in the Creed, and if it incorporates diversity, then diversity must have the same status as locality; it must belong to the theological definition of a local church.

Komonchak's treatment of catholicity shows that he is a master of balance. He realizes that the positive value he ascribes to socio-cultural particularities may lead to local churches closing in on themselves and to various kinds of exclusivism. His proposal for deemphasizing the particularities among the local churches and conceiving catholicity as a redemptive integration appears to be necessary to maintain the *via media* between the extremes of uniformity stemming from a universalistic ecclesiology that does not see value in socio-cultural particularity, and radical fragmentation and exclusivism which is a possibility in an ecclesiology that focuses on local churches.

The way Komonchak thinks of locality and catholicity finds support in the work of Jean-Marie Roger Tillard (1927–2000), the foremost authority on the local church in the period after the council. Tillard's reflections on the catholicity of the local church display a rich understanding of locality. For Tillard, the church of God exists only in and through the local churches. He describes each local church as, "the human space (geographic, cultural, historical, and sociological) where the Gospel of God—"effected" in Jerusalem by the suffering of Christ and by Pentecost which manifests its effects—can be grasped as including both *homo* (human being) and *humus* (the earth) from which it sprouts, *homo* as *humus*, *homo* and his *humus*."[90] Locality for Tillard is not just a geographical category, but has an anthropological dimension touching upon the totality of the human condition.

Tillard understands the church to be catholic precisely because it is local. It is in the local church where one witnesses the interplay of various elements, possibly contradictory at first sight. It is in the interplay among

88. Komonchak, "Culture and History," 59.
89. Komonchak, "Catholicity and the Redemption of History," 611–12.
90. Tillard, *L'Église locale*, 53.

them that the catholicity, the fullness of the church of God, is realized.[91] Tillard ultimately argues that the church is catholic because it is of God who is catholic in his design of salvation: "The essence of the local church is found in its catholicity without which it would no longer be *of God*. It is the catholic church *of God* in this place."[92]

For Tillard, catholicity is the opposite of uniformity. Catholicity is unity-in-diversity and is synonymous with his understanding of communion, which already characterized the church that emerged at Pentecost. As he explains:

> The Pentecostal community—the basic cell of the Church—thus appears as the manifestation, the *epiphaneia*, of the opening up of the era of Salvation. This is so in the coming together, radically unbreakable, of three elements: the Spirit, the apostolic witness which centers on the Lord Jesus Christ, and the *communion* in which the human multitude and its diversity are contained within this unity and where the unity is expressed in the multitude and its diversity. These three elements belong to the very essence of the Church.[93]

This understanding of catholicity as unity-in-diversity allows Tillard to eliminate tensions between unity and diversity arising when catholicity is equated with mere universality. Like Komonchak, Tillard shows that neither unity and diversity nor catholicity and locality are mutually exclusive.

Church Local and Universal

The re-validation of the local church at Vatican II, in terms of its full ecclesial reality, raised the question of the relationship of the church local and universal. But the council's treatment of this issue is less than satisfying. There is only one explicit statement concerning this relationship which asserts that the particular churches are formed in the image of the universal church, and that the universal church exists in and out of the particular churches.[94] This raises more questions than it answers. It appears that the council wanted to affirm mutual interiority and reciprocity between the church local and universal but the articulation is confusing. It consists of two assertions: one seemingly stating the priority of the universal church, and the other the

91. See Tillard, *L'Église locale*, 125.
92. Tillard, *L'Église locale*, 141.
93. Tillard, *Church of Churches*, 8.
94. LG 23.

priority of the local church. How these two competing priorities amount to mutual interiority between the local churches and the universal church is not clear. After the council, ecclesiologists spilled plenty of ink trying to interpret what those two assertions mean. Some have advocated the priority of the universal church[95]; affirmations of the priority of the local church have been rare.[96] Others have rejected the whole question as misguided and argued that the relationship of the local church and the universal church ought to be envisioned in terms of simultaneity or reciprocity.[97]

The relationship of the local church and the universal church has usually been envisioned in terms of the relationship of the bishops to the pope. The question has profound practical consequences. The decades since the close of Vatican II have shown that the way one negotiates this question has enormous impact on such matters as liturgy, episcopal conferences, synods of bishops, evangelization, ecumenism, and the Petrine ministry. There is hardly anything in the life of the church that is unaffected by this question. After more than two decades of theological discussions, the Congregation for the Doctrine of the Faith weighed in on the issue in 1992 and took a stand on the side of the priority of the universal church over the local church. It stated:

> Particular churches, insofar as they are "part of the one church of Christ," have a special relationship of "mutual interiority" with the whole, that is, with the universal church, because in every particular church "the one, holy, catholic and apostolic church of Christ is truly present and active. For this reason, "the universal church cannot be conceived as the sum of the particular churches or as a federation of particular churches." It is not the result of the communion of the churches, but in its essential mystery it is a reality ontologically and temporally prior to every individual particular church.
>
> Indeed, according to the fathers, ontologically the church-mystery, the church that is one and unique, precedes creation

---

95. For instance, Bandera, "Iglesia particular e Iglesia universal," 80–87; Boff, *Ecclesiogenesis*, 19; Carlo Colombo, "La teologia della chiesa locale," 261–65; Mondin, *La Chiesa primicia del Regno*, 405–18; Ratzinger, *Called to Communion*, 43–44.

96. For instance, Forte, *Church*, 68–77. An affirmation of the priority of the local church should not be confused with a methodological insistence that ecclesiology as a systematic reflection on the church ought to start with the local church.

97. For instance, Tillard, *L'Église locale*, 228; Zizioulas, *Being as Communion*, 217, 237; Antón, "Local Church/Regional Church," 571–72; Granfield, "Priority Debate," 160–61. Hervé Legrand lists over thirty ecclesiologists writing in major European languages who hold the simultaneity position, see Legrand, "La théologie des Églises sœurs," 495.

> and gives birth to the particular churches as daughters. She expresses herself in them; she is the mother and not the offspring of the particular churches. Furthermore, the church is manifested temporally on the day of Pentecost in the community of the 120 gathered around Mary and the Twelve Apostles, the representatives of the one unique church and the founders-to-be of the local churches, who have a mission directed to the world: from the first the church speaks all languages.
>
> From the church, which in its origins and its first manifestation is universal, have arisen the different local churches as particular expressions of the one unique church of Jesus Christ. Arising within and out of the universal church, they have their ecclesiality in her and from her. Hence the formula of the Second Vatican Council: *The Church in and formed out of the churches (ecclesia in et ex ecclesiis)* is inseparable from this other formula, *the churches in and formed out of the church (ecclesiae in et ex ecclesia)*. Clearly the relationship between the universal church and the particular churches is a mystery and cannot be compared to that which exists between the whole and the parts in a purely human group or society.[98]

The letter sparked a vigorous debate, probably best known through the back-and-forth exchanges between Cardinals Ratzinger and Kasper.[99] As Brian Flanagan rightly points out, the heavy reliance of the letter on the private writings of Joseph Ratzinger has made its interpretation especially challenging.[100]

Komonchak has attributed the persistence of the priority question to the ambiguous treatment of the relationship of the local and universal church at Vatican II. But in his view, the question should not even arise, and merely posing it is problematic since it tends to lead to one of two unacceptable conclusions; either that local churches are simply subdivisions of the universal church, or that they come first and the universal church is simply a confederation of prior independent local churches. Both of these positions he considers inadequate.[101]

As with the question of the theological significance of locality, Komonchak has distinguished between two approaches that are operative in

---

98. CN 9.

99. For a summary and evaluation, see McDonnell, "Ratzinger/Kasper Debate," 227–50.

100. Flanagan, *Communion, Diversity, and Salvation*, 42.

101. Komonchak, "Local Church," 325; "Theology of the Local Church," 39.

conceiving the relationship of the local and universal church.[102] The "descending" approach envisions the relationship between the universal church and the local churches in terms of a whole to its parts. The whole precedes the parts, and the parts participate in the nature that only the whole fully possesses. Komonchak likens this view to a modern transnational corporation in which all authority is centralized in its headquarters (Rome) and dispersed into regional branches (dioceses). In contrast, in an "ascending" approach, the whole is not conceived prior to its parts but it, "comes to be, is constituted by, in, and out of the realizations of its many constituents. *All the intrinsic and distinctive elements that constitute the reality are realized individually, and the relationships that make the individual realizations a single whole are grounded in a common participation in one reality constitutive of them all.*"[103] In this view, the universal church does not exist apart from the local churches; rather, it *is* the communion of local churches. In the differences between these approaches, Komonchak sees a partial explanation of the different ecclesiological visions of the First and Second Vatican Councils, where the former represents the descending and the latter the ascending approaches. He sees the descending approach as the basis for Roman centralization in the second millennium and Vatican II as the effort to retrieve the ascending view both theoretically and practically. While Komonchak considers the ascending approach superior, he sees both views present in the documents of Vatican II and in the post-conciliar debates about the relationship of the local and universal church.[104]

Conceiving the universal church as the communion of the local churches, Komonchak has argued that the relationship of the local and the universal church ought to be conceived in terms of mutual interiority and has illustrated it with an example from human anatomy:

> The body's cells are alive only with the life of the whole organism, separated from which they are no longer living members, but inorganic tissue. On the other hand, the body is alive and functioning only in the living cells and as articulated in differentiated organs and members. In the same way, the life of the local Churches is the life of the whole Church, which has no existence except as realized and functioning in the varied and diverse local Churches.[105]

---

102. Komonchak, "Church Universal," 30.
103. Komonchak, "Church Universal," 30.
104. Komonchak, "Church Universal," 31.
105. Komonchak, "Local Church," 327.

This example shows well that the universal church is not something separate from the local churches; they are interdependent.

Komonchak has found the reasoning of the CDF concerning the ontological and chronological priority of the universal church over any individual particular church unconvincing. He considers asserting the priority of either the universal or the local church to be a mistake on both theological and historical grounds.[106] Theologically, the CDF asserted the ontological priority of the universal church on the basis that the Church Fathers conceived the church-mystery as preceding creation.[107] Since this claim was met with heavy criticism, the Congregation and Joseph Ratzinger, its prefect, subsequently addressed and further clarified it. In addition to providing scriptural warrants for the contested view, three further points were made.[108] First, an affirmation of the ontological priority of the universal church means that the church does not owe its existence to some accidental historical developments. As Ratzinger explained, the Fathers followed rabbinic interpretations, according to which the Torah and Israel were preexistent, and since they considered Israel and the church to be ultimately identical, "they could not regard the Church as something that came into being at a late hour, *by chance*."[109] Second, the ontological priority of the universal church refers to God's idea of the church. Ratzinger explained that for him, the ontological priority of the universal church over the local church is so clear that objections against it seem possible

> only if one refuses to see God's *great idea*, the Church—perhaps through despair at her inadequacy here on earth—if one will

---

106. Komonchak, "Local Church and the Church Catholic," 431. See also Komonchak, "Local Church," 324.

107. CN 9. Two texts are referenced: one from St. Clement of Rome and one from the Shepherd of Hermas.

108. A year after the publication of *Communionis notion*, an article which responded to the critics appeared in the Vatican newspaper, *L'Osservatore Romano*. The article is signed with three asterisks, which has traditionally designated a particularly significant text. Since the language and the content of the argument resemble closely that of Joseph Ratzinger, the article might have been prepared by the CDF. As regards the ontological priority, it explained that even though the expression "ontologically prior" does not appear in Scripture, the affirmation of the ontological priority of the universal church over the individual particular churches can be discerned in the letters to the Ephesians and Colossians. See CDF, "Church Unity," 4. A few years later, Ratzinger said that the New Testament warrant for the ontological priority of the universal church can be found not only in the Deutero-Pauline letters and the Apocalypse, but also in Paul's letter to the Galatians (Gal 4:26), where Paul "talks to us about the heavenly Jerusalem, and indeed not as an eschatological entity, but as one that comes before us: 'the Jerusalem above . . . is our mother'" (Ratzinger, "Ecclesiology of the Constitution," 135–36).

109. Ratzinger, "Ecclesiology of the Constitution," 134 (italics mine).

no longer and can no longer see it at all; it then appears as the product of a fit of theological enthusiasm, and all that remains is the empirical structure of the Church, her elements side-by-side in all their confusion and contradiction. Yet that means that the Church is ruled out as a theme of theology at all. If you can no longer see the Church except as existing in human organizations, then hopelessness is in fact all there is left.[110]

Third, Ratzinger provided further arguments for the priority of the universal church from the theology of baptism, Eucharist, and apostolic ministry. He argued that baptism is entirely a theological process, not just socialization into a local church. As such, baptism "does not spring from the individual congregation; rather, in baptism the door is opened for us into the one Church: baptism is the presence of the one Church and can come only from her—from the Jerusalem that is above, from our new mother.... In baptism the universal Church always takes priority over the local Church and is creating her."[111] In regard to the Eucharist, Ratzinger contended that it neither originates from nor does it end in the local church. Like Christ who comes to us from without, passing through the locked doors, so the Eucharist "comes to us from without, from the whole, one body of Christ, and draws us into that body."[112] This *extra nos* dimension of the sacraments Ratzinger also elucidated in relation to the office of bishop and of priest. He explained that "the office of bishop arises from the one Church and leads into her."[113] Within the local church, the bishop represents the one church and builds it up by building up the local church.

Komonchak has found it problematic to speak of the church as pre-existing creation since it appears to imply that the church pre-exists its members, which is at odds not only with the CDF's own definition of the universal church as "the world wide community of the disciples of the Lord,"[114] but also with one of Komonchak's foundational ecclesiological points: that with regards to statements about the church, one should always be able to explain in whom or of whom they are true.[115] Since only God can pre-exist creation in any real sense, and based on Ratzinger's later clarification that the church's pre-existing creation refers to God's idea of the church,

---

110. Ratzinger, "Ecclesiology of the Constitution," 134 (italics mine). See also Ratzinger, Introduction to *Lettera*, 9.

111. Ratzinger, "Ecclesiology of the Constitution," 141. See also Ratzinger, "Local Church and the Universal Church," 11.

112. Ratzinger, "Ecclesiology of the Constitution," 143.

113. Ratzinger, "Ecclesiology of the Constitution," 143.

114. CN 7.

115. Komonchak, *Who Are the Church?*, 9.

Komonchak considers the claim that the universal church precedes creation a case of reification of the church.[116] Ratzinger's affinity for Plato and the primacy of ideas,[117] coupled with his tendency to conceive the church either as something that comes from God or as something that we make, makes Ratzinger susceptible to downplaying, even compromising, the human and social dimensions of the church.

Komonchak has also been critical of the way *Communionis notio* interprets the event of Pentecost (Acts 2:1–13) to support the historical priority of the universal church. The letter claims that the church originates as the universal church and relates to the local churches like the mother to her offspring. Komonchak argues that the church born at Pentecost ought to be thought of as simultaneously local and universal (or catholic), and that *this* Pentecost church of Jerusalem is a mother in relation to other local churches, from which they were propagated "as if by cuttings and replanting."[118] Komonchak does not think that the maternal analogy in *Communionis notio* is compatible with the *in et ex quibus* phrase of *Lumen gentium* 23, according to which the universal church exists in and out of the particular churches. He considers the analogy consistent only with the phrase *ecclesiae in et ex ecclesia*,[119] and finds it unclear why this new phrase is necessary since what it communicates is already expressed in the council's affirmation that the particular churches are made in the image of the universal church.[120] Ultimately, Komonchak thinks that *Communionis notio* represents poorly the principle that apart from the local churches the universal church has only a notional existence leading to the disappearance of the dialectical balance of *Lumen gentium* 23.[121]

Komonchak suggests that the maternal analogy needs to be carefully studied, and he doubts that referring to the universal church as the mother of particular churches is in line with the tradition of the early church. He contends that, historically, it was the local Church of Jerusalem which was considered to be the mother of all other churches, and jurisdictionally, it was the local Church of Rome. He also points out that in the debates preceding the schism between Catholics and the Orthodox the relationship

---

116. Komonchak, "Epistemology of Reception," 198. See also Komonchak, "À propos de la priorité," 253, 265–66

117. See Kasper, "On the Church," 930.

118. Komonchak, "Local Church and the Church Catholic," 432. See also Komonchak, "Theology of the Local Church," 43.

119. CN 9.

120. Komonchak, "Theology of the Local Church," 42

121. Komonchak, "À propos de la priorité," 263.

between these two maternities was often an issue, yet neither side turned to the notion of the universal church as the mother of both of them.[122]

Komonchak argues that the question of priority should not even arise, especially when the CDF's letter itself affirms the relationship of mutual interiority between the local and the universal church. As he explains,

> if local church and universal church exist within one another, how is it possible to set them over-and-against one another as if they were distinct and the problem were how to relate them. Ontologically, (1) there cannot be a church except in time and place, gathering specific men and women in communion of faith, hope and love; and (2) a local community is not a church unless it is also universal or catholic in its constitutive principles: catholic both because the whole of the mystery of the church is realized in it and because the mystery that makes it a communion in Christ is the same mystery that makes every other community a communion in Christ.[123]

The influence of Komonchak's conception of the church's ontology can be detected here clearly, but his seeming conflation of the church's universality and catholicity might prove to be a vulnerability.

Komonchak has also defended ecclesiologists for whom the notion of mutual recognition or reception is an integral component of their ecclesiology of communion.[124] *Communionis notio* disapproved of a conception according to which the universal church results from a reciprocal recognition on the part of the particular churches.[125] Komonchak has argued that the theologians who speak about reciprocal reception and recognition do not imagine them as some second moment in the realization of the ecclesial communion, wherein there are first independent particular churches which subsequently decide to form a federation. Komonchak notes that if beneath the CDF's concern lies a concern over the notion of the universal church as a federation of local churches, then the theologians who have used the language of reciprocal recognition would agree with the congregation. Instead, he explains, the language of reciprocal recognition aims to communicate that "the mystery of communion that makes the church to be the church, whether locally or universally, consists in the common incorporation of its members, together, into Christ."[126] In Komonchak's view, communion and reception/recognition

---

122. Komonchak, "À propos de la priorité," 263–64.
123. Komonchak, "Theology of the Local Church," 42–43.
124. For instance, J-M R. Tillard.
125. See CN 8.
126. Komonchak, "Theology of the Local Church," 43.

are synonymous. For him, the universal church *is* the communion of local churches, not the result of their communion; it *is* the reciprocal reception on the part of the local churches. Apart from communion and reception, the universal church is merely something abstract.[127]

Komonchak contends that the question of the priority of the universal church over the local church is closely related to the exercise of the Petrine ministry.[128] He explains that a few years before the CDF's letter *Communionis notio*, the Congregation for Bishops issued a draft statement on episcopal conferences. It stated that the "Petrine primacy, understood as *plenitudo potestatis*, has no theological sense and coherence unless within the primacy of the one and universal church over particular and local churches."[129] Komonchak points out that one finds the same claim in one of Ratzinger's writings where it says that the "office of Peter and its responsibility could not exist if the universal Church had not existed before it. Otherwise it would be grasping at emptiness and would represent an absurd claim."[130] Komonchak observes that such statements come close to implying that "if the priority of the universal church were denied, the pope would have nothing to do."[131]

This is a perceptive observation indeed; it seems to point out the key concern that the proponents of the priority of the universal church over the local church intend to safeguard. The concern is understandable since papal primacy is not a marginal Catholic belief. The conception of papal primacy as it is exercised at present developed within the framework of a universalist ecclesiology, in which the universal church is seen as a single diocese that spans the whole world. The pope is envisioned as having a quasi-monarchical, supra-episcopal authority over all other bishops, and as relating to the universal church like a bishop relates to his diocese. In

---

127. Komonchak, "Theology of the Local Church," 43–44.

128. See Komonchak, "Local Church and the Church Catholic," 430–31; "Theology of the Local Church," 40; "À propos de la priorité," 248–49; "What Ecclesiology?," (2010) 148–49.

129. Congregation for Bishops, "Draft Statement on Episcopal Conferences," 735. This draft statement is an *Instrumentum laboris* (a working paper) titled "Theological and Juridical Status of Episcopal Conferences," and it was sent to all the bishops in the beginning of 1988. The focus of the statement is twofold: (1) the extent to which the actions of episcopal conferences are an exercise of collegiality, and (2) the nature of their teaching authority. The statement is a result of a study called for by the 1985 extraordinary Synod of Bishops. The draft statement was issued by the Congregation for Bishops but it was prepared in collaboration with the Congregations for the Doctrine of the Faith, for Eastern Churches, and for the Evangelization of Peoples, as well as by the General Secretariat of the Synod of Bishops. The original of the draft statement is in Italian.

130. Ratzinger, "Ecclesiology of the Constitution," 144.

131. Komonchak, "What Ecclesiology?," 149.

actual practice, this ecclesiology treats bishops as the pope's vicars and local churches as administrative units of the universal church, even though the former has been denied in theory.[132] With its rediscovery and revalidation of the local church, the Second Vatican Council made an important step toward a retrieval of an ecclesiological vision which predated the East-West schism. The council taught explicitly that bishops are not to be regarded as vicars of the pope but vicars of Christ,[133] and it affirmed the sacramentality of episcopal ordination.[134] The cumulative effect on Catholic ecclesiology of the council's teachings about episcopal collegiality, a connection between a bishop and the Eucharist, and about catholicity has amounted to an affirmation of the full ecclesial reality of a local church. As a result, the universal church cannot be conceived as a trans-national corporation or a world-wide diocese with local churches as its regional branches or parts. This new vision of the church—which is in fact rather old, and which has been referred to as *communio* ecclesiology—is in tension with universalist ecclesiology, and a key question is whether communion ecclesiology can accommodate the Petrine ministry in terms of *plenitudo potestatis* as it has been practiced since the latter part of the nineteenth century. As William Henn aptly expressed it, "Can papal primacy be conceived in such a way that it does not derogate from the proper dignity and ministry of the bishops, either taken singly or as a college? Can the authority of bishops be understood in such a way that it does not essentially compromise the fullness of authority that is necessary to an effective ministry of primacy?"[135]

While an affirmation of the ontological and chronological priority of the universal church over the local churches can ground the primacy of jurisdiction of the pope, it compromises the ecclesiological vision of Vatican II.[136] This is a precarious situation in which the Catholic Church has found itself. In recent decades there have been proposals to re-read and re-receive the dogmas of Vatican I, which defined papal primacy and infallibility. Theologians who undertook such studies typically concluded that the dogmas of Vatican I have been exaggerated and that in order to rediscover the council's true meaning exaggerations of papal primacy and

---

132. See "Collektiv-Erklärung," 209–13. English translation of the entire statement is available in Küng, *Council Reform and Reunion*, 194–99. This declaration of the German bishops was issued to counter the view that the teachings of Vatican I reduced bishops to the status of mere papal officials. Pope Pius IX gave an approval to this statement in an apostolic brief (March 6, 1975).

133. LG 27.

134. LG 26.

135. Henn, "Historical-Theological Synthesis," 224.

136. Cf. Kasper, "Zur Theologie und Praxis," 43–44.

infallibility ought to be curtailed.¹³⁷ Yet it is not clear that even a minimalist interpretation of Vatican I is compatible with the notion of the mutual inherence and simultaneity of the universal church and the local churches and with the demand it places on the exercise of the Petrine ministry—a demand which appears to point in the direction of robust synodality and the collegiality of bishops. If the priority of the universal church (or of the local church) is not coherent with an understanding of the universal church as existing only in and out of the local churches, what implications does this have for papal primacy and its *plenitudo potestatis*? The task Catholic ecclesiology faces is to construct a theology of the Petrine ministry that is grounded in an understanding of the simultaneity between the church local and universal. Significant contributions in this regard have already been made,¹³⁸ but their insights have not yet become part of the official Catholic teaching on the ministry of the pope.¹³⁹ Joint ecumenical statements also offer constructive attempts at envisioning the ministry of unity of the Bishop of Rome within the framework of communion ecclesiology.¹⁴⁰

Komonchak's interpretation of the relationship of the local and universal church preserves the balance of *Lumen gentium* 23. He has argued that the affirmation that the particular churches are constituted after the image of the universal church should be understood in terms of the generative principles of the church. Agreeing with Hervé Legrand, Komonchak does not think that the assertion that local churches are constituted after the model of the universal church should be interpreted in a Platonic sense as if the local churches were reproductions of some ideal church, but in the sense of "the normative pattern that must be realized in any concrete community if it is rightly to be called the Church."¹⁴¹ As he explains, the generative principles "pre-exist any particular church only in the fashion in which the divine intention pre-exists the Church *tout court* or in which a "form" may be said to pre-exist the matter in which it is received; but [reception of these principles] is precisely what is needed for a concrete reality called

---

137. See, for instance, Kasper, "Introduction to the Theme," 7–23; Pottmeyer, *Towards a Papacy in Communion*; O'Gara, "Three Successive Steps," 208–23.

138. For instance, Tillard, *Bishop of Rome*; *Church of Churches*; *L'Église locale*; Granfield, *Limits of the Papacy*; Quinn, *Reform of the Papacy*; Pottmeyer, "Primacy in Communion," 15–18; Gaillardetz, "Reflections on the Future," 52–66.

139. It ought to be noted that the way Pope Francis conducted the synods on the Family in 2014 and 2015 is an encouraging sign of serious attempts at the practice of synodality.

140. For instance, Anglican-Roman Catholic International Commission, "Gift of Authority," s.v. "nos. 45–48"; Bilateral Working Group, *Communio Sanctorum*, s.v. "nos. 153–200"; Joint International Commission, *Ecclesiological and Canonical Consequences*.

141. See Komonchak, "Towards a Theology," 17; "Epistemology of Reception," 198. Cf. Legrand, "La réalisation," 152.

the Church to exist, and this happens only in the churches."[142] Komonchak explains that by generating every local church, these principles also generate the universal church.[143]

Komonchak has shown in a compelling way that advocating for the priority of the universal church results in the demise of Vatican II's teaching on the full ecclesial reality of the local church. He has interpreted fairly the teaching of *Lumen gentium* 23 against efforts to revise the impact of the *in et ex quibus* phrase and its implications for Catholic ecclesiology. He has rightly pointed out that Joseph Ratzinger and the CDF have at times privileged the universal church to an extent that they have *de facto* reduced the local church to a sphere where only the universal church is at work and in this way have nearly divested the local church of theological significance. His observation that the writings of Ratzinger and of the CDF contain a valid criticism and correction of one-sidedness of some post-conciliar ecclesiological stances is also perceptive.[144]

There are two areas of Komonchak's theology of the local church that could be strengthened. First, in my view, Komonchak has not applied the intersubjective ontology consistently in his interpretation of the church. This is noticeable when he makes statements about the (universal) church as being realized *in* the local church(es). Below are several examples:

> The focus will be on the genesis of the Church in the local Churches.[145]

> But this single Church exists and acts only in the many local Churches.[146]

> The universal Church is not something accessory to the local Church; it is precisely what is being realized in a local Church. The universal Church, in turn, is not something which existed or now exists prior to or independent of the local Churches, as if the latter were administrative sub-divisions of the former, on the analogy, say, of a multi-national corporation which from a central office establishes branch offices in major cities and

---

142. Komonchak, "Epistemology of Reception," 192.
143. Komonchak, "Local Church," 326.
144. See Komonchak, "À propos de la priorité," 265.
145. Komonchak, "Toward a Theology," 21.
146. Komonchak, "Preparing for the New Millennium," 52.

> retail shops in smaller localities. There is nothing which constitutes the universal Church which is not realized in the local Churches.[147]

> This self-actualization of the Church in assemblies of believers is always and everywhere a concrete hermeneutical and historical event.[148]

> It is indeed the one church of Christ that is present in all of the individual churches.[149]

As I discussed in the previous chapter, Komonchak has argued that the church's ontology ought to be conceived in terms of intersubjectivity. But if so, it must be true of the church local and universal even though they are not the same realities. I think that the preposition *in* obscures the intersubjective ontology of the church. Saying that the universal church is realized *in* the local churches still seems to suggests that the universal church exists apart from the local churches and is anterior to them—the notion Komonchak rejects.[150] If, as Komonchak argues, the referent of the word "church" is *congregatio fidelium*, if "church" always refers to people, can people (the universal church) be realized *in* people (the local churches)? It appears that when Komonchak says that the (universal) church is realized *in* the local churches, by the universal church he does not mean people but the generative principles of the church, as the following examples illustrate:

> More important than the Council's vocabulary are its major theological concerns in its statements about the local churches. These seem to me to be twofold: first, the assertion that the distinctive and constitutive principles of the Church's existence are realized in the local church.[151]

> In its distinctive and constitutive principles, the Church is realized in local Churches.[152]

> I will discuss two themes that emerged from the ecclesiology of Vatican II, the generative and constitutive principles of the church as realized in the many churches and . . . [Vatican II

---

147. Komonchak, "Local Church," 326.
148. Komonchak, "Local Church," 327.
149. See Komonchak, "Theology of the Local Church," 46.
150. See, for instance, Komonchak, "Church Universal," 30; "Local Church," 326; "Local Church and the Church Catholic," 433.
151. Komonchak, "Ministry and the Local Church," 57.
152. Komonchak, "Toward a Theology," 16.

> revalidated the local church] by its renewed attention to the distinctive spiritual principles of the church as realized in local communities.[153]

The generative principles in these examples are not what the church is, provided that the ontology of the church is intersubjective. If not as a Platonic idea, conceiving the universal church as being realized in the local churches seems to suggest that it exists as something abstracted from the local churches, namely, as that which exists in all of them and what they all share in common. The preposition *in* thus fits Platonic and Aristotelian metaphysics, but it does not seem to fit the ontology of the church that Komonchak advocates.

I think that a better way of expressing the mutual relationship between the universal church and the local churches while affirming the intersubjective ontology of the church is to use the preposition *as* instead of *in*. The universal church exists *as* a communion of local churches; it is the communion existing among the local churches; it is the church of churches. My suggestion is not entirely absent from Komonchak's writings. The title of his very first article on the local church is "The Church Universal as the Communion of Local Churches." I would thus modify the statements from above in this way:

> The focus will be on the genesis of the Church *as* the local Churches.
>
> But this single Church exists and acts only *as* the many local Churches.
>
> The universal Church is not something accessory to the local Church; it is precisely what is being realized *as* a local Church. The universal Church, in turn, is not something which existed or now exists prior to or independent of the local Churches, as if the latter were administrative sub-divisions of the former, on the analogy, say, of a multi-national corporation which from a central office establishes branch offices in major cities and retail shops in smaller localities. There is nothing which constitutes the universal Church which is not realized *as* the local Churches.
>
> This self-actualization of the Church *as* assemblies of believers is always and everywhere a concrete hermeneutical and historical event.

---

153. Komonchak, "Theology of the Local Church," 35–37.

> It is indeed the one church of Christ that is present *as* all of the individual churches.

A further consequence of this proposal is that it implies a modification of the *in et ex quibus* formulation of *Lumen gentium* 23.

Komonchak's theology of the local church would be strengthened further if there was more clarity with regard to what the term "universal church" designates. This point applies to contemporary writings in ecclesiology in general, whether by individual theologians or the magisterium. The term is sometimes employed in the binary of the "universal" and the "particular," or in the binary of the "one" and the "many." Other times, "universal" seems to mean "whole" as in the distinction between the "whole" and its "parts." "Universal," in the sense of "whole," can also refer to the sum total of believers as it is in *Communionis notio*, which in one place defines the universal church as "the worldwide community of the disciples of the Lord."[154] Still other times theologians speak of "the one church" or "the catholic church," "the church of Christ," "the church of God," or just "the church." The lack of terminological clarity is further exacerbated by the fact that Latin, which is typically the original language of the documents issued by the pope and the curia, knows both *universus* (whole) and *universalis* (universal).

The statement in *Lumen gentium* 23 about the relationship of the local and the universal church aptly illustrates this terminological ambiguity: "The individual bishops are the visible source and foundation of unity in their own particular Churches, which are constituted after the model of the universal Church; it is in these and formed out of them that the one and unique Catholic Church exists." If the council wanted to affirm the mutuality between the particular churches and the universal church, why is there a terminological change from the "universal church" in the first assertion to the "one and unique Catholic Church" in the second assertion? Are these churches the same realities? It seems that "universal" in the expression "the model of the universal church" carries the philosophical meaning of essence. This essence, however, is an abstraction. It refers to what is found in all the particular churches; namely the generative principles of the church. This universal church, which is the model for the particular churches, is not made up of believers. The "one and Catholic Church," however, exists in and out of the particular churches; hence it is made of believers. Thus, the "universal church" and "one and Catholic Church" appear to refer to distinct realities, even though there is no evidence that the council intended this to be the case.

---

154. CN 7.

The different referents of the term "universal church" imply different conceptions of the relationship between the local and the universal church. If "universal" refers to what is abstracted from the particulars, the universal church would be an abstraction, and it would be difficult to determine what it means to ask about the relationship of the church local and universal. If "universal" refers to the "whole church" as the sum total of its parts, then only the universal/whole church is fully church, and local churches lack full ecclesial reality. If the universal church is understood as the communion of local churches, then one would speak about the relationship of mutuality and interiority between the local and the universal church.

Komonchak shows awareness of these issues when he writes:

> There remains the question of terminology. Everyone knows the debate, which is more than semantic, over whether to speak of the "local" Church or the "particular" Church. Much less attention has been given to how the one Church should be referred to. Should it be *ecclesia universalis* or *ecclesia universa*? . . . The question would appear not to be trivial. In some languages at least, and in some contexts to ask about the relationship between the whole Church (*universa Ecclesia*) and the particular or local Churches is very different from asking about the relationship between the universal Church (*Ecclesia universalis*) and the local or particular Churches. With the first way of posing the question one more easily avoids the danger of hypostasizing the universal Church, of forgetting that the distinction is, as scholastics say, an inadequate one, because the one Church, the whole Church, the Church as a whole, does not exist apart from the many Churches.[155]

One might wish that Komonchak had expanded these observations further. Nevertheless, they illustrate the need for ecclesiologists not only to sort through the terminological options with regard to the "universal church," but also, and perhaps more importantly, to work out a metaphysics for relating the local churches and the universal church in terms of mutual interiority.

As concerns this last point, the work of philosophical theologian Joseph Bracken may hold valuable insight for ecclesiologists. Bracken has attempted to articulate the philosophical paradigm that underlies the conception of the universal church as a communion of local churches.[156]

155. Komonchak, "À propos de la priorité," 267–68.
156. See Bracken, "Ecclesiology and the Problem," 298–311. In this article, he directly engages Komonchak's theology of the local church as articulated in Komonchak, "Ministry and the Local Church."

He believes that the dynamic understanding of reality as worked out by Alfred North Whitehead is key to unlocking the elusive puzzle of how the many churches are one church—a puzzle Bracken conceives in terms of the perennial problem of the one and the many. He argues that Whitehead's notion of "society" corresponds well to what ecclesiologists call the universal church envisioned as the church of churches, where "unity emerges out of the ongoing interaction of constituent parts or members within society."[157] As Bracken explains, Whitehead defines society in terms of the interrelationship of its constituent actual entities, which he understands as "the final real things of which the world is made up."[158] While remaining ontologically themselves, by virtue of their interrelationship, the actual entities constitute the new reality of a society. It can be said that they are at the same time the many and the one. On this account, the universal church is "a structured society, a society of subsocieties (yet with a common element of form for the entire structured society); for each of the local churches is itself a society composed of individual human beings who are equivalently its member actual entities."[159]

Although not using the same terminology, Bracken's account coheres well with Komonchak's conception of the intersubjective ontology of an (individual) church and extends it to the level of the universal church. As discussed in the previous chapter, Komonchak envisions the church's reality as a process in which the church comes-to-be when human beings respond by grace to God's offer of self through the shared acts of faith, hope, and love. In Bracken's terms, individual believers are the actual entities; they are the final real things whose interrelationship gives rise to sub-societies such as two or three gathered in Christ's name, a small community, a parish, or a diocese, and ultimately their interrelationship constitutes the church universal. The parish, the diocese, and the universal church are different realities. The interrelationship among the parishes constitutes a diocese, and the interrelationship among the dioceses constitutes the universal church, but neither a diocese nor the universal church exists concretely apart from those interrelationships. On every level, the church is an event in process and is made of believers. Bracken's philosophical paradigm corresponds well with Komonchak's understanding of the universal church as a concrete universal, in which "the whole is not conceived prior to the parts; rather, the one whole comes to be, is constituted by, in, and out of the realizations of its many constituents."[160]

157. Bracken, "Ecclesiology and the Problem," 301.
158. Whitehead, *Process and Reality*, 18.
159. Bracken, "Ecclesiology and the Problem," 304.
160. Komonchak, "Church Universal," 30.

The philosophical framework Bracken proposes could be used to sort out the terminological and conceptual ambiguity and confusion that marks the discourse related to the local and the universal church. If the universal church is the new reality that emerges out of the interrelationship of the local churches, then it follows that one church in the absence of any other churches cannot be referred to as the universal church. This has ramifications for the priority debate, since representatives on both sides of the issue have argued their position by appealing to the church born at Pentecost. The proponents of the priority of the universal church over the local churches claimed that the Pentecost church was the universal church, and the proponents of the simultaneity of the local church and the universal church claimed that the Pentecost church should be conceived as both local and universal. A close look at their understanding of the Pentecost church reveals, however, a seeming conflation of catholicity and universality. For instance, the CDF argued in *Communionis notio* that the Pentecost church originated as the universal church:

> The Church is manifested temporally on the day of Pentecost in the community of the 120 gathered around Mary and the Twelve Apostles, the representatives of the one unique church and the founders-to-be of the local churches, who have a mission directed to the world. From the first the church speaks all languages. From the church, which in its origins and its first manifestation is universal, have arisen the different local churches as particular expressions of the one unique church of Jesus Christ.[161]

Joseph Ratzinger has expressed the same position in his personal writings:

> The image of Pentecost presented in the Acts of the Apostles shows the interplay of plurality and unity.... The Church embraces the many languages, that is, the many cultures, that in faith understand and fecundate one another. In this respect it can be said that we find here a preliminary sketch of a Church that lives in manifold and multiform particular Churches but that precisely in this way is the one Church. At the same time, Luke expresses with this image the fact that at the moment of her birth, the Church was already catholic, already a world Church. Luke thus rules out a conception in which a local Church first arose in Jerusalem and then became the base for the gradual establishment of other local Churches that eventually grew into a federation. Luke tells us that the reverse is true: what first exists is the one Church, the Church that speaks in all tongues—the

---

161. CN 9.

ecclesia universalis; she then generates Church in the most diverse locales, which nonetheless are all always embodiments of the one and only Church. The temporal and ontological priority lies with the universal Church.[162]

Komonchak has argued, however, that the Pentecost church should be conceived as both local and universal: "The Church which first emerges at Pentecost is at once local and catholic, gathered in Jerusalem but already speaking the one message in all languages, and because the churches generated from that mother-church are the same Church, becoming catholic now concretely, in various other places."[163]

One more example:

> If local church and universal church exist within one another, how is it possible to set them over-and-against one another as if they were distinct and the problem were how to relate them. Ontologically, (1) there cannot be a church except in time and place, gathering specific men and women in communion of faith, hope and love; and (2) a local community is not a church unless it is also universal or catholic in its constitutive principles: catholic both because the whole of the mystery of the church is realized in it and because the mystery that makes it a communion in Christ is the same mystery that makes every other community a communion in Christ. Historically, the paradigmatic case of Pentecost makes it clear that the church was born both local and universal. The assembly gathered in Jerusalem and yet it included representatives of all the nations, all of whom heard the one message in their various native languages. It was in this Jerusalem assembly that the universal church was already realized, and it was as a development and realization of this original catholicity that other particular and local churches were founded.[164]

While Walter Kasper has pointed out the limitations of constructing the church's historical origins solely on the account of Pentecost and isolating it from the rest of Acts,[165] he has not questioned the assertion that such details in Luke's account of Pentecost as the church from its inception speaking in all languages and embracing many cultures indicate that the Pentecost

---

162. Ratzinger, *Called to Communion*, 43–44. See also Ratzinger, "Ecclesiology of the Constitution," 136–38.
163. Komonchak, "Church Local and the Church Catholic," 431–32.
164. Komonchak, "Theology of the Local Church," 42–43.
165. Kasper, "On the Church," 929.

church was the universal church. Kasper only insisted that it ought to be conceived also as local.[166]

This sampling of examples shows that the CDF, Ratzinger, Komonchak, and Kasper have employed the terms "catholic" and "universal" interchangeably with regard to the church born at Pentecost. "Catholic," which comes from the Greek *kat'holon*, means "as regards the whole" (*universus* in Latin) and has been used to communicate the notion of geographic universality of the church. In addition to this quantitative dimension, catholicity also has a qualitative aspect and expresses the idea of what kind of unity one predicates about the church: not uniformity, but unity that integrates diversity. A single church in the absence of any other churches, such as the Pentecost church, can be said to be catholic in terms of qualitative catholicity but not in terms of quantitative catholicity, since this latter notion requires that there be not only more than one church, but also that the churches exist all over the world.

Like qualitative catholicity, which integrates diversity into unity, the notion of universality, understood in the metaphysical terms of Bracken, also expresses the idea that the many are the one. Furthermore, while the notion of qualitative catholicity can be predicated of both a single church in the absence of any other churches and of several churches in communion with one another, the philosophical notion of universality applies only to the communion of churches in the sense of society of sub-societies, but not to a single church when no other church is in existence. This last point becomes obscured when catholicity and universality are conflated.

Furthermore, "catholic" designates a property or a characteristic of the church, whether local or universal. "Universal" is not a characteristic of the church but designates a different reality than the "local" church. Thus, if the distinctions outlined here were accepted, the church born at Pentecost would be conceived as catholic in the qualitative but not quantitative sense, and it would not be seen as the universal church. Consequently, referring to the Pentecost church could not resolve the issue of the priority of the

---

166. "In principle, there is no objection to the formula 'Ecclesiae in et ex Ecclesia. It applies, of course, to the *una, sancta, catholica et apostolica Ecclesia*, with all the magnificent images the Church Fathers describe her. This formula can therefore be accepted, provided that it is clear that the church or the universal church refer to something concrete. If it is meant to be taken historically in the sense of the primordial Jerusalem community, it is correct in the sense that Luke describes it in the Acts of the Apostles. It was at once the universal and the local church. This, of course, is a Lucan construction since historically there were probably several communities from the beginning, communities in Galilee in addition to the Jerusalem community. The one church, therefore, existed from the beginning 'in and out' of the local churches" (Kasper, "Zur Theologie und Praxis," 44).

universal church over the local churches since the category of universality was not yet present at Pentecost.[167]

In a universalistic ecclesiology, which dominated Catholic theology prior to Vatican II, the priority of the universal church over the local churches was defended not by appealing to the pre-existence of the universal church or by asserting that the church was universal from its very origins, but on the basis of Aristotle's theory of matter and form and his political philosophy. As Bracken explains, form for Aristotle, although only a part of the composite reality, functions as the principle of unity and intelligibility of the whole reality.[168] Bracken points out, however, that Aristotle's metaphysics suffer from a shortcoming in that it reifies form and treats it as a part of an entity, even though a superior part in relation to other parts. But the form, Bracken explains, "is not a 'part,' since as an immaterial principle of being and activity it is operative within the entity as a whole and in each of its constituent parts. Similarly, the 'matter' of the entity is not simply to be identified with the 'elements' or component parts but likewise with the total entity as a material reality."[169] Bracken notes that the tendency to reify form marks also Aristotle's political philosophy, which considers monarchy as the ideal form of government and conceives the king as representing form. Even though the king is only one member of a society, he is the one and stands over the rest of the society's members who are the many.[170]

Catholic ecclesiology in the second millennium gradually developed a theology of the papacy akin to Aristotle's king.[171] The pope became superior to all other bishops. The unity of the bishops became grounded not in their relationship to one another, but in the person of the pope and in their relationship to him. Bracken observes that "as the king is regarded as the organizing principle and source of unity for the state in the political philosophy of Aristotle and Aquinas, the pope as the visible head of the Church exercises immediate jurisdiction over all the other members, in-

---

167. A letter published on the first anniversary of *Communionis notio*, likely by the CDF, likewise affirmed that one cannot apply categories "universal" and "particular" to the church of Pentecost because they were not yet developed, but it does not seem that the Congregation thought that this should affect its affirmation of the priority of the universal church. The letter stated: "At Pentecost there is no 'mutual interiority' between universal and particular Church, because these two dimensions are not yet distinct" (CDF, "Church Unity," 4).

168. Bracken, "Ecclesiology and the Problem," 301.

169. Bracken, "Ecclesiology and the Problem," 306.

170. Bracken, "Ecclesiology and the Problem," 307.

171. For an excellent discussion of Aristotle's influence on Aquinas's conception of the common good and in its impact on his conception of papal primacy, see Tillard, *L'Église locale*, 489–501.

cluding his brother bishops."[172] This view of papal ministry is at home in the universalistic ecclesiology in which the universal church has precedence over the local churches.

Vatican II's theology of the local church, however, does not fit this framework, for it presupposes a dynamic understanding of the relationship of the one and the many. It is this understanding that grounds the notion of the simultaneity of the church local and universal. Komonchak has called it the ascending approach to ecclesiology, in which "the whole is not conceived prior to its parts; rather the one whole comes to be, is constituted by, in, and out of the realizations of its many constituents."[173] The task Catholic ecclesiology faces is to reconceive papal ministry so that it would cohere with an understanding of the universal church as a communion of local churches.

Conclusion

The Second Vatican Council made a vital step toward restoring appreciation for the local church. Although the council's treatment of the local church was unsystematic and fragmentary, it introduced a new flavor into Catholic ecclesiology and proposed that Catholics reconfigure their thinking about the church. In the five decades following the council, the theology of the local church has been at the center of such matters as liturgy, inculturation, evangelization, the role of synods and episcopal conferences, and the appointment of bishops. Being central to the council's ecclesiology of communion, one can agree with Christopher Ruddy that "the theology of the local church represents both a cornerstone in, and a stumbling block to, the church's reception of Vatican II."[174]

The embryonic nature of the council's treatment of the local church meant that it was left to theologians after the council to construct accounts of the local church that would be faithful to the council and the larger theological tradition. Joseph Komonchak has made a distinctive contribution in this respect. His writings on the local church address three issues that the council left unresolved, namely: (1) what should constitute the theological definition of a local church, (2) what impact should the enlarged understanding of the church's catholicity have for the church's unity, and (3) what is the relationship between the local and the universal church.

172. Bracken, "Ecclesiology and the Problem," 309.
173. Komonchak, "Universal Church," 30.
174. Ruddy, *Local Church*, 3.

By arguing that locality and diversity ought to enter into the theological definition of a local church, by conceiving the universal church as the communion of local churches, and by rejecting the idea of the priority of either the universal or the local church and thinking instead of their relationship in terms of mutual interiority or inclusivity, Komonchak constructed an account of the church thoroughly from below. It stands in contrast to the universalistic ecclesiology that dominated Catholic ecclesiology in the second millennium and in large part informs the documents of Vatican II.

Komonchak's theology of the local church, although not comprehensive in nature, is a significant contribution to contemporary ecclesiology. It shows how to think of the church consistently as a communion that is realized concretely from the most elemental local levels to the global level of the church universal. In this way, Komonchak's theology of the local church advances the ecclesiological project of Vatican II. It sidesteps universalistic ecclesiology—something that the council was not able to do.

Komonchak's theology of the local church thus holds a promise not only for the Catholic Church, but also for ecumenism. As for the former, it offers conceptual tools for the reception of the elements of Vatican II's ecclesiology that have not yet been realized adequately. Chief among them are the collegiality of bishops and the synodality of the whole church. If collegiality and synodality were allowed to plant deeper roots in the fabric of the church, the local churches would become a more genuine communion and a more effective witness of the gospel. Under the pontificate of Pope Francis, synodality has made a come-back in Catholic consciousness. The pope has made a significant effort to revive synodality at all levels of the church. While this is something that will undoubtedly take a long time to realize effectively, Komonchak's theology of the local church could be invoked to offer robust theological support for this endeavor. As for the latter, a more collegial and synodal Catholicism would be in a better position to engage in ecumenical dialogue with other Christians and be more likely to achieve tangible results on issues pertaining to the nature, structure, and mission of the church.

5

Authority in the Church

A CRISIS OF AUTHORITY has marked the last five decades in the life of the Catholic Church. It was precipitated by the release of the encyclical *Humanae vitae* (July 29, 1968), which affirmed the Catholic teaching condemning artificial means of preventing conception. The encyclical taught that any such means were illicit.[1] For most Catholics who were invigorated by the Second Vatican Council, the decision of Pope Paul VI to reaffirm the conclusions of his predecessors came as a disappointment and a surprise. It was even more so since the Pontifical Commission on Birth Control, which John XXIII created in 1963 to study the issue and which Paul VI expanded, recommended that the teaching on birth control be allowed to evolve, and that the pope approve some form of contraception for married couples. Instead of accepting the proposal of the commission's majority, which consisted of bishops, theologians, and laity, the pope adopted the view of the minority.[2] While the commission was only consultative and its recommendations were not binding, those who disagreed with the pope's decision perceived it as a failure to exercise collegiality. As Bernard Sesboüé explains,

> A major reason for the malaise provoked by the encyclical comes from the fact that, as it happened, one man decided alone. This was resented in the Church the more strongly because the Council and the proclamation of episcopal collegiality were such recent events.... It appeared very surprising that a

---

1. See Paul VI, "*Humane vitae*," nos. 11–14, in Carlen, *Papal Encyclicals*, 5: 226–27.

2. For an account of the commission's deliberations, including the text of the majority report, see McClory, *Turning Point*, 38–128. For the minority report, see Callahan, *Catholic Case for Contraception*, 174–211.

single man decided alone a point so difficult and delicate, which so closely touched the personal lives of the Catholic faithful.[3]

Collegiality was a signature teaching of Vatican II. It was one of the so-called novelties that the council (re)introduced into Catholic ecclesiology. Collegiality was central to the council's understanding of the church as communion. In essence, collegiality refers to the idea that all bishops together, including the pope, rule the universal church. Collegiality is thus about cooperation and communal governance of the church. Bishops who at the council advocated for collegiality hoped that it would bring about the much-needed decentralization of the church. They saw collegiality as a corrective to the understanding of the church as an absolute monarchy.

Humanae vitae was also perceived as a departure from the "spirit of Vatican II." Most Catholics saw the council as a positive change, as bringing the church closer to the modern world with its emphasis on personal responsibility. In contrast, the encyclical was seen as contradicting this more open and self-responsible way of being a Catholic. It was met with criticism not only from theologians and ordinary faithful, but also from some national conferences of bishops.[4] After some time it became evident that the majority of Catholics did not receive the encyclical's teaching, and this became the flashpoint of the crisis. The non-reception of *Humanae vitae* fatally undermined authority in the church and complicated the reception of Vatican II, which was in its infancy. The crisis of authority that *Humanae vitae* triggered became a wound unable to heal, for new injuries continued to reopen it, such as controversies over the ordination of women, the authority of episcopal conferences, the censorship of theologians, or the investigation of women religious in the US. Perhaps the most painful in this series of injuries has been the scandal of sexual abuse of minors by clergy.

Surely, problems with authority in the church are not a recent phenomenon. Disputes over the understanding and exercise of ecclesial authority are as old as the church. They arise periodically for various reasons and are addressed with different degrees of success. The past fifty years have witnessed a sustained engagement with questions pertaining to authority in the church, producing many volumes of analyses and proposals for dealing with the current crisis.[5] Joseph Komonchak has entered the discussion of author-

---

3. Sesboüé, "Autorité du magistère," 360, quoted in Komonchak, "*Humanae Vitae* and Its Reception" (1978) 228n27.

4. Canadian, Austrian, English, German, and Belgian.

5. See, for instance, Lash, *Voices of Authority*; De George, *Nature and Limits of Authority*; Stagaman, *Authority in the Church*; Hoose, *Authority in the Roman Catholic Church*; Oakley and Lacey, *Crisis of Authority*; Carroll et al., *Towards a Kenotic Vision*.

ity in the church in several essays.[6] Although his contribution in this area is less extensive than in method in ecclesiology or the theology of the local church, it nevertheless deserves to be included in the study of Komonchak's ecclesiology, for his reflections on authority further expound his understanding of the church and advance the contemporary discussion of how authority in the church should be conceived of and exercised.

As in his foundations in ecclesiology, so in his writings on authority Komonchak has employed an approach that aims at a theoretical understanding of the matter. He has provided a series of analytical reflections, which aim to clarify and define the terms of discussion: what it means to be an authority in general and a teaching authority in particular; how authority functions in the church; and what its limits are. While Komonchak has not attempted to resolve particular controversies troubling the church, he believes that his reflections provide sets of questions that may suggest ways of going beyond the present impasses.[7]

Authority as a Social Relationship

Komonchak has approached the topic of authority with a basic assumption that one cannot address it adequately without raising questions about community and about the relationship between community and authority; he sees the two as being two sides of the same coin. Komonchak believes that in order to make real progress regarding the crisis of authority in the church and arrive at some resolution, it is necessary to overcome the assumption that authority and community are antithetical and that "authority can be understood and exercised without reference to community."[8]

The conception of authority as a social relationship is for Komonchak a hermeneutical entry point into the subject. Authority is essentially a relationship between two parties: an A and a B. Komonchak defines social relationships as being constituted by "the reciprocal and mutually reinforcing knowledge, agreement, decisions, expectations, and actions of the two parties. A knows what is expected of herself and of B. B knows what is expected of himself and of A. Each knows that the other knows. These

---

6. Komonchak, "Ordinary Papal Magisterium," (1969) 101–26; "*Humanae Vitae* and Its Reception" (1978) 221–57; "Authority and Magisterium," (1987) 103–14; "Magisterium and Theologians," (1990) 307–29; "Authority and Its Exercise," (1999) 29–46; "Authority and Conversion," (2000) 207–29.

7. Cf. Komonchak, "Authority and Magisterium," 103, 113.

8. Komonchak, "*Humanae Vitae* and Its Reception," 257.

mutually reinforcing expectations *are* the social relationship."[9] To say that authority is a social relationship thus means that it is not a one-directional phenomenon, but rather that authority "resides in the mutual knowledge and expectations of the two parties."[10] On this understanding, no one is an authority for oneself.

Komonchak understands the authority relationship as asymmetrical— it is not a relationship of equals. If A is an authority for B, the latter is not an authority for the former in the same way and concerning the same matter. In the absence of asymmetry, one is not dealing with authority but with persuasion, which assumes equality between the parties.[11]

Komonchak relates authority to power and defines the latter as the ability to impose one's will on someone else. He understands authority as legitimate power in the sense of being grounded in something other than force, threat, or a promise of reward. Komonchak distinguishes between the notions of authority as legitimate power and as mere power; the former respects both the intelligence and freedom of the other, while the latter may not.[12]

Komonchak understands the authority relationship as operating with an assumption that there is some level of community between the two parties. They share something in common, and it is within this realm that A is an authority for B. The way the authority relationship functions is that B acknowledges that A has the ability to contribute something that B needs but cannot provide for himself. By understanding and accepting this dynamic, B legitimizes A's power. The key is that in an authority relationship one party acknowledges the capacity of the other party to provide direction. It is this acknowledgement of the capacity on the part of B that makes A an authority for B. Komonchak calls this acknowledgement B's trust in A.[13]

Essentially, an authority relationship exists in so far as there is a B who trusts an A to provide direction. Both parties constitute the authority relationship. An A constitutes it by her capacity to supply direction and B does the same by his acknowledgement and acceptance of the capacity. B thus does not make A an authority by supplying her with the capacity, but by acknowledging and accepting her capacity.[14] What makes A a genuine authority is that she can be trusted intelligently, reasonably, and

9. Komonchak, "Authority and Conversion," 210.

10. Komonchak, "Authority and Magisterium," 103.

11. Komonchak, "Authority and Magisterium," 103; "Authority and Conversion," 210.

12. Komonchak, "Authority and Magisterium," 103; "Authority and Conversion," 210.

13. Komonchak, "Authority and Magisterium," 104.

14. Komonchak, "Authority and Conversion," 211.

responsibly. Authority, for Komonchak, is thus not only a legitimate but also a trustworthy power.[15]

Komonchak argues that "there is in fact no A at all, genuine or not, if there is no B who trusts A, however genuine A may be."[16] He explains that if B questioned every act of A, the former would no longer trust the latter, and the authority relationship between the two had either ceased or was about to cease. Lack of trust is a sign that the authority relationship has reached a crisis.[17]

This understanding of authority as a social relationship contributes two important insights to the discussion of authority in the church. First, it suggests that theological categories alone provide an incomplete account of authority and that understanding authority through the categories of the social sciences broadens the understanding of what authority is and how it functions. The phenomenon of authority is not unique to the church but is a component of any organized human setting. Since the church is a human and social reality, the understanding of authority provided by the human and social sciences should enter into the conversation of the exercise of authority in the church in order to understand the issue more comprehensively and avoid theological reductionism.

Second, the understanding of authority as a social relationship shows why merely formal understanding of authority is unlikely to be of much avail in resolving the current crisis of authority in the church. In Catholic understanding, bishops are entrusted with a unique type of authority, dissimilar from authority in other settings. The bishops' authority is said to be objective in the sense that: it is not derived from the community; it is of divine origin and consists of participation in the authority of Christ; it is guided by the Holy Spirit and is embodied through institutional structures and canonical norms. While these points may be taken well theologically, the issue of the exercise of authority is more complex than that. As Gerard Mannion argues, the crisis the Catholic Church has faced for decades now is fundamentally about the legitimation of authority and it is fueled by "the continued assumption by many bishops, clergy, and other church leaders that respect is theirs *by right* and that they are entitled to expect and even demand obedience and deference to their decisions."[18] It is not difficult to see that this view is in tension with the understanding of authority as a social relationship: it conceives of authority in one-directional terms,

---

15. Komonchak, "Authority and Magisterium," 105.
16. Komonchak, "Authority and Conversion," 212.
17. Komonchak, "Authority and Conversion," 212.
18. Mannion, "'Haze of Fiction,'" 162.

not as a relationship between two parties; and it does not see authority as a phenomenon grounded in reciprocity and trust, but in static terms as a possession with which an office holder is endowed once for all. The merely formal conception of authority does not operate with an understanding that authority is fundamentally a relationship in which one party acknowledges the capacity of the other party to provide direction. The key ramification for authority in the church is that unless those in positions of ecclesial leadership understand and acknowledge that authority is based on trust that needs justification and validation, it is difficult to expect that much progress will be made about the infelicitous state of authority in the church.

Lastly, understanding authority as a social relationship conditions one to think about authority in ways that make it easier to avoid its reification. In chapter three, I discussed Komonchak's criticism of reification of the church, that is, bestowing on the church an ontological status independent of human activity. The problem with reification is that it misrepresents what the church is, namely, a human and social reality constituted by the shared intentionalities of its members.[19] Authority in the church is also susceptible to reification. As Komonchak explains,

> to say that God wills certain structures of authority in the Church is to describe a divine intention; but what exists by that will is a set of social relationships and institutions that, however normative they are, have substantive existence only in the shared intentionalities of the members of the Church. If God wills that some members of the Church be recognized by other members to have authority from him to teach and to lead, this divine will is not realized in some reified realm of divinely empowered "objective" authority, but only when that authority is recognized and received by others.[20]

Conceiving of authority in terms of trust existing between the bearers of authority and its subjects indicates the kind of ontology one has in mind when thinking of authority. As the church, authority is a reality that is constituted by shared intentionalities between human beings. Apart from them, it is merely an abstraction.

---

19. See chapter 3, pp. 86 and 97.
20. Komonchak, "Epistemology of Reception," 195.

Authority and Its Exercise

The notion of authority as a social relationship functions for Komonchak as an entry point into theological considerations of the exercise of authority in the church. They address three main issues: limits of authority, authority and conversion, and obedience as response to teaching authority.

Limits of Authority

Komonchak argues that all human authority is conditional because it is essentially a form of trust between two parties. If trust deteriorates—for example, through betrayals—it will have an adverse effect on the relationship of authority. One way of understanding a crisis of authority is to conceive of it as an inability to maintain trust. As in any other human community, so also in the church, all human authority is conditional.[21]

Komonchak explains that official authority in the church is rooted in the communion of faith and in the belief that there are offices in the church willed by Christ. Yet the exercise of authority in the church also depends on trustworthiness, competence, and respectfulness. Similarly, authority should not be seen as "a substitute for the exercise of intelligence, reason, and responsibility in either the bearers or the subjects of authority."[22] As Komonchak explains, Catholics

> have canonical rules governing the appointment of people to offices of responsibility, because what is called "the grace of office" is not trusted to supply for stupidity, sinfulness, or irresponsibility.... We have some rules for removing inept people from offices of responsibility. All these are necessary and part of the larger institutional framework for the retention of trust in authority. Violate these rules frequently enough, and people will cease to trust the whole framework.[23]

The key point is that genuine authority cannot be guaranteed simply by virtue of an office; rather, it depends on the community to bestow it. As a social relationship, authority is constituted by shared intentionality between the persons in authority and those under authority. Both of these co-constitute authority.[24] Mere appeals to formal authority of office cannot suffice, espe-

---

21. Komonchak, "Authority and Magisterium," 105; "Authority and Conversion," 213.

22. Komonchak, "People of God," (1998) 100.

23. Komonchak, "People of God," 100.

24. Komonchak, "People of God," 99. See also Komonchak, "Epistemology of Reception," 195.

cially when trust has been disturbed. To maintain trust in the office requires that the office holders elicit it and that they know how and what to teach. If the teaching office becomes occupied repeatedly by people who are not suitable teachers, it will eventually cease to be trusted.[25] Komonchak thinks that in such case tests and oaths of fidelity are unlikely to substitute for the breakdown of trust.[26]

Komonchak articulates several criteria that define the limits for the exercise of authority in the church: "It must be exercised within the community of faith and with respect to its defining concerns. It must be in accordance with the constitutive faith of the Church, respect the Church's distinctive spiritual reality, and serve the realization of its proper goals."[27] Komonchak points out that there is ample historical evidence that ordinations and subsequent appointments to offices do not guarantee meeting these criteria. He argues that the authority of the official office holders in the church will be considered trustworthy in as much as persons who are capable to carry out official roles are appointed and in as much as they show that they deserve the trust.[28]

Authority and Conversion

For Komonchak, a balanced theory of authority in the church should include the notion of conversion of both the subjects and the bearers of authority. He notes, however, that while the need for conversion of the former is brought up regularly, a similar need on the part of those who exercise authority is discussed much less frequently.[29] He points out that when discussing tensions between the magisterium and theologians, the magisterium is often approached abstractly and theologians concretely. Theologians are reminded of the need of conversion, subordination, and of fostering ecclesial communion. Reminders of similar obligation on the part of bishops and popes are rare. Komonchak argues that it is not acknowledged adequately that the magisterial task is undertaken by limited and sinful people, and that it is undertaken concretely, not in the abstract. Komonchak believes that real progress will be made only if both the magisterium and theologians are approached concretely.[30]

25. Komonchak, "Authority and Its Exercise," 38.
26. Komonchak, "Authority and Conversion," 219, 221.
27. Komonchak, "Authority and Magisterium," 108.
28. Komonchak, "Authority and Magisterium," 108.
29. Komonchak, "Authority and Conversion," 221–28.
30. Komonchak, "Theologians in the Church," 84.

For Komonchak, maintaining trust in the bearers of authority requires that those who get appointed to leadership roles in the church be committed to the pursuit of all aspects of conversion. He explains that repeated appointments of people who lack such commitment, for which there is ample historical evidence, will eventually erode trust in the institutions and offices. Authority is no substitute for conversion.[31] As he puts it:

> Tests and oaths of fidelity and new canons in a Code of Canon Law will never be anything but a superficial solution even to a genuine problem. Recourse to them is less the remedy than the sign that something needs healing. They are at best somewhat like the brace that sustains a broken leg. The real healing has to come from within, with the reknitting of the bones and strengthening of the sinews of ecclesial communion, of admiration, trust, and love of Christ and his church, and these are the work of the Spirit effecting conversion in all concerned, and for that no authority can substitute.[32]

That conversion should apply to the bearers of authority in the church and not only to its subjects may at first seem a theologically trivial point. Who would object to the need for conversion? Yet upon careful consideration, one could see that talk of conversion on the part of the bearers of authority in the church presents a theological challenge, for it implies a possibility that those endowed with magisterial authority, if not converted, might stand in the way of the Holy Spirit's guidance of the church. Acknowledging this point would likely make at least some Catholics uncomfortable.

While matters of truth should not be decided simply on the basis of which position has the majority on its side, one can hardly not be puzzled by the fact that a substantial majority of self-identified Catholics rejected the teaching of *Humanae vitae* regarding the immorality of artificial contraception, especially if part of the majority were priests, religious, and even some bishops, not only theologians and "well-informed" laity.[33] One is tempted to wonder whether the majority report presented to the pope recommending that the magisterium relax its prohibition on artificial contraception for married couples was the Holy Spirit's prompting to the church that was not listened to.

While I agree with Komonchak that commitment to all aspects of conversion is essential in order to maintain trust, commitment to intellectual

---

31. Komonchak, "Authority and Conversion," 224–27.
32. Komonchak, "Authority and Conversion," 228.
33. It would be much more difficult today than in 1968 to find a bishop, who would be willing to be openly critical of *Humanae vitae*.

conversion appears to be particularly relevant for the discussion of authority in the church.³⁴ The magisterial documents that greatly contributed to the current crisis of teaching authority in the church seem to have one thing in common,³⁵ namely, the perception that their conclusions had been predetermined and that the arguments provided to support them were tailored to those conclusions. It is not difficult to see why such perception could erode trust between the magisterium and the rest of the faithful. A firm commitment to intellectual conversion by all the faithful appears to be a critical step toward overcoming the crisis of teaching authority in the church.

Magisterium and Obedience

Another important issue, in Komonchak's view, pertaining to the discussion of teaching authority in the church is a lack of proper distinction between teaching and legislating. He argues that conceiving the response to a teaching authority in terms of obedience is problematic because it conflates teaching with legislating, as illustrated in the expression "*obeying* the church *teaching*," which Komonchak finds odd.³⁶ The problem, as he sees it, is that ordinarily the response we give to teachings is agreement or assent, and we respond to laws or commands with obedience or respect. Komonchak explains that conflating teaching with legislating has carried over to the present from neoscholastic manuals, which did not distinguish appropriately between the role of the mind and the role of the will in responding to a teaching. Komonchak finds the conflation particularly concerning if it is accompanied by a voluntaristic conception of truth, in which case truth is considered to be whatever the authority happens to be teaching.³⁷

    Komonchak explains that although in Catholic understanding there is a unique kind of authority in the church, this does not mean that the way teaching authority functions sidesteps the logic of authority, that is, trustworthiness. For Komonchak, it is an oversimplification to think of the magisterium of bishops as being authoritative in the sense of binding for the faithful, and of everyone else's teaching role in the church as merely scientific, that is, depending on the strength of the arguments. While it is true that the magisterium of bishops ought to be trusted because of the Christ's

---

    34. Intellectual conversion refers to the idea of cognitive integrity in one's intellectual positions and reveals itself in the love of truth for its own sake.

    35. For instance, *Humanae vitae*, *Veritatis splendor*, *Inter insigniores*, *Ordinatio sacerdotalis*, *Apostolos suos*, and *Communionis notio*.

    36. Komonchak, "Authority and Its Exercise," 35.

    37. Komonchak, "Ordinary Papal Magisterium," 118.

promise not to abandon the church into error, this does not mean that bishops and popes do not need to provide reasons for their teachings, and that this is the task proper to theologians.[38]

Komonchak's distinction between obeying laws and assenting to teachings is well taken and illumines the discussion of the crisis of the teaching authority in the church. The key point, which could be seen as a diagnosis of the crisis, is that the mind cannot be compelled to assent to a teaching that has not been argued credibly. Conceiving of teaching authority in terms of legislating was typical of pre-Vatican II Catholicism and continues to have a grasp on the Catholic imagination in the present. Its description by Walter Burkhardt illustrates the idea well: "Authority does not have to explain, prove, convince, appeal to human intelligence. The Church is not a democracy or a debating society. The Church proclaims—proclaims the truth; and there it stands.... Those who hold office make the decisions; the faithful in the ranks submit to the decisions, execute the orders."[39] "Submission" of the will rather than "assent" of the mind defines this view of teaching authority and is its main liability. It might have worked well in the past, but times have changed. Many Catholics today will withhold assent to a teaching that they do not find argued persuasively. Knowledge of the tradition and especially the experience of the Second Vatican Council is evidence for them that the magisterium can and has changed some of its teachings.[40] It appears that the way forward in overcoming the crisis of teaching authority is for the magisterium to allow and promote open discussion of disputed teachings and to listen to the faithful who have not received them. Moreover, as Peter Phan argues, the bishops should acknowledge, especially in our time of paradigm shifts, that they too—not only theologians or the faithful in general—are learners.[41] The idea that episcopal ordination confers theological competence is not credible. In the end, conflation of teaching with legislating closely relates to intellectual conversion since at bottom it raises the issue of providing compelling arguments for a teaching.

Conclusion

Joseph Komonchak's reflections on authority in the church contribute several critical points to the overall discussion of the topic and suggest ways of

---

38. Komonchak, "Authority and Magisterium," 109–11.

39. Burghardt, *Long Have I Loved You*, 332–33.

40. For instance, on slavery, usury, religious freedom, the role of love and pleasure in marital sexual relations, ecumenism, and salvation of non-Christians.

41. Phan, "Teaching as Learning," 75–87.

resolving the present impasses. First, Komonchak argues that the discussion of authority ought not take place in isolation from the overall discussion of the dynamics of community. Second, Komonchak suggests that it would be a mistake to conceive of the crisis of authority in the church exclusively in theological terms, such as lack of faith commitment or virtue. Instead, the crisis should be understood essentially as a breakdown of a social relationship, namely, as an inability to maintain trust between the bearers and the subjects of authority. Understanding how trust is established and maintained is key to a meaningful solution to the current crisis of authority in the church. Third, Komonchak argues that a commitment to all aspects of conversion on the part of all the faithful, including the bearers of authority, is indispensable to maintaining trust between the bearers and the subjects of authority. Lastly, Komonchak proposes that bishops not conceive of responding to their teaching magisterium in terms of obedience to laws. The conflation of legislating with teaching is part of the problem of why the crisis of authority developed and why it has continued.

Komonchak's reflections on authority reinforce central features of his foundations in ecclesiology. They operate with an understanding of the church as a human and social reality. They understand the church as a community of meaning and value, *congregatio fidelium*, and simultaneously as God's gift and our task. By portraying the nature of authority in relational terms, Komonchak's view of authority fits well within ecclesiologies of communion.

Conclusion

REFLECTING ON THE CHURCH theologically is not an easy task; at least that has been my experience. Frankly, I have found ecclesiology strange at times. The lofty, theological language designating the church as the mystical body of Christ, the temple of the Holy Spirit, mystery, sacrament, communion, the bride of Christ, or our mother, which has been typical in contemporary ecclesiological discourse, made me wonder where I could encounter this reality. At times, it seemed as if this church was a mythical creature hovering somewhere above in a supra-historical realm, and at times it was clear that "the church" was simply a synonym for the hierarchy. Not until I encountered the writings of Joseph Komonchak did the strangeness of ecclesiology begin to fade away. While the theologians whose writings on the church I had studied before did not deny that the church is essentially a group of people, they did not give adequate attention to this basic affirmation of ecclesiology. In Komonchak, however, it took center stage. He argued that any statement about the church must be true of some Christian *congregatio fidelium*, if it were to be true at all. Coupled with his account of the church's ongoing genesis in history and of the church's ontology, Komonchak provided conceptual clarity for the "church talk" I found lacking elsewhere.

In the multilayered landscape of twentieth-century Catholic ecclesiology, Komonchak appears as a visionary, deserving a distinguished place. Being a student of Lonergan taught him to be a tough-minded systematic thinker, capable of re-envisioning ecclesiology as a critical, systematic discipline—a challenge posed by the shift in ecclesiology made at Vatican II. While most theologians after the council provided largely descriptive or image-based accounts of the church, Komonchak took up the challenge and constructed theory-based foundations for ecclesiology. At their center is the distinctive trademark of his ecclesiological vision, namely, his call to incorporate the human and social sciences into the task of interpreting the church. Attending to a theory of history and the metaphysics of social realities, Komonchak worked out general categories for ecclesiology, without which a theory-based understanding of the church would not be possible. This enabled him to avoid theological reductionism—an interpretation of the church that draws almost exclusively on religious or theological language, resulting often in the mystification of the church. It also helped him avoid being methodologically naïve and idealizing the church.

Furthermore, in the scene of post-Vatican II ecclesiology, Komonchak can be seen as a heavy lifter delivering a definitive resolution to the central problem of ecclesiology, which is to explain how the visible and invisible dimensions of the church comprise a single reality. For centuries these two dimensions were disjointed: the former dominated institutional approaches to ecclesiology and the latter came to the fore in highly spiritual and theological approaches. Understanding the two dimensions analogically with the Incarnation, which became typical in the nineteenth century and was espoused by Vatican II, did not offer the desired clarity. Komonchak's proposal to conceive of the visible, human dimension of the church as being simultaneously a response to God's offer of self and a mediation of God's saving love before the world offered such clarity. The key lies in invoking the sacramental imagination and in identifying the human aspect of the church as the locus of unity of the visible and the invisible aspects of the church.

As an ecclesiologist, Komonchak is a master of balance, brilliantly discerning the *via media* among theological positions, not overplaying his hand. His thinking about the church stands out among contemporary theologians as skillfully weaving together the old and the new into a cohesive whole. On one hand, his ecclesiology is firmly rooted in the spiritual and theological dimensions of the church that Vatican II validated and reinserted into Catholic ecclesiology. On the other hand, his thinking about the church remains "traditional" as far as it focuses on the visible church and does not downplay its institutional character. In this regard, he is in continuity with pre-Vatican II ecclesiologists. Komonchak differs from them, however, in the way he approaches the visible church. While they addressed the "visible" juridically or canonically, Komonchak has done this through the lenses of the human and social sciences.

Komonchak's great service to contemporary Catholic ecclesiology is not in providing a comprehensive systematic treatise on the church, but in navigating through the methodological exigencies of such a project. As the last paragraph of his *Foundations in Ecclesiology* indicates, Komonchak is aware that his work is unfinished:

> I do not pretend that these essays represent a complete ecclesiology. Several areas need much further development: the constitutive role of liturgy and sacrament, the foundations and role of ministry, and, perhaps above all, the incidence upon the Church itself of the dialectic of progress, decline, and recovery, that is, the question of the sinfulness of the Church. I remain convinced, however, that all these themes can be developed coherently from the foundations I have tried to lay here. And perhaps time and energy will permit them to be taken up in the future.[1]

Unfortunately, Komonchak has not realized the wish expressed in the last sentence, perhaps waiting for his students to pick up the mantle.

Komonchak's thinking about the church has some important ramifications for church practice. His attention to the church's human dimension and his insistence on understanding the church as the gathering of the faithful (*congregatio fidelium*) makes it clear that the church is all the baptized. The church does not exist in the abstract nor is it just clergy and religious. The future of the church is thus in everyone's hands.

Furthermore, Komonchak's theology of the local church envisions a church that is more participatory and synodal. In the current climate shaped by the papacy of Francis, Komonchak's foundations for ecclesiology, which underpin his thinking on the local church and on authority, could be used to realize the pope's desire for bishops to discern the signs of the times in local contexts and respond to them with the gospel. Unfortunately, the pope's call has been mostly unheeded. It seems that bishops have been conditioned to simply implement directives coming from Rome. Following the stunning resignation of Pope Benedict XVI, Catholics should draw the conclusion that has not been easy to draw in the recent past: "the church is not the pope, and the pope is not the church."[2] Perhaps Pope Francis ought to be more emphatic in encouraging and allowing the laity, the religious, and the clergy "to assume their responsibilities for the difference the church is supposed to make in the world."[3]

It is my sincere hope that this study has helped the reader realize the distinctive contribution Joseph Komonchak has made to Catholic ecclesiology and presented a compelling case for the ways in which his thinking about the church holds a promise that ought to be realized more fully.

---

1. Komonchak, *Foundations in Ecclesiology*, 188–89.
2. Komonchak, "Benedict's Act of Humility," (2013) 8.
3. Komonchak, "Benedict's Act of Humility," 8.

Bibliography of Joseph A. Komonchak

1967

"The Problem of a Religious *a priori*." *The Dunwoodie Review* 7 (1967) 199–214.

1969

"Ordinary Papal Magisterium and Religious Assent." In *Contraception: Authority and Dissent*, edited by Charles E. Curran, 101–26. New York: Herder and Herder, 1969. Reprinted in *The Magisterium and Morality*. Vol. 3 of *Readings in Moral Theology*, edited by Charles E. Curran and Richard A. McCormick, 67–90. New York: Paulist, 1982.

1971

(with William Ryan, et al.). "The Liberation of Men and Nations: The Role of the Church in the Americas." *The Catholic Mind* 69 (1971) 13–29. Reprinted in *Studies in the International Apostolate of Jesuits* 1 (1972) 39–64.

1972

"Preaching and Social Development." *ComPassion* 1 (1972) 2–6.
"Redemptive Justice: An Interpretation of the *Cur Deus Homo*." *The Dunwoodie Review* 12 (1972) 35–55.

1973

"A Theology of Liberation." *The Catholic Charities Review* 57 (1973) 1–8. Reprinted in *The Catholic Mind* 71 (1973) 21–29.

"Towards a Theology of Liberation." In *The Social Mission of the Church: A Theological Reflection*, edited by Edward J. Ryle, 5–28. Washington: National Catholic School of Social Service, 1973.

1974

"The Church." In *The Catholic Encyclopedia for School and Home: The Contemporary Church*, edited by George E. Tiffany, 47–49. New York: Grolier, 1974.
"John Courtney Murray." In *The Catholic Encyclopedia for School and Home: The Contemporary Church*, edited by George E. Tiffany, 163–64. New York: Grolier, 1974.
"Membership in the Church." In *The Catholic Encyclopedia for School and Home: The Contemporary Church*, edited by George E. Tiffany, 160. New York: Grolier, 1974.
"Mystical Body of Christ." In *The Catholic Encyclopedia for School and Home: The Contemporary Church*, edited by George E. Tiffany, 164. New York: Grolier, 1974.
"Response to Professor Tavard (II)." *Proceedings of the Catholic Theological Society of America* 29 (1974) 389–95.
"Salvation Outside the Church." In *The Catholic Encyclopedia for School and Home: The Contemporary Church*, edited by George E. Tiffany, 219. New York: Grolier, 1974.
"Theology, Transcendental." In *The Catholic Encyclopedia for School and Home: The Contemporary Church*, edited by George E. Tiffany, 235–36. New York: Grolier, 1974.

1976

"Réflexions théologiques sur l'autorité enseignante dans l'Eglise." *Concilium* 117 (1976) 89–99.
"Theological Questions on the Ordination of Women." In *Women and Catholic Priesthood: An Expanded Vision*, edited by Anne Marie Gardiner, 241–59. New York: Paulist, 1976. Reprinted in *The Catholic Mind* 75 (1977) 13–28.

1977

"The Permanent Diaconate and the Variety of Ministries in the Church." *Diaconal Quarterly* 3.3 (1977) 15–23; 3.4 (1977) 29–40; 4.1 (1978) 13–25.

1978

"*Humanae Vitae* and its Reception: Ecclesiological Reflections." *Theological Studies* 39.2 (1978) 221–57.

1979

"Authority, Ecclesiastical." In *Supplement: Change in the Church*. Vol. 17 of *The New Catholic Encyclopedia*, edited by the Catholic University of America, 31–32. Washington: McGraw-Hill, 1979.
"Church and World." In *Supplement: Change in the Church*. Vol. 17 of *The New Catholic Encyclopedia*, edited by the Catholic University of America, 125–26. Washington: McGraw-Hill, 1979.
"Community and Mankind." In *Supplement: Change in the Church*. Vol. 17 of *The New Catholic Encyclopedia*, edited by the Catholic University of America, 148–49. Washington: McGraw-Hill, 1979.
"Society (Theology)." In *Supplement: Change in the Church*. Vol. 17 of *The New Catholic Encyclopedia*, edited by the Catholic University of America, 618. Washington: McGraw-Hill, 1979.

1980

"Christ's Church in Today's World: Medellin, Puebla, and the United States." *The Living Light* 17 (1980) 108–20.
"'Non-ordained' and 'Ordained' Ministers in the Church." In *The Right of a Community to a Priest*, edited by Edward Schillebeeckx and Johann Baptist Metz. *Concilium* 133 (1980) 44–50.
"A Response to Fr. Sobrino." In *Theology and Discovery: Essays in Honor of Karl Rahner, SJ*, edited by William J. Kelly, 228–30. Milwaukee: Marquette University Press, 1980.

1981

"Celibacy and Tradition." *Chicago Studies* 20 (1981) 5–17.
"The Church Universal as the Communion of Local Churches." In *Where Does the Church Stand?*, edited by Giuseppe Alberigo and Gustavo Gutierrez. *Concilium* 146 (1981) 30–35.
"Clergy, Laity and the Church's Mission in the World." *The Jurist* 41 (1981) 422–47.
"Ecclesiology and Social Theory: A Methodological Essay." *The Thomist* 45 (1981) 262–83. Reprinted in *Foundations in Ecclesiology*, edited by Fred Lawrence, 57–76. Boston: Lonergan Workshop, 1995.
"History and Social Theory in Ecclesiology." *Lonergan Workshop* 2, 1–53. Chico, CA: Scholars, 1981. Reprinted in *Foundations in Ecclesiology*, edited by Fred Lawrence, 3–46. Boston: Lonergan Workshop, 1995.
"Lonergan and the Task of Ecclesiology." In *Creativity and Method: Essays in Honor of Bernard Lonergan, SJ*, edited by Matthew L. Lamb, 265–73. Milwaukee: Marquette University Press, 1981. Reprinted in *Foundation in Ecclesiology*, edited by Fred Lawrence, 47–56. Boston: Lonergan Workshop, 1995.
"Ministry and the Local Church." *Proceedings of the Catholic Theological Society of America* 36 (1981) 56–82.
"Moral Pluralism and the Unity of Faith." In *One Faith, One Church, Many Moralities?*, edited by Jacques Pohier and Dietmar Mieth. *Concilium* 150 (1981) 89–94.

"A New Law for the People of God: A Theological Evaluation." In *Canon Law Society of America: Proceedings of the Forty-second Annual Convention*, 14–23. Washington: Canon Law Society of America, 1981.

"Research and the Church: A Theologian's View." *The Living Light* 18 (1981) 112–20.

"The Status of the Faithful in the Revised Code of Canon Law." In *The Revised Code of Canon Law: A Missed Opportunity?*, edited by Peter Huizing and Knut Walf. *Concilium* 147 (1981) 37–45.

1982

"The Church and Religious Education in the 1980s." *The Living Light* 19 (1982) 200–10.

1983

"Church and Ministry." *The Jurist* 43 (1983) 273–88.

"The Church is a Communion." *Liturgy* 3.2 (1983) 7–11.

"The Ecumenical Council in the New Code of Canon Law." In *The Ecumenical Council: Its Significance in the Constitution of the Church*, edited by Peter Huizing and Knut Walf. *Concilium* 167 (1983) 100–105.

"Kingdom, History, and Church." In *Catholics and Nuclear War*, edited by Philip J. Murnion, 106–15. New York: Crossroad, 1983.

"Reflections on the New York Forum." *Theological Education* 20.1 (1983) 60–64.

"The Return of Yves Congar." *Commonweal* 110.13 (1983) 7–11.

1985

"The Ecclesial and Cultural Roles of Theology." *Proceedings of the Catholic Theological Society of America* 40 (1985) 15–32.

"The Enlightenment and the Construction of Roman Catholicism." *Annual of the Catholic Commission on Intellectual and Cultural Affairs* 4 (1985) 31–59.

"What Is Happening to Doctrine?" *Commonweal* 112.17 (1985) 456–59.

1986

Introduction to *Synode extraordinaire: Célébration de Vatican II*, 9–32. Paris: Cerf, 1986.

"The Theological Debate." In *Synod 1985: An Evaluation*, edited by Giuseppe Alberigo and James Provost. *Concilium* 188 (1986) 53–63.

"Towards a Theology of the Local Church." In *Federation of Asian Bishops' Conferences Papers* 42 (1986) 1–43.

"Vatican II and the New Code." *Archives de sciences sociales des religions* 62 (1986) 107–17.

1987

"Authority and Magisterium." In *Vatican Authority and American Catholic Dissent: The Curran Case and Its Consequences*, edited by William W. May, 103-14. New York: Crossroad, 1987.
"The Church: God's Gift and Our Task." *Origins* 16.2 (1987) 735-41.
"Interpreting the Second Vatican Council." *Landas: Journal of Loyola School of Theology* 1 (1987) 81-90.
"Issues behind the Curran Case." *Commonweal* 114.2 (1987) 43-47.
"The Local Realization of the Church." In *The Reception of Vatican II*, edited by Giuseppe Alberigo, et al., 77-90. Washington: Catholic University of America Press, 1987.
(with Mary Collins and Dermot Lane, eds.). *The New Dictionary of Theology*. Wilmington, DE: Michael Glazier, 1987.
(with Giuseppe Alberigo and Jean-Pierre Jossua, eds.). *The Reception of Vatican II*. Washington: Catholic University of America Press, 1987.
"The Synod of 1985 and the Notion of the Church." *Chicago Studies* 26 (1987) 330-45.
"Vatican Council II." In *The New Dictionary of Theology*, 1072-77. Wilmington, DE: Michael Glazier, 1987.

1988

"Bishops, Conferences, and Collegiality." *America* 158.11 (1988) 302-4.
"The Church." In *The Desire of the Human Heart: An Introduction to the Theology of Bernard Lonergan*, edited by Vernon Gregson, 222-36. New York: Paulist, 1988. Reprinted under the title "Lonergan and the Church," in *Foundations in Ecclesiology*, edited by Fred Lawrence, 77-94. Boston: Lonergan Workshop, 1995.
"Episcopal Conferences." *Chicago Studies* 27.3 (1988) 311-28.
"La subsidiarité dans l'Eglise." *Documents-épiscopat* 1 (1988) 1-10.
(With James Provost). "Ready for Rome: Defining Episcopal Conferences." *Commonweal* 115.4 (1988) 102-5.
"Subsidiarity in the Church: The State of the Question." *The Jurist* 48 (1988) 298-349.

1989

"The Church in the United States." In *The Spirit Moving the Church in the United States*, edited by Francis A. Eigo, 1-31. Villanova, PA: Villanova University Press, 1989.
"Congar, Yves Marie-Joseph." In *Supplement 1978-1988*. Vol. 18 of *The New Catholic Encyclopedia*, edited by the Catholic University of America, 104-5. Washington: Catholic University of America, 1989.
"Defending our Hope: On the Fundamental Task of Theology." In *Faithful Witness: Foundations of Theology for Today's Church*, edited by Leo J. O'Donovan and T. Howland Sanks, 14-26. New York: Crossroad, 1989.
"Introduction: Episcopal Conferences under Criticism." In *Episcopal Conferences: Historical, Canonical, and Theological Studies*, edited by Thomas J. Reese, 1-22. Washington: Georgetown University Press, 1989.
"The Local Church." *Chicago Studies* 28.3 (1989) 320-35.

"The Roman Working Paper on Episcopal Conferences." In *Episcopal Conferences: Historical, Canonical, and Theological Studies*, edited by Thomas J. Reese, 177–204. Washington: Georgetown University Press, 1989.
"Synod of Bishops (Second Extraordinary, 1985)." In *Supplement 1979-1988*. Vol. 17 of *The New Catholic Encyclopedia*, edited by the Catholic University of America, 495–97. Washington: Catholic University of America, 1989.

1990

"The Magisterium and Theologians." *Chicago Studies* 29.3 (1990) 307–29.
"Marie-Dominique Chenu: A Tribute." *Commonweal* 117.8 (1990) 252–54.
"Newman's Infallible Instincts." *Commonweal* 117.14 (1990) 445–48.
"Theology and Culture at Mid-Century: The Example of Henri de Lubac." *Theological Studies* 51.4 (1990) 579–602.
"What They Said before the Council: How the US Bishops Envisioned Vatican II." *Commonweal* 117.21 (1990) 714–17.

1991

"Modernity and the Construction of Roman Catholicism." In *Modernism as a Social Construct*, edited by George Gilmore, et al., 11–41. Mobile, AL: Spring Hill College, 1991.

1992

"The Coldness of Clarity, the Warmth of Love: The Measure of John Courtney Murray." *Commonweal* 119.4 (1992) 14–17.
"The Local Church and the Church Catholic: The Contemporary Theological Problematic." *The Jurist* 52 (1992) 416–47.
"Recapturing the Great Tradition: *In Memoriam* Henri de Lubac." *Commonweal* 119.2 (1992) 14–17.

1993

"The Authority of the *Catechism of the Catholic Church*." *The Living Light* 29 (1993) 39–49. Reprinted in *Introducing the Catechism of the Catholic Church: Traditional Themes and Contemporary Issues*, edited by Berard L. Marthaler, 18–31. New York: Paulist, 1994.
"The Catholic University in the Church." In *Catholic Universities in Church and Society*, edited by John P. Langan, 35–55. Washington: Georgetown University Press, 1993.
"*Ex Corde Ecclesiae* and its Ordinances." *Commonweal* 120.20 (1993) 22–23.
"The Initial Debate about the Church." In *Vatican II commence*, edited by Étienne Fouilloux, 320–52. Leuven: Bibiliotheek van de Faculteit der Godgeleerdheid, 1993.
"*Veritatis Splendor*." *Commonweal* 120.18 (1993) 22–23.

1994

"Lonergan's Early Essays on the Redemption of History." *Lonergan Workshop* 10 (1994) 159-77.
"US Bishops' Suggestions for Vatican II." *Cristianesimo nella Storia* 15 (1994) 313-71.
"Vatican II and the Encounter between Catholicism and Liberalism." In *Catholicism and Liberalism: Contributions to American Public Philosophy*, edited by R. Bruce Douglas and David Hollenbach, 76-99. New York: Cambridge University Press, 1994.

1995

"Concepts of Communion, Past and Present." *Cristianesimo nella Storia* 16 (1995) 321-40.
Foundations in Ecclesiology. Edited by Fred Lawrence. Lonergan Workshop 11. Supplementary issue. Boston: Lonergan Workshop, 1995.
"A Hero of Vatican II: Yves Congar." *Commonweal* 122.21 (1995) 15-17.
(with Giuseppe Alberigo, eds.). *Toward a New Era in Catholicism*. Vol. 1 of *History of Vatican II*. Maryknoll, NY: Orbis, 1995.
"Interpreting the Council: Catholic Attitudes toward Vatican II." In *Being Right: Conservative Catholics in America*, edited by Mary Jo Weaver and R. Scott Appleby, 17-36. Bloomington, IN: Indiana University Press, 1995.
"The Struggle for the Council in the Preparation of Vatican II." In *Toward a New Era in Catholicism*. Vol. 1 of *History of Vatican II*, 167-356. Maryknoll, NY: Orbis, 1995
"Theologians in the Church." In *Church and Theology: Essays in Memory of Carl J. Peter*, edited by Peter C. Phan, 63-87. Washington: Catholic University of America Press, 1995.
"What is the Pope Saying?" *Church* 11 (1995) 25-27.

1996

"Conversion and Objectivity." *Method: Journal of Lonergan Studies* 14 (1996) 99-105.
"Das II. Vatikanum und die Auseinandersetzung zwischen Katholizismus und Liberalismus." In *Vatikanum II und Modernisierung: Historische, theologische and soziologische Perspektiven*, edited by Franz-Xaver Kaufmann and Arnold Zingerle, 147-69. Paderborn: Ferdinand Schöningh, 1996.
"John Courtney Murray and the Redemption of History: Natural Law and Theology." In *John Courtney Murray and the Growth of Tradition*, edited by J. Leon Hooper and Todd D. Whitmore, 60-81. Kansas City: Sheed & Ward, 1996.
"Responses to Rome." *Commonweal* 123.2 (1996) 15-16.
"The Secretariat for Promoting Christian Unity and the Preparation of Vatican II." *Centro pro Unione Semi-annual Bulletin* 50 (1996) 11-17.
"The Silencing of John Courtney Murray." *Cristianesimo nella Storia: Saggi in onore di Giuseppe Alberigo*, edited by A. Melloni, et al., 657-702. Bologna: Il Mulino, 1996.
"The Theology of the Local Church: State of the Question." In *Multicultural Church: A New Landscape in US Theologies*, edited by William Cenkner, 35-49. New York: Paulist, 1996.

1997

"Catholicity and the Redemption of History." In *Ecclesia Tertii Millenii Advenientis: Omaggio al P. Angel Antón*, edited by F. Chica, et al., 602–13. Casale Monferrato: Piemme, 1997.

"The Epistemology of Reception." In *La recepción y la comunión entre las Iglesias. Actas de Coloquio Internacional de Salamanca, 8–14 Abril 1996*, edited by Hervé Legrand, et al., 240–57. Salamanca: Departamento de Publicaciones de la Universidad Pontificia, 1997. Reprinted in *The Jurist* 57 (1997) 180–203; *Reception and Communion and Churches*, edited by Hervé Legrand, et al., 180–203. Washington: Canon Law Department (CUA), 1997.

"Fenton, Joseph." In *The Encyclopedia of American Catholic History*, edited by Michael Glazier and Thomas J. Shelley, 505–6. Collegeville, MN: Liturgical, 1997.

(with Giuseppe Alberigo, eds.). *The Formation of the Council's Identity*. Vol. 2 of *History of Vatican II*. Maryknoll, NY: Orbis, 1997.

"Mission and Identity in Catholic Universities." In *Theological Education in the Catholic Tradition: Contemporary Challenges*, edited by Patrick W. Carey and Earl C. Muller, 34–48. New York: Crossroad, 1997.

"Modernity and the Construction of Roman Catholicism." *Cristianesimo nella Storia* 18 (1997) 353–85.

"Murray, John Courtney." In *The Encyclopedia of American Catholic History*, edited by Michael Glazier and Thomas J. Shelley, 993–96. Collegeville, MN: Liturgical, 1997.

"On the People of God as a Theological and Sociological Reality: The Case for Dialogue." *National Catholic Register*, June 8–14, 1997, 5.

"Preparing for the New Millennium." *Logos* 1 (1997) 34–55.

"Riflessioni storiografiche sul Vaticano II come evento." In *L'evento e le decisioni: Studi sulle dinamiche del concilio Vatican II*, edited by Maria Teresa Fattori and Alberto Melloni, 417–49. Bologna: Il Mulino, 1997.

1998

"Das II. Vatikanum und die nordamerikanische Kultur am Beispiel von John Courtney Murray." In *Das II. Vatikanum: Christlicher Glaube im Horizont globaler Modernisierung; Einleitungsfragen*, edited by Peter Hünermann, 211–25. Paderborn: Schöningh, 1998.

"On the Authority of Bishops' Conferences." *America* 179.6 (1998) 7–10.

"People of God, Hierarchical Structure, and Communion: An Easy Fit?" In *Canon Law Society of America: Proceedings of the Sixteenth Annual Convention* (1998) 91–102.

"The Redemptive Identity and Mission of a Catholic University." In *Catholic Theology in the University: Source of Wholeness*, edited by Virginia M. Shaddy, 73–89. Milwaukee: Marquette University Press, 1998.

"Thomism and the Second Vatican Council." In *Continuity and Plurality in Catholic Theology: Essays in Honor of Gerald A. McCool, SJ*, edited by Anthony J. Cernera, 53–73. Fairfield, CT: Fairfield University Press, 1998.

1999

"Authority and its Exercise." In *Church Authority in American Culture: The Second Cardinal Bernardin Conference*, 29–46. New York: Crossroad, 1999.
"Catholic Principle and the American Experiment: The Silencing of John Courtney Murray." *US Catholic Historian* 17 (1999) 28–45.
"Convening Vatican II: John XXIII Calls for a Council." *Commonweal* 126.3 (1999) 10–11.
"'The Crisis in Church-State Relationships in the USA' A Recently Discovered Text by John Courtney Murray." *The Review of Politics* 61 (1999) 675–714.
"Ecclesiology of Vatican II." *Origins* 28.44 (1999) 763–68.
"La redazione della Gaudium et Spes." *Il Regno* 44 (1999) 446–55.
"Renewing Authority: The Lesson of *Dei Verbum*." *Commonweal* 126.20 (1999) 21–22.
"Returning from Exile: Catholic Theology in the 1930s." In *The Twentieth Century: A Theological Overview*, edited by Gregory Baum, 35–48. Maryknoll, NY: Orbis: 1999.
"Vatican II as an 'Event.'" *Theology Digest* 46.4 (1999) 337–52. Reprinted in *Vatican II: Did Anything Happen?*, edited by David G. Schultenover, 24–51. New York: Continuum, 2007.

2000

"Authority and Conversion or: The Limits of Authority." *Cristianesimo nella Storia* 21 (2000) 207–29.
"Culture and History as the Material Conditions of the Genesis of the Local Church." In *Changing Churches: The Local Church and the Structures of Changes*, edited by Michael Warren, 48–65. Portland, OR: Pastoral, 2000.
"La valutazioni sulla *Gaudium et Spes*: Chenu, Dossetti, Ratzinger." In *Volti di fine Concilio: Studi di storia e teologia sulla conclusione del Vaticano II*, edited by Joseph Doré and Alberto Melloni, 115–53. Bologna: Il Mulino, 2000.
(with Giuseppe Alberigo, eds.). *The Mature Council*. Vol. 3 of *History of Vatican II*. Maryknoll: NY: Orbis, 2000.
"Religious Freedom and the Confessional State: The Twentieth-Century Discussion." *Revue d'Historie Ecclésiastique* 95 (2000) 634–50.
"Remembering Good Pope John." *Commonweal* 127.14 (2000) 11–15.
"The Significance of Vatican Council II for Ecclesiology." In *The Gift of the Church: A Textbook in Ecclesiology in Honor of Patrick Granfield, OSB*, edited by Peter C. Phan, 69–92. Collegeville, MN: Liturgical, 2000.

2001

"All Dressed in Scarlet: Avery Dulles Goes to College." *Commonweal* 128.4 (2001) 9.
"Roots and Branches: Studying the History of Vatican II." In *Vatican II au Canada: enracinement et réception*, edited by Gilles Routhier, 503–24. Québec: Fides, 2001.

2002

"40 Years after Vatican II: The Ongoing Challenge." *Liguorian* (2002) 11–14.
"Christians Must Make a Difference." *The Tablet*, September 28, 2002, 4–5.
"Vatican II as an Ecumenical Council: Yves Congar's Vision Realized." *Commonweal* 129.20 (2002) 12–14.
"What Road to Joy?" *The Tablet*, November 30, 2002, 11–12.

2003

"Augustine, Aquinas or the Gospel *sine glossa*: Divisions over *Gaudium et Spes*." In *Unfinished Journey: The Church 40 Years after Vatican II. Essays for John Wilkins*, edited by Austen Ivereigh, 102–18. New York: Continuum, 2003.
"Canon Law in the Service of Communion: The Example of James H. Provost." *The Jurist* 63 (2003) 1–21.
(with Giuseppe Alberigo, eds.). *Church as Communion*. Vol. 4 of *History of Vatican II*. Maryknoll, NY: Orbis, 2003.
"Is Christ Divided? Dealing with Diversity and Disagreement." *Origins* 33.9 (2003) 140–47.
"Toward an Ecclesiology of Communion." In *Church as Communion*. Vol. 4 of *History of Vatican II*, 1–93. Maryknoll, NY: Orbis, 2003.
"What if the Church Is Not a Pyramid? We the People of God, the Body of Christ." *Church* 19.2 (2003) 5–10.

2005

"The Church in Crisis: Pope Benedict's Theological Vision." *Commonweal* 132.11 (2005) 11–14.
"The Future of Theology in the Church." In *New Horizons in Theology*, edited by Terrence W. Tilley, 16–39. Maryknoll, NY: Orbis, 2005.
"The Violence of the Cross: A Mystery, not a Punishment." *Commonweal* 132.2 (2005) 19–22.

2006

"The American Contribution to *Dignitatis Humanae*: The Role of John Courtney Murray, SJ." *US Catholic Historian* 24.1 (2006) 1–20.
"À propos de la priorité de l'Église universelle: analyse et questions." In *Nouveaux apprentissages pour l'Église: Mélanges en l'honneur de Hervé Legrand, OP*, edited by Gilles Routhier and Laurent Villemin, 245–68. Paris: Cerf, 2006.
"The Council of Trent at the Second Vatican Council." In *From Trent to Vatican II: Historical and Theological Investigations*, edited by Raymond F. Bulman and Frederick J. Parella, 61–80. New York: Oxford University Press, 2006.
(with Giuseppe Alberigo, eds.). *The Council and the Transition*. Vol. 5 of *History of Vatican II*. Maryknoll: NY: Orbis, 2006.

2007

"Benedict XVI and the Interpretation of Vatican II." *Cristianesimo nella Storia* 28 (2007) 323-37. Translated into Italian as "Benedetto XVI e l'interpretazione del Vaticano II." In *Chi ha paura del Vatican II?* edited by Alberto Melloni and Giuseppe Ruggieri. Rome: Carocci, 2009.
"One Cheer." *Commonweal* 134.14 (2007) 15-16.
"A Response to Gilles Routhier." *Proceedings of the Catholic Theological Society of America* 62 (2007) 16-18.

2008

"The 'Legislative History' of *Gaudium et Spes*: An Original Tension in Views of Vatican II and Implementation of Catholic Social Thought." *Journal of Law, Philosophy, and Culture* 2 (2008) 53-112.[1]
"Lonergan and Post-Conciliar Ecclesiology." *Lonergan Workshop* 20 (2008) 165-83.
Who Are the Church? Milwaukee: Marquette University Press, 2008.

2009

"Novelty in Continuity." *America* 200.3 (2009) 10-16. Reprinted in edited form in *The Tablet* 263, January 31, 2009, 5-6. Translated into German as "Erneuerung in Kontinuität." In *Vatikan und Pius-Brüder: Anatomie einer Krise*, edited by Wolfgang Beinert, 163-74. Freiburg: Herder, 2009.
"A Postmodern Augustinian Thomism?" In *Augustine and Postmodern Thought: A New Alliance against Modernity?*, edited by Lieven Boeve, et al., 123-46. Leuven: Peeters, 2009.

2010

"'The American Schema': John Courtney Murray and the Elaboration of *Dignitatis Humanae*." In *Religionsfreiheit und Pluralismus: Entwicklungslinien eienes katholischen Lernprozesses*, edited by Karl Gabriel, et al., 155-76. Paderborn: Ferdinand Schöningh, 2010.
"Dall'intransigentismo alla libertà religiosa." In *Libertà religiosa e diritti dell'uomo: Introduzione a Dignitatis Humanae*, edited by Silvia Scatena and Marco Ronconi, 21-37. Milan: Periodoci San Paolo, 2010.
"John Courtney Murray." In *Libertà religiosa e diritti dell'uomo: Introduzione a Dignitatis Humanae*, edited by Silvia Scatena and Marco Ronconi, 109-19. Milan: Periodoci San Paolo, 2010.
"Tacking Toward the Truth: The Wisdom of Cardinal Newman." *Commonweal* 137.16 (2010) 14-16, 18-19.

---

1. This is a slightly altered version of "Le valutazioni sulla *Gaudium et Spes*: Chenu, Dossetti, Ratzinger."

"What Ecclesiology for Petrine Ministry?" In *How Can Petrine Ministry be a Service to the Unity of the Universal Church?*, edited by James. F. Puglisi, 145–54. Grand Rapids: Eerdmans, 2010.

2011

"Benedict XVI and the Interpretation of Vatican II." In *The Crisis of Authority in Catholic Modernity*, edited by Michael J. Lacey and Francis Oakley, 93–110. New York: Oxford University Press, 2011.[2]

2012

"*Humani Generis* and *Nouvelle Théologie*." In *Ressourcement: A Movement for Renewal in Twentieth-Century Catholic Theology*, edited by Gabriel Flynn and Paul D. Murray, 138–56. New York: Oxford University Press, 2012.

"Interpreting the Council and Its Consequences: Concluding Reflections." In *After Vatican II: Trajectories and Hermeneutics*, edited by James L. Heft with John O'Malley, 164–72. Grand Rapids: Eerdmans, 2012.

2013

"Benedict's Act of Humility." *Commonweal* 140.5 (2013) 7–8.

2015

"Interpreting the 'Event' of Vatican II." In *The Contested Legacy of Vatican II: Lessons and Prospects*, edited by Lieven Boeve, et al., 1–33. Louvan Theological & Pastoral Monographs 43. Leuven: Peeters, 2015.

2016

"Theological Perspectives on the Exercise of Synodality." In *A cinquant' anni dall' Apostolica sollicitudo Il Sinodo dei Vescovi al servizio di una Chiesa sinodale. Atti del Seminario di studio organizzato dalla Segreteria generale del Sinodo dei Vescovi*, edited by Lorenzo Baldisseri, 349–68. Vatican City: Libreria Editrice Vaticana, 2016.

2018

"Performative Ecclesiology." *Cristianesimo nella Storia* 39.2 (2018) 427–41.

---

2. This is a slightly revised version of "Benedict XVI and the Interpretation of Vatican II."

Bibliography

Acta Synodalia Sacrosancti Concilii Oecumenici Vaticani II. 6 vols. Vatican City: Typis polyglottis Vaticanis, 1970–1996.
Alberigo, Giuseppe. "The Local Church in the West (1500–1945)." *Heythrop Journal* 28.2 (1987) 125–43.
Alberigo, Giuseppe, et al., eds. *The Reception of Vatican II.* Washington, DC: Catholic University of America Press, 1987.
Alberigo, Giuseppe, and Joseph A. Komonchak, eds. *History of Vatican II.* 5 vols. Maryknoll, NY: Orbis, 1995–2006.
Anderson, Floyd, ed. *Council Daybook: Vatican II. Sessions 1 and 2.* Washington, DC: National Catholic Welfare Conference, 1965.
Anglican-Roman Catholic International Commission. "The Gift of Authority: Authority in the Church III (1999)." In *Looking towards a Church Fully Reconciled: The Final Report of the Anglican-Roman Catholic International Commission 1983–2005 (ARCIC II)*, edited by Adelbert Denaux, et al., 123–74. New York: Paulist, 2016.
Antón, Angel. "Iglesia Universal—Iglesias particulares." *Estudios Eclesiásticos* 47 (1972) 409–35.
———. "Local Church/Regional Church: Systematic Reflections." *The Jurist* 52 (1992) 553–76.
Bandera, Armando. "Iglesia particular e Iglesia universal." *Ciencia tomistica* 105 (1978) 67–112.
Baum, Gregory. "Sociology and Theology." In *The Church as Institution*, edited by Gregory Baum and Andrew Greeley, 22–31. Concilium 91. New York: Herder and Herder, 1974.
———. "The Impact of Sociology on Catholic Theology." *Proceedings of the Catholic Theological Society of America* 30 (1975) 1–47.
Beal, Rose M. *Mystery of the Church, People of God: Yves Congar's Total Ecclesiology as a Path to Vatican II.* Washington, DC: Catholic University of America Press, 2014.
Becker, Karl Joseph. "The Church and Vatican II's '*Subsistit in*' Terminology." *Origins* 35.31 (2006) 514–22.
Bede, the Venerable. "*Explanatio Apocapolypsis.*" In *Patrologie cursus completus: Series Latina*, edited by Jacque P. Migne. Vol. 93, 129–206. Paris: n.p., 1862.

Bellarmine, Robert. *Controversies of the Christian Faith*. Translated by Kenneth Baker. Saddle River, NJ: Keep the Faith, 2016.

———. *Disputationes de controversiis Christianae fidei adversus huius temporis haereticos*. Vol. 2. Naples: n.p., 1872.

Berger, Peter, and Thomas Luckman. *The Social Construction of Reality: A Treatise in the Sociology of Knowledge*. Garden City, NY: Doubleday, 1967.

Bilateral Working Group of the German National Bishops' Conference and the Church Leadership of the United Lutheran Church of Germany. *Communio Sanctorum: The Church as the Communion of Saints*. Translated by Mark Jeske, et al. Collegeville, MN: Liturgical, 2004.

Bluett, Joseph. "The Mystical Body of Christ: 1890–1940." *Theological Studies* 3 (1942) 261–89.

Boersma, Hans. *Nouvelle Théologie and Sacramental Ontology*. New York: Oxford University Press, 2009.

Boff, Leonardo. *Ecclesiologenesis: The Base Communities Reinvent the Church*. Translated by Robert Barr. Maryknoll, NY: Orbis, 1986.

Bracken, Joseph. "Ecclesiology and the Problem of One and the Many." *Theological Studies* 43.2 (1982) 298–311.

Brown, Raymond E. "New Testament Background for the Concept of Local Church." *Proceedings of the Catholic Theological Society of America* 36 (1981) 1–14.

Burghardt, Walter. *Long Have I Loved You: A Theologian Reflects on His Church*. Maryknoll, NY: Orbis, 2000.

Callahan, Daniel, ed. *The Catholic Case for Contraception*. London: Macmillan, 1969.

Camelot, Pierre-Thomas. *Die Lehre von der Kirche: Väterzeit bis asschließlich Augustinus*. Vol. 3.3b of *Handbuch der Dogmengeschichte*. Edited by Michael Schmaus, et al. Freiburg: Herder, 1970.

Carlen, Claudia, ed. *The Papal Encyclicals*. 5 vols. Ann Arbor, MI: Pierian, 1990.

Carroll, Anthony, et al., eds. *Towards a Kenotic Vision of Authority in the Catholic Church*. Washington, DC: Council for Research in Values and Philosophy, 2015.

"Collektiv-Erklärung des deutschen Episkopates, betreffend die Circular-Depesche des Deutschen Reichskanzlers hinsichtlich der Künfligen Papstwahl." *Der Katholik* 55 (1875) 209–13.

Colombo, Carlo. "La teologia della Chiesa locale." *Vita e pensiero* 54 (1971) 261–65.

Comblin, Jose. *The People of God*. Maryknoll, NY: Orbis, 2004.

Congar, Yves. *Chrétiens désunis: principes d'un "oecumenisme" catholique*. Unam Sanctam 1. Paris: Cerf, 1937

———. *Divided Christendom: A Catholic Study of the Problem of Reunion*. Translated by M. A. Bousfield. London: Geoffrey Bles, 1939.

———. "The Idea of the Church in St. Thomas Aquinas." *The Thomist* 1.3 (1939) 331–59.

———. *Jalons pour une théologie du laïcat*. Unam Sanctam 23. Rev. ed. Paris: Cerf, 1964.

———. *Lay People in the Church: A Study for a Theology of Laity*. Translated by Donald Attwater. Rev. ed. Westminster, MD: Newman, 1965.

———. *L'Église. De saint Augustin à l'époque moderne*. Vol. 3.3 of *Historie des dogmes*. Paris: Cerf, 1970.

———. "Mother Church." In *The Church To-day*, edited by Joseph Ratzinger, et al., 37–44. Translated by M. Ignatius. Cork: Mercier, 1968.

———. "Moving toward a Pilgrim Church." In *Vatican II Revisited by Those Who Were There*, edited by Alberic Stacpoole, 129–52. Minneapolis, MN: Winston, 1986.

———. "Peut-on définir l'Église?" In *Sainte Église: Études et approches ecclésiologiques*, edited by Yves Congar, 21–44. Unam Sanctam 41. Paris: Cerf, 1963.

———. *Vraie et fausse réforme dans l'Eglise*. Unam Sanctam 20. Paris: Cerf, 1950.

———. *True and False Reform of the Church*. Translated by Paul Philibert. Collegeville, MN: Liturgical, 2011.

Congregation for Bishops. "Draft Statement on Episcopal Conferences." *Origins* 17.43 (1988) 731–37.

Congregation for the Doctrine of the Faith. "Church Unity Rooted in the Eucharist." English edition. *L'Osservatore Romano*, July 7, 1993, 4, 10.

———. "*Communionis notio* [Letter to the Bishops of the Catholic Church on Some Aspects of Church Understood as Communion], May 28, 1992." *Origins* 37.9 (2007) 134–36.

———. "Responses to Certain Aspects of the Doctrine of the Church." *Origins* 37.9 (2007) 134–36.

Cooke, Bernard. *Ministry to Word and Sacraments: History and Theology*. Philadelphia: Fortress, 1976.

Dadosky, John D. "Who/What Is/Are the Church (es)?" *Heythrop Journal* 52.5 (2011) 785–801.

De George, Richard T. *The Nature and Limits of Authority*. Lawrence: University Press of Kansas, 1985.

De Lubac, Henri. *Catholicisme: les aspects sociaux du dogme*. Paris: Cerf, 1938.

———. *Catholicism: A Study of Dogma in Relation to the Corporate Destiny of Mankind*. Translated by Lancelot C. Sheppard and Elizabeth Englund. San Francisco: Ignatius, 1988.

———. *Corpus Mysticum: The Eucharist in the Middle Ages; Historical Survey*. Edited by Laurence Paul Hemming and Susan Frank Parsons. Translated by Gemma Simmonds, et al. Notre Dame, IN: University of Notre Dame Press, 2006.

———. *Corpus Mysticum: L'Eucharistie et L'Église au moyen âge*. Paris: Aubier, 1944.

———. *Les églises particulières dans l'Église universelle, suivi de La maternité de l'église*. Paris: Aubier Montaigne, 1971.

———. *Méditation sur l'Église*. Paris: Montaigne, 1953.

———. *The Motherhood of the Church followed by Particular Churches in the Universal Church*. Translated by Sergia Englund. San Francisco: Ignatius, 1982.

———. *The Splendor of the Church*. Translated by Michael Mason. New York: Sheed and Ward, 1956.

Denny, Christopher D., et al., eds. *A Realist's Church: Essays in Honor of Joseph A. Komonchak*. Maryknoll, NY: Orbis, 2015.

Dias, Patrick V. *Kirche in der Schrift und im 2. Jahrhundert*. Vol. 3.3a of *Handbuch der Dogmengeschichte*. Edited by Michael Schmaus, et al. Freiburg: Herder, 1974.

Doyle, Dennis M. *Communion Ecclesiology: Visions and Versions*. Maryknoll, NY: Orbis, 2000.

Dulles, Avery. "The Church according to Thomas Aquinas." In *A Church to Believe In: Discipleship and the Dynamics of Freedom*, by Avery Dulles, 149–69. New York: Crossroads, 1982.

———. "A Half Century of Ecclesiology." *Theological Studies* 50.3 (1989) 419–42.

———. *Models of the Church*. 1974. Exp. ed. New York: Doubleday, 1987.

Durkheim, Émile. *Formes élémentaires de la vie religieuse*. Paris: F. Alan, 1912.

Extraordinary Synod of Bishops (1985). "Final Report: The Church, in the Word of God, Celebrates the Mystery of Christ for the Salvation of the World." *Origins* 15.27 (1985) 444–50.

Faggioli, Massimo. *True Reform: Liturgy and Ecclesiology in* Sacrosanctum Concilium. Collegeville, MN: Liturgical, 2012.

Feník, Juraj. *Given to the Church: An Exegetical Analysis of Christology and Anthropology in Eph 1:20–23 and 2:5–6*. Brno: Tribun EU, 2014.

Flanagan, Brian. *Communion, Diversity, and Salvation: The Contribution of Jean-Marie Tillard to Systematic Ecclesiology*. Ecclesiological Investigations 12. Edited by Gerard Mannion. New York: Bloomsbury, 2011.

Flynn, Gabriel. *Yves Congar's Vision of the Church in a World of Unbelief*. Burlington, VT: Ashgate, 2004.

Flynn, Gabriel, and Paul D. Murray, eds. *Ressourcement: A Movement for Renewal in Twentieth-Century Catholic Theology*. New York: Oxford University Press, 2012.

Forte, Bruno. *The Church: Icon of the Trinity*. Translated by Robert Paolucci. Boston: St. Paul Books & Media, 1991.

Gaillardetz, Richard R. *The Church in the Making: Lumen Gentium, Christus Dominus, Orientalium Ecclesiarum*. New York: Paulist, 2006.

———. *Teaching with Authority: A Theology of the Magisterium*. Collegeville, MN: Liturgical, 1997.

———. "Reflections on the Future of Papal Ministry." *New Theology Review* 13 (2000) 52–66.

Gaillardetz, Richard R., and Catherine E. Clifford. *Keys to the Council: Unlocking the Teaching of Vatican II*. Collegeville, MN: Liturgical, 2012.

Ghirlanda, Gianfranco. "Universal Church, Particular Church, and Local Church at the Second Vatican Council and in the New Code of Canon Law." In *Vatican II: Assessment and Perspectives. Twenty-five Years After (1962–1987)*, edited by René Latourelle, 233–71. Vol. 2. New York: Paulist, 1989.

Gilkey, Langdon. *How the Church Can Minister to the World Without Losing Itself*. New York: Harper & Row, 1964.

Gleeson, Philip. "Mystery." In *The New Dictionary of Theology*, edited by Joseph A. Komonchak, et al., 688–92. Collegeville, MN: Liturgical, 1990.

González de Cardenal, Olegario. "Development of a Theology of the Local Church from the First to the Second Vatican Council." *Jurist* 52 (1992) 11–43.

Granfield, Patrick. "The Church as 'Societas Perfecta' in the Schemata of Vatican I." *Church History* 48.4 (1979) 431–46.

———. *The Limits of Papacy: Authority and Autonomy in the Church*. New York: Crossroads, 1987.

———. "The Local Church as a Center of Communication and Control." *Proceedings of the Catholic Theological Society of America* 35 (1980) 256–63.

———. "The Priority Debate: Universal or Local Church?" In *Ecclesia Tertii Millennii Advenientis. Omaggio al P. Angel Anton*, edited by F. Chica, et al., 152–61. Monferrato: Piemme, 1997.

———. "The Rise and Fall of *Societas Perfecta*." In *May Church Ministers Be Politicians?*, edited by Peter Huizing and Walf Knut, 3–8. Concilium 157.7. New York: T & T Clark, 1982.

Grootaers, Jan. "The Drama Continues between the Acts: The 'Second Preparation' and Its Opponents." In *History of Vatican II*, edited by Giuseppe Alberigo and Joseph A. Komonchak, 359–514. Vol. 2. Maryknoll, NY: Orbis, 1997.

Grosche, Robert. *Pilgernde Kirche*. Freiburg: Herder, 1938.

Gustafson, James. *Treasure in Earthen Vessels: The Church as a Human Community*. Chicago: University of Chicago, 1961.

Hahnenberg, Edward P. *A Concise Guide to the Documents of Vatican II*. Cincinnati, OH: St. Anthony Messenger, 2007.

———. *Ministries: A Relational Approach*. New York: Herder and Herder, 2003.

Haight, Roger. *Christian Community in History*. 3 vols. New York: Continuum, 2004–2008.

———. "Critical Witness: The Question of Method." In *Faithful Witness: Foundations of Theology for Today's Church*, edited by Leo J. O'Donovan and T. Howland Sanks, 185–204. New York: Crossroads, 1989.

———. *Dynamics of Theology*. 1990. Reprint, Maryknoll, NY: Orbis: 2001.

———. "Historical Ecclesiology. Part I: An Essay on Method in the Study of the Church." *Science et Esprit* 39.1 (1987) 27–46.

———. "On Systematic Ecclesiology." *Toronto Journal of Theology* 8.2 (1992) 220–38.

———. "Systematic Ecclesiology." *Science et Esprit* 45 (1993) 253–81.

Hamer, Jerome. *The Church Is a Communion*. Translated by Ronald Matthews. New York: Sheed and Ward, 1964

———. *L'Église est un communion*. Paris: Cerf, 1962.

Healy, Nicholas M. *Church, World, and the Christian Life: Practical-Prophetic Ecclesiology*. New York: Cambridge University Press, 2000.

———. "Communion Ecclesiology: A Cautionary Note." *Pro Ecclesia* 4.4 (1995) 442–53.

———. "Ecclesiology and Communion." *Perspectives in Religious Studies* 31.3 (2004) 273–90.

Henn, William. "Historical-Theological Synthesis of the Relation between Primacy and Episcopacy during the Second Millennium." In *Il primato del successore di Pietro: Atti del simposio teologico, Roma, dicembre 1996*, 222–80. Vatican City: Libreria Editrice Vaticana, 1997.

Himes, Michael J. "The Development of Ecclesiology: Modernity to the Twentieth Century." In *The Gift of the Church: A Textbook on Ecclesiology*, edited by Peter Phan, 45–67. Collegeville, MN: Liturgical, 2000.

———. *Ongoing Incarnation: Johann Adam Möhler and the Beginning of Modern Ecclesiology*. New York: Crossroads, 1997.

Hinze, Bradford. "Releasing the Power of the Spirit in a Trinitarian Ecclesiology." In *Advents of the Spirit: An Introduction to the Current Study of Pneumatology*, edited by Bradford Hinze and D. Lyle Dabney, 347–81. Milwaukee: Marquette University Press, 2001.

Hoose, Bernard, ed. *Authority in the Roman Catholic Church: Theory and Practice*. Burlington, VT: Ashgate, 2002.

International Theological Commission. "'Sensus Fidei' in the Life of the Church." *Origins* 44.9 (2014) 133–55.

Izbicki, Thomas M. *Protector of the Faith: Cardinal Johannes de Turrecremata and the Defense of the Institutional Church*. Washington, DC: Catholic University of America Press, 1981.

Jay, Eric. *The Church: Its Changing Image through Twenty Centuries*. Atlanta: John Knox, 1980.

Joint International Commission for the Theological Dialogue between the Roman Catholic Church and the Orthodox Church. "Ecclesiological and Canonical Consequences of the Sacramental Nature of the Church: Ecclesial Communion, Conciliarity and Authority." October 13, 2007. http://www.vatican.va/roman_curia/pontifical_councils/chrstuni/ch_orthodox_docs/rc_pc_chrstuni_doc_20071013_documento-ravenna_en.html.

Journet, Charles. *The Church of the Word Incarnate: An Essay in Speculative Theology*. Vol. 1 of *The Apostolic Hierarchy*. Translated by A. H. C. Downes. New York: Sheed and Ward, 1955.

———. *L'église du verbe incarné: Essai de théologie spéculative*. 3 vols. Bruges: Desclée de Brouwer, 1941.

Jungmann, Andreas. "Constitution on the Sacred Liturgy." In *Commentary on the Documents of Vatican II*, edited by Herbert Vorgrimler, 1–87. Vol. 1. New York: Herder and Herder, 1967.

Kasper, Walter. *The Catholic Church: Nature, Reality, and Mission*. New York: Bloomsbury, 2015.

———. "Introduction to the Theme and Catholic Hermeneutics of the Dogmas of the First Vatican Council." In *The Petrine Ministry: Catholics and Orthodox in Dialogue*, edited by Walter Kasper, 7–23. New York: Newman, 2006.

———. "On the Church." *The Tablet* 255 (2001) 927–30.

———. "Zur Theologie und Praxis des bischöflichen Amtes." In *Auf neue Art Kirche Sein: Wirklichkeiten—Herausforderungen—Wandlungen. Festschrift für Bischof Dr. Josef Homeyer*, edited by Werner Schreer and Georg Steins, 32–48. Munich: Berward bei Don Bosco, 1999.

Kilian, Sabbas J. "The Meaning and Nature of the Local Church." *Proceedings of the Catholic Theological Society of America* 35 (1980) 244–55.

Kloppenburg, Bonaventure. *Ecclesiology of Vatican II*. Translated by Matthew J. O'Connell. Chicago: Franciscan Herald, 1974.

Klostermann, Ferdinand. "Desiderate zur Reform des Laienrechtes." *Theologisch-Praktische Quartalschrift* 115 (1967) 334–48.

Knox, John. *The Early Church and the Coming Great Church*. London: Epworth, 1957.

Koster, Mannes D. *Ekklesiologie im Werden*. Paderborn: Bonifacius-Druckerei, 1940.

Küng, Hans. *The Church*. London: Burns & Oates, 1967.

———. *The Council Reform and Reunion*. Translated by Cecily Hastings. New York: Sheed and Ward, 1961.

———. *My Struggle for Freedom: Memoirs*. Grand Rapids, MI: Eerdmans, 2003.

Küng, Hans, et al., eds. *Council Speeches of Vatican II*. Glen Rock, NJ: Paul, 1964.

Lanne, Emmanuel. "The Local Church: Its Catholicity and Apostolicity." *One in Christ* 6 (1970) 288–313.

Lash, Nicholas. *Voices of Authority*. London: Sheed and Ward, 1976.

Lawler, Michael G., et al. *The Church in the Modern World: Gaudium et Spes Then and Now*. Collegeville, MN: Liturgical, 2014.

Legrand, Hervé-Marie. "La réalisation de l'Église en un lieu." In *Initiation à la pratique de la théologie*, edited by Bernard Lauret and François Refoulé, 143–345. Vol. 3. Paris: Cerf, 1983.

———. "La théologie des Églises sœurs: Réflexions ecclésiologiques autour de la Declaration de Balamand." *Revue des sciences Philosophiques et théologiques* 88.3 (2004) 461–96.
Leo XIII. "*Satis cognitum* [Encyclical on the Unity of the Church], June 29, 1896." In *The Papal Encyclicals*, edited by Claudia Carlen, 387–404. Vol. 2. New York: McGrath, 1981.
Lindbeck, George. *The Nature of Doctrine: Religion and Theology in a Postliberal Age*. Philadelphia: Westminster, 1984.
Lombard, Peter. *The Sentences*. 4 vols. Translated by Giulio Silano. Toronto: Pontifical Institute of Mediaeval Studies, 2008.
Lonergan, Bernard J. F. *De Deo trino*. 2 vols. Rome: Gregorian University, 1961.
———. *De verbo incarnato*. 4 vols. Rome: Gregorian University, 1960.
———. *Grace and Freedom: Operative Grace in the Thought of St. Thomas Aquinas*. Edited by J. Patout Burns. New York: Herder and Herder, 1971.
———. *Insight: A Study in Human Understanding*. New York: Philosophical Library, 1957.
———. *Method in Theology*. 1972. Reprint, Toronto: University of Toronto Press, 1999.
Looney, Thomas P. "*Koinonia* Ecclesiology: How Solid a Foundation?" *One in Christ* 36 (2000) 145–66.
MacDonald, Timothy I. *The Ecclesiology of Yves Congar: Foundational Themes*. Lanham, MD: University Press of America, 1984.
Madar, Martin. "An Alternative Middle Position: The Contribution of Joseph A. Komonchak to the Hermeneutics of Vatican II." *Cristianesimo nella Storia* 36.3 (2015) 643–69.
———. "The Contribution of Joseph A. Komonchak to the Theology of the Local Church in Light of *Lumen Gentium*." PhD diss., Catholic University of America, 2014.
Malanowski, Gregory E. "The Christocentrism of Émile Mersch and Its Implications for a Theology of Church." PhD diss., Catholic University of America, 1988.
Mannion, Gerard. "'A Haze of Fiction': Legitimation, Accountability, and Truthfulness." In *Governance, Accountability, and the Future of the Catholic Church*, edited by Francis Oakley and Bruce Russett, 161–77. New York: Continuum, 2004.
Mansi, Ioannes D. *Sacrorum conciliorum nova et amplissima collectio*. 53 vols. Leipzig, 1926.
Markey, John J. *Creating Communion: The Theology of the Constitutions of the Church*. Hyde Park, NY: New City, 2003.
Maritain, Jacques. *De L'Eglise du Christ: La Personne de l'église et son personnel*. Paris: Desclée de Brouwer, 1970.
———. *On the Church of Christ: The Person of the Church and Her Personnel*. Translated by Joseph W. Evans. Notre Dame IN: University of Notre Dame Press, 1973.
McBrien, Richard. *The Church: The Evolution of Catholicism*. New York: HarperCollins, 2009.
McCarthy, Timothy G. *The Catholic Tradition: The Catholic Church in the Twentieth Century*. Rev. and exp. ed. Chicago: Loyola, 1998.
McClory, Robert. *Turning Point: The Inside Story of the Papal Birth Control Commission, and How Humanae Vitae Changed the Life of Patty Crowley and the Future of the Church*. New York: Crossroads, 1995.

McDonnell, Killian. "The Ratzinger/Kasper Debate: The Universal Church and Local Churches." *Theological Studies* 63.2 (2002) 227–50.

McLoughlin, David. "*Communio* Models of Church—Rhetoric or Reality?" In *Authority in the Roman Catholic Church: Theory and Practice*, edited by Bernard Hoose, 181–90. Burligton, VT: Ashgate, 2002.

McNamara, Kevin. "From Möhler to Vatican II: The Modern Movement in Ecclesiology." In *Vatican II: The Constitution on the Church; A Theological and Pastoral Commentary*, edited by Kevin McNamara, 9–35. Chicago: Franciscan Herald, 1968.

McPartlan, Paul. *The Eucharist Makes the Church: Henri de Lubac and John Zizioulas in Dialogue*. 2nd ed. Fairfax, VA: Eastern Christian, 2006.

Melloni, Alberto. "The Beginning of the Second Period: The Great Debate on the Church." In *History of Vatican II*, edited by Giuseppe Alberigo and Joseph A. Komonchak, 1–115. Vol. 3. Maryknoll, NY: Orbis, 2000.

Mersch, Émile. *La théologie du corps mystique*. 2 vols. Paris: Desclèe, 1944.

———. *Le Corps mystique du Christ: etudes de théologie historique*. 2 vols. Paris: Desclèe, 1933.

———. *The Theology of the Mystical Body*. Translated by Cyril Vollert. St. Louis, MO: Herder, 1951.

———. *The Whole Christ: The Historical Development of the Doctrine of the Mystical Body in Scripture and Tradition*. Translated by John R. Kelly. Milwaukee: Bruce, 1938.

Mettepenningen, Jürgen. *Nouvelle Théologie—New Theology: Inheritor of Modernism, Precursor of Vatican II*. New York: T & T Clark, 2010.

Möhler, Johann A. *Die Einheit in der Kirche, oder, die Princip des Katholisizmus: Dargestellt in Geiste der Kirchenvater der drei ersten Jahrhunderte*. Tübingen: Heinrich Laupp, 1925.

———. Review of *Des errsten Zeitalters der Kirchengeschichte erste Abtheilung: die Zeit der Verfolgungen*, by Theodor Katerkampp. *Theologische Quartalschrisft* 5.3 (1823) 484–532.

———. *Symbolik: oder Darstellung der dogmatischen Gegensatze der Katholiken und Protestanten nach ihren offentlichen Bekenntnisschriften*. Mainz: F. Kupferberg, 1832.

———. *Symbolism: Exposition of the Doctrinal Differences between Catholics and Protestants as Evidenced by Their Symbolical Writings*. Translated by James Burton Robinson. New York: Crossroad, 1997.

———. *Unity in the Church or the Principle of Catholicism: Presented in the Spirit of the Church Fathers of the First Three Centuries*. Edited and Translated with an Introduction by Peter C. Erb. Washington, DC: Catholic University of America Press, 1996.

Mondin, Battista. *La Chiesa primicia del Regno*. Bologna: Dehoniane, 1986.

———. *La nuove eclesiologie: un'immagine attuale della Chiesa*, Theologia 29. Rome: Edizioni Paoline, 1980.

Oakley, Francis. *The Western Church in the Later Middle Ages*. Ithaca, NY: Cornell University Press, 1979.

Oakley, Francis and Michael Lacey, eds. *The Crisis of Authority in Catholica Modernity*. New York: Oxford, 2011.

O'Donnell, Christopher. *Ecclesia: A Theological Encyclopedia of the Church*. Collegeville, MN: Liturgical, 1996.

O'Gara, Margaret. "Three Successive Steps Toward Understanding Papal Primacy in Vatican I." *The Jurist* 64 (2004) 208–23.

O'Malley, John W. *What Happened at Vatican II*. Cambridge, MA: Harvard University Press, 2008.

O'Meara, Thomas. "Philosophical Models in Ecclesiology." *Theological Studies* 39 (1978) 3–21.

———. *Romantic Idealism and Roman Catholicism: Schelling and the Theologians*. Notre Dame, IN: Notre Dame University Press, 1982.

———. "Theology of Church." In *The Theology of Thomas Aquinas*, edited by Rik van Nieuwenhove and Joseph Wawrykow, 303–25. Notre Dame, IN: University of Notre Dame Press, 2005.

Ormerod, Neil. "Ecclesiology and the Social Sciences." In *The Routledge Companion to the Christian Church*, edited by Gerard Mannion and Lewis S. Mudge, 639–54. New York: Routledge, 2008.

———. *Re-Visioning the Church: An Experiment in Systematic Historical Ecclesiology*. Minneapolis: Fortress, 2014.

———. "The Structure of Systematic Ecclesiology." *Theological Studies* 63.1 (2002) 3–30.

———. "A Voice Cries in the Wilderness: The Place of the Social Sciences in Ecclesiology." In *A Realist's Church: Essays in Honor of Joseph A. Komonchak*, edited by Christopher D. Denny, et al., 203–19. Maryknoll, NY: Orbis, 2015.

Ott, Ludwig. *Fundamentals of Catholic Dogma*. 6th ed. Edited by James Canon. Translated by Patrick Lynch. St. Louis, MO: Herder, 1964.

Pannenberg, Wolfhart. *Theology and Philosophy of Science*. Philadelphia: Westminster, 1976.

Papal Teachings: The Church. Selected and arranged by the Benedictine Monks of Solesmes. Translated by E. O'Gorman. Boston: Daughters of St. Paul, 1962.

Paul VI. "*Humanae vitae* [Encyclical on the Regulation of Birth], July 25, 1968." In *The Papal Encyclicals*, edited by Claudia Carlen, 223–36. Vol. 5. New York: McGrath, 1981.

———. "Opening General Congregation, September 29, 1963." In *Council Daybook: Vatican II. Sessions 1 and 2*, edited by Floyd Anderson, 141–50. Washington, DC: National Catholic Welfare Conference, 1965.

Pelz, Karl. *Der Christ als Christus: der Weg meine Forschens*. Berlin: n.p., 1939.

Phan, Peter. "Contemporary Theology of Inculturation in the United States." In *Multicultural Church: A New Landscape in US Theologies*, edited by William Cenkner, 109–30. New York: Paulist, 1996.

———. "Teaching as Learning: An Asian View." In *Theology and Magisterium*, edited by Susan A. Ross and Felix Wilfred, 75–87. Concilium 2. London: SCM Press, 2012.

Pius X. "*Vehementer nos* [Encyclical on the French Law of Separation], February 11, 1906." In *The Papal Encyclicals*, edited by Claudia Carlen, 45–51. Vol. 3. New York: McGrath, 1981.

Pius XI. "*Mortalium animos* [Encyclical on Religious Unity], January 6, 1928." In *The Papal Encyclicals*, edited by Claudia Carlen, 313–19. Vol. 3. New York: McGrath, 1981

Pius XII. "*Humani generis* [Encyclical Concerning Some False Opinions Threatening to Undermine the Foundations of Catholic Doctrine], August 12, 1950." In *The Papal Encyclicals*, edited by Claudia Carlen, 175-83. Vol. 4. New York: McGrath, 1981.

———. "*Mystici corporis* [Encyclical on the Mystical Body of Christ], June 29, 1943." In *The Papal Encyclicals*, edited by Claudia Carlen, 37-63. Vol. 4. New York: McGrath, 1981

Plumer, Eric. "The Development of Ecclesiology: Early Church to the Reformation." In *The Gift of the Church: A Textbook on Ecclesiology*, edited by Peter Phan, 23-44. Collegeville, MN: Liturgical, 2000.

Pottmeyer, Herman J. "Primacy in Communion: What Must Happen to a Centralist Papacy to Become a Papacy in Communion?" *America* 182.20 (2000) 15-18.

———. *Towards a Papacy in Communion: Perspectives from Vatican Councils I and II*. Translated by Matthew J. O'Connell. New York: Crossroads, 1998.

Prusak, Bernard P. *The Church Unfinished: Ecclesiology through the Centuries*. New York: Paulist, 2004.

———. "The Theology of the Local Church in Historical Development." *Proceedings of the Catholic Theological Society of America* 35 (1980) 287-308.

Puyo, Jean. *Une vie pour la vérité: Jean Puyo interroge le Père Congar*. Paris: Centurion, 1975.

Quinn, John R. *The Reform of the Papacy: The Costly Call to Christian Unity*. New York: Crossroads, 1999.

Rahner, Karl. *The Church and the Sacraments*. Translated by W. J. O'Hara. Freiburg: Herder, 1963.

———. *Kirche und Sakramente*. Questiones Disputate 10. Freiburg: Herder, 1960.

———. *Theology of Pastoral Action*. New York: Herder and Herder, 1968.

Ratzinger, Joseph. *Called to Communion: Understanding the Church Today*. Translated by Adrian Walker. San Francisco: Ignatius, 1996.

———. "The Ecclesiology of the Constitution *Lumen Gentium*." In *Pilgrim Fellowship of Faith: The Church as Communion*, edited by Stephen Otto Horn and Vinzenz Pfnür, 123-52. Translated by Henry Taylor. San Francisco: Ignatius, 2005.

———. "The Ecclesiology of the Second Vatican Council." *Communio* 13 (1986) 239-52.

———. Introduction to *Lettera* "Communionis Notio": *Su alcuni aspetti della Chiesa Intesa come communion (28 maggio 1992); Testo e commenti*. Città del Vaticano: Libreria editrice Vaticana, 1994.

———. "The Local Church and the Universal Church." *America* 185.16 (2001) 7-11.

———. *Zur Gemeinschaft gerufen: Kirche heute verstehen*. Freiburg im Breisgau: Herder, 1991.

Ratzinger, Joseph with Vittorio Messori. *The Ratzinger Report: An Exclusive Interview on the State of the Church*. Translated by Salvator Attanasio and Graham Harrison. San Francisco: Ignatius, 1985.

Riga, Peter. "The Ecclesiology of Johann Adam Möhler." *Theological Studies* 22.4 (1961) 563-87.

Rikhof, Herwi. *The Concept of the Church: A Methodological Inquiry into the Use of Metaphors in Ecclesiology*. London: Sheed and Ward, 1981.

———. "Thomas on the Church: Reflections on a Sermon." In *Aquinas on Doctrine: A Critical Introduction*, edited by Thomas Weinandy, et al., 199-223. New York: Continuum, 2004.

Rosato, Philip J. "Between Christocentrism and Pneumatocentrism: An Interpretation of Johann Adam Möhler's Ecclesiology." *Heythrop Journal* 19.1 (1978) 46–70.
Ruddy, Christopher J. *The Local Church: Tillard and the Future of Catholic Ecclesiology.* New York: Herder & Herder, 2006.
Routhier, Gilles. "'Église locale' ou 'Église particulière': querelle sémantique ou option théologique?" *Studia Canonica* 25 (1991) 277–334.
―――. "Finishing the Work Begun: The Trying Experience of the Fourth Period." In *History of Vatican II*, edited by Giuseppe Alberigo and Joseph A. Komonchak, 49–184. Vol. 5. Maryknoll, NY: Orbis, 2006.
―――. "Reception in the Current Theological Debate." *The Jurist* 57 (1997) 17–52.
Ruggieri, Giuseppe. "Beyond an Ecclesiology of Polemics: The Debate on the Church." In *History of Vatican II*, edited by Giuseppe Alberigo and Joseph A. Komonchak, 281–357. Vol. 2. Maryknoll, NY: Orbis, 1997.
―――. "First Doctrinal Clash." In *History of Vatican II*, edited by Giuseppe Alberigo and Joseph A. Komonchak, 233–66. Vol. 2. Maryknoll, NY: Orbis, 1997.
Sabra, George F. *Thomas Aquinas's Vision of the Church: Fundamentals of Ecumenical Ecclesiology.* Mainz: Mathias Grünewald Verlad, 1987.
Salaverri, Joachim. "On the Church of Christ." In *Sacrae theologiae summa*, by Joachim Salaverri and Michaele Nicolau, 1–552. Vol 1.B. Translated by Kenneth Baker. 3rd ed. Ramsey, NJ: Keep the Faith, 2015.
Sanks, T. Howland. *Authority in the Church: A Study in Changing Paradigms.* Missoula, MT: Scholars, 1974.
Schatz, Klaus. "The Gregorian Reform and the Beginning of a Universal Ecclesiology." *The Jurist* 57 (1997) 123–36.
Scheeben, Matthias J. *Die Mysterien des Christentums.* Freiburg, 1865.
―――. *The Mysteries of Christianity.* Translated by Cyril Vollert. St. Louis, MO: Herder, 1946.
Schelkens, Karim. "*Lumen Gentium*'s '*Subsistit in*' Revisited: The Catholic Church and Christian Unity after Vatican II." *Theological Studies* 69.4 (2008) 875–93.
Schillebeeckx, Edward. *Christ the Sacrament of the Encounter with God.* Translated by Paul Barett. New York: Sheed and Ward, 1963.
―――. *The Church with a Human Face.* Translated by John Bowden. New York: Crossroad, 1987.
―――. *De Christusontmoeting als sacrament van de Godsontmoeting: theologishe begrijpelijkheid van het heilsfeit der sacramenten.* Bilthoven: H Nelissen, 1957.
Schineller, Peter. *A Handbook on Inculturation.* New York: Paulist, 1990.
Schmaus, Michael. *Dogma.* Vol. 4 of *The Church: Its Origins and Structure.* Translated by Mary Ledderer. New York: Sheed and Ward, 1972.
Schüssler Fiorenza, Francis. *Foundational Theology: Jesus and the Church.* New York: Crossroads, 1984.
―――. "Systematic Theology: Task and Methods." In *Systematic Theology: Roman Catholic Perspectives*, edited by Francis Schüssler Fiorenza and John P. Galvin, 1–78. 2nd ed. Minneapolis: Fortress, 2011.
Scully, J. Eileen. "The Theology of the Mystical Body of Christ in French Language Theology 1930–1950." *Irish Theological Quarterly* 58.1 (1992) 58–74.
Searle, John R. *The Construction of Social Reality.* New York: Simon & Schuster, 1995.
Semmelroth, Otto. *Church and Sacrament.* Translated by Emily Schossberger. Notre Dame, IN: Fides, 1965.

———. *Die Kirche als Ursakrament*. Frankfurt: Knecht, 1953.

———. *Vom Sinn der Sakramente*. Frankfurt: Knecht, 1960.

Shakespeare, Steven. "Ecclesiology and Philosophy." In *The Routledge Companion to the Christian Church*, edited by Gerard Mannion and Lewis S. Mudge, 655–73. New York: Routledge, 2008.

Stagaman, David. *Authority in the Church*. Collegeville, MN: Liturgical, 1999.

Sullivan, Francis A. *Questiones theologiae fundamentalis*. Vol. 1 of *De ecclesia*. Rome: Gregorian University, 1963.

———. "Further Thoughts on the Meaning of *Subsistit in*." *Theological Studies* 71.1 (2010) 133–47.

———. "The Meaning of *Subsistit in* as Explained by the Congregation for the Doctrine of the Faith." *Theological Studies* 69.1 (2008) 116–24.

Supreme Sacred Congregation of the Holy Office. "*Ecclesia Catholica* [Instruction to Local Ordinaries about the 'Ecumenical Movement'], December 20, 1949." *The Jurist* 10 (1950) 206–13.

"*Supremi pastoris* [Schema of a Dogmatic Constitution on the Church Prepared for the Examination of the Fathers of the Vatican Council]." In *Papal Teachings: The Church*, selected and arranged by the Benedictine Monks of Solesmes, 809–23. Translated by E. O'Gorman. Boston: Daughters of St. Paul, 1962.

Synod of Bishops (15th Ordinary General Assembly). "Young People, the Faith, and Vocational Discernment." Preparatory Document. http://www.vatican.va/roman_curia/synod/documents/rc_synod_doc_20170113_documento-preparatorio-xv_en.html.

Tagle, Luis Antonio G. "'The Black Week' of Vatican II (November 12–21, 1964)." In *History of Vatican II*, edited by Giuseppe Alberigo and Joseph A. Komonchak, 387–452. Vol. 4. Maryknoll, NY: Orbis, 2003.

Talar, Charles J. T. "'The Synthesis of All Heresies'—100 Years On." *Theological Studies* 68.3 (2007) 491–514.

Tan, Richard. "'Every day the Church Gives Birth to the Church.' The Ongoing Genesis of the Church with a Special Reference to the Mission of the Laity: The Contributions of Yves Congar, Severino Dianich, and Joseph Komonchak." STD diss., Pontifical Gregorian University, 2013.

Tanner, Norman. *The Church and the World. Gaudium et Spes, Inter Mirifica*. New York: Paulist, 2005.

———. "The Church in the World (*Ecclesia ad extra*)." In *History of Vatican II*, edited by Giuseppe Alberigo and Joseph A. Komonchak, 270–386. Vol. 4. Maryknoll, NY: Orbis, 2003.

Tanquerey, Adolphe. *Synopsis theologiae dogmatiae fundamentalis ad mentem S. Thomae Aquinatis hodiernis moribus accomodata*. 11th ed. Rome: Desclée & Socii, 1907.

Tierney, Brian. *Foundations of the Conciliar Theory: The Contribution of the Medieval Canonists from Gratian to the Great Schism*. Cambridge: University Press, 1955.

Tillard, Jean-Marie R. *The Bishop of Rome*. Translated by John de Satgé. Wilmington, DE: Michael Glazier, 1983.

———. *Church of Churches: The Ecclesiology of Communion*. Translated by R. C. De Peaux. Collegeville, MN: Liturgical, 1992.

———. *Église d'églises: L'ecclésiologie de communion*. Paris: Cerf, 1987.

———. *L'Église locale: Ecclésiologie de communion et catholicité*. Paris: Cerf, 1995.

Torquemada, John of. *Summa de ecclesia*. Venice, 1561.
Tracy, David. *Blessed Rage for Order: New Pluralism in Theology*. New York: Seabury, 1975.
Tromp, Sebastian. *Corpus Christi quod est ecclesia*. 4 vols. 1937. Revised, Rome: Gregorian University, 1972.
———. *Corpus Christi quod est ecclesia*. Translated by Ann Condit. New York: Vantage, 1960.
Van Noort, Gerard. *Christ's Church*. Vol. 2 of *Dogmatic Theology*. Translated and revised by John J. Castelot and William R. Murry. Westminster, MD: Newman, 1957.
Vilanova, Evangelista. "The Intersession (1963–1964)." In *History of Vatican II*, edited by Giuseppe Alberigo and Joseph A. Komonchak, 347–490. Vol. 3. Maryknoll, NY: Orbis, 2000.
Von Allmen, Jean-Jacque. "L'Église local parmi les autres Églises locales." *Irénikon* 43 (1970) 512–37.
Wackenheim, Gérard. "Ecclesiology and Sociology." In *Sociology of Religion: The Church as Institution*, edited by Gregory Baum and Andrew Greeley, 32–41. Concilium 91. New York: Herder and Herder, 1974.
Wang, Lisa. "*Sacramentum Unitatis Ecclesiasticae*: The Eucharistic Ecclesiology of Henri de Lubac." *Anglican Theological Review* 85.1 (2003) 143–58.
Watkins, Clare. "Objecting to *Koinonia*: The Question of Christian Discipleship Today– And Why Communion Is not the Answer." *Louvain Studies* 28.4 (2003) 326–43.
Welch, Claude. *The Reality of the Church*. New York: Scribners, 1958.
Welch, Lawrence J., and Guy Mansini, O.S.B. "*Lumen Gentium* no. 8, and *Subsistit in*, Again." *New Blackfriars* 90.1029 (2009) 602–17.
Whitehead, Alfred North. *Process and Reality: An Essay in Cosmology*. Corrected ed. Edited by David Ray Griffin and Donald W. Sherburne. New York: Free Press, 1978.
Wood, Susan K. "Continuity and Development in Roman Catholic Ecclesiology." *Ecclesiology* 7 (2011) 147–72.
Zapelena, Timotheus. *De ecclesia Christi*. 2 vols. Rome: Gregorian University, 1950.
Zizioulas, John D. *Being as Communion: Studies in Personhood and the Church*. Crestwood, NY: St. Vladimir's Seminary Press, 1985.

Index

Acts of the Apostles, 40, 135, 146–47
Ad gentes ("Decree on the Church's Missionary Activity"), 45, 106, 111–12
Alberigo, Giuseppe, 55, 56
Albert the Great, 5
Alexander of Hales, 5
Alfaro, Juan, 52
Allmen, Jean-Jacques von, 104
Alszeghy, Zoltan, 53
apologetic ecclesiology. *See* perfect society ecclesiology
Apostolicam actuositatem ("Decree on the Apostolate of the Laity"), 47
Apostolos suos (John Paul II), 102
Aquinas, Thomas, 4, 5, 53, 93
Aristotelian causes and redemption, 58
Aristotle, 149
Augustine of Hippo, 43–44, 82n65, 93, 111
authority, in the church
    conversion and, 159–161
    generally, 162–63
    Humanae vitae and, 152–53
    limits of, 158–59
    magisterium and obedience, 161–62
    as a social relationship, 154–57
Avignon papacy, 5–6

baptism, 134
Bede, Venerable, 81
Bellarmine, Robert, 8–10, 18
Benedict XVI, Pope, 166. *See also* Ratzinger, Joseph
Berger, Peter, 63–64, 83, 83n72, 86
Bernstein, Richard, 64
birth control, 152
Bishop of Rome, 118, 126, 139. *See also* papacy; *specific Popes by name*
bishops
    authority of, 156–57
    Christus Dominus, 106, 108, 115
    the church and, 107–10
    collegiality of, 38, 48–49, 113, 138, 152–53
    Congregation for Bishops, 137, 137n129
    Extraordinary Synod of Bishops (1985), 72
    local church and, 112–15
    Lumen gentium on, 108
    as vicars of Christ, 138
Bonaventure, 5
Boniface VIII, Pope, 5
Bracken, Joseph, 144–46, 148, 149
Burkhardt, Walter, 162

canon law, 4–5, 8
Cardenal, González de, 105
Catholic Action movement, 33, 47
Catholic church. *See* Roman Catholic Church
Catholicism (Lubac), 28
catholicity, 110–12, 110n29, 125–29

Christ and Culture (Niebuhr), 69
Christological doctrine, 19–20, 61
Christus Dominus ("Decree on the Pastoral Office of Bishops"), 106, 108, 115
Church, World and the Christian Life (Healy), 76
The City of God (Augustine), 44
collegiality of bishops, 38, 48–49, 113, 138, 152–53
Colombo, Giuseppe, 117
Colossians, Letter to, 22n84, 133n108
common sense, 91–92
communion
  church as, 38–39
  ecclesial, 42
  ecclesiology of, 34–35, 100, 135
  reciprocal recognition and, 136–37
Communionis notio (CDF letter), 133n108, 135, 136
community
  authority and, 154
  classic approach, 118–19
  of disciples, 77–78
  meaning and mediated by value, 78–79
  redemptive, 87
comparative ecclesiology, 69
conciliarist ecclesiology, 6, 7, 8
concreteness, of Komonchak's ecclesiology, xvii, 100–101
Congar, Yves, 3, 4, 16, 28–31, 85, 88
congregatio fidelium (meaning of church), 77–78, 98–99
Congregation for Bishops, 137, 137n129
Congregation for the Doctrine of the Faith (CDF), 102, 130–31, 133, 140
  Communionis notion (CDF letter), 133n108, 135, 136, 146, 149n167
  "Theological and Juridical Status of Episcopal Conferences," 137n129
Constitution on the Sacred Liturgy (*Sacrosanctum concilium*), 35, 39–40, 40n144, 47, 106, 110–11
continual incarnation, 19–21
conversion
  authority and, 159–161
  intellectual conversion, 161, 161n34, 162
  intentionality, 93
Corinthians, First Letter to, 22n84
Corpus Mysticum (Lubac), 28
Council of Basel (1431–1437),, 6
Council of Chalcedon (451), 75
Council of Constance (1414–1418), 7
Council of Trent (1545–1563), 10, 103
counter-reformation ecclesiology
  generally, 8–10
  perfect society ecclesiology, 10–16

Dadosky, John, 78
De ecclesia (Vatican II schema), 32–34, 39, 42, 47
De ecclesiastica potestate (Giles of Rome), 5
De fontibus revelationis (Vatican II schema), 34
De potestate regia et papalis (John of Paris), 5
De regimine christiano (Viterbo), 5
"Decree on Ecumenism" (*Unitatis redintegratio*), 35, 41–43, 45, 106, 110–11
"Decree on the Apostolate of the Laity" (*Apostolicam actuositatem*), 47
"Decree on the Church's Missionary Activity" (*Ad gentes*), 45, 106, 111–12
"Decree on the Pastoral Office of Bishops" (*Christus Dominus*), 106, 108, 115
Decreta (Gratian), 5
Dianich, Severino, 98n140, 124
Dignitatis humanae (declarations on religious liberty), 45
dioceses
  local church and, 103, 109
  as particular church, 106, 116–19
Divided Christendom (Congar), 29–30
Dogmatic Constitution on the Church. *See Lumen gentium* (Dogmatic Constitution on the Church)
Drey, Johann Sebastian, 17, 92–93
Dulles, Avery, 69–70, 77, 98n140

Duperron, Jacque, 9
Durkheim, Émile, 97

ecclesial communion, 42
ecclesiological monophysitism, 88–89
ecclesiology
    central challenge for, 75–76
    of communion, 34–35, 100
    comparative ecclesiology, 69
    conciliarist ecclesiology, 6, 7, 8
    counter-reformation ecclesiology, 8–16
    formal ecclesiology, 5–8
    foundations in, 66
    generally, 3–5, 98
    methodological shift in, 93–94
    methods in, 66–67
    objective of, 94
    renewal prior to Vatican II, 16–31
    shift in, 1–2
    social sciences and, 95–97
    solutions for central challenge for, 88–89, 99
    as theory about practice, 94–95
    at Vatican II, 31–49
ecumenical movement, 33, 41, 41n153
ecumenism, 41–43, 45, 151
Ephesians, Letter to, 22n84, 73, 133n108
episcopal collegiality, 38, 48–49, 113, 138
Eucharist, the church and, 27–28, 134
eucharistic ecclesiology, 104
Execrabilis (Pius II), 7
Extraordinary Synod of Bishops (1985), 72

Fiorenza, Francis Schüssler, 67
First Letter to Corinthians, 22n84
Flanagan, Brian, 131
Flick, Maurizio, 53
formal ecclesiology, 5–8
foundations, in ecclesiology, 66–67
Francis, Pope, 102, 139n139, 151
Franzelin, Johann Baptist, 21
fundamental theology, 31–32

Gaillardetz, Richard, 8, 108, 110

Galatians, Letter to, 133n108
Gaudium et spes ("The Pastoral Constitution on the Church in the Modern World"), 35, 45, 47
general categories, 96
Giddens, Anthony, 64
Giles of Rome, 5
Gilkey, Langdon, 59, 59n22, 62–63
God
    church as gift from, 87
    as mystery, 37
    people of God, 24–25, 39–41, 72
    self-communication in Christ and the Spirit, 88–89
grace, 93–94
Granfield, Patrick, 21–22, 49
Great Western Schism (1378–1417), 5–6
Gregorian Reforms, 1–2, 4–5, 11, 103
Gregory VII, Pope, 4–5
Gregory XVI, Pope, 14
Gustafson, James, 59, 59n22, 61–62, 74

Hahnenberg, Edward, 47
Haight, Roger, 18, 66–67, 80, 98n140
Hamer, Jerome, 10
Healy, Nicholas, 76, 98n140
Henn, William, 138
Himes, Michael, 17, 92
History of Vatican II (Alberigo & Komonchak), 55
Holy Spirit, role in the church, 18–19
How the Church Can Minister to the World without Losing Itself (Gilkey), 62–63
human and divine dimensions of church, 59–60, 63, 75–76, 79–80
human nature of Christ, 61, 63
human reality of the church, 59–60, 63
Humanae vitae (Paul VI), 152–53, 160
Humani generis, xvn1
Hus, John, 8
hypostatic union, 19–20

Incarnation, 88–89
Insight (Lonergan), 53, 57–58, 66, 87
institutional view of the church, 1, 8, 16, 26, 68, 165

intellectual conversion, 161, 161n34, 162
intentionality and conversion, 93
International Theological Commission, 101
intersubjectivity, 85–86
Izbicki, Thomas, 7

James of Viterbo, 5
John of Paris, 5
John of Torquemada, 6–7
John Paul II, Pope, 72, 102
John XXIII Foundation for Religious Sciences, 56
John XXIII, Pope, 31, 32, 152
Jungmann, Josef, 111

Kasper, Walter, 131, 147–48
Kleutgen, Joseph, 12, 21
Knox, John, 59, 59n22, 60
Koster, Mannes, 24
Küng, Hans, 105

laity, 46–48
Laity in the Church (Congar), 30–31
Lanne, Emmanuel, 109
Latourelle, René, 52
Legrand, Hervé, 122, 139
Lindbeck, George, 67
liturgical reform, 102, 102n1
local church
  bishops and, 112–15
  catholicity, meaning of, 125–29
  church local and universal, 129–150
  Komonchak on, 115–150
  post Vatican II, 102
  pre Vatican II on, 103
  terminology, 106
  theological significance of locality, 116–124
  Vatican I on, 103–4, 138, 138n132
  Vatican II on, 43, 103–15, 150–51
Lombard, Peter, 4
Lonergan, Bernard
  on common sense and theory, 91–92
  critical exigence, 78
  on grace, 93–94

Insight, 53, 57–58, 66, 87
intentionality and conversion, 93
Komonchak and, 52–53, 57–59, 67, 87
Method in Theology, 57
Lubac, Henri de, 23, 26–28, 116–17
Luckman, Thomas, 63–64, 83, 83n72, 86
Lumen gentium (Dogmatic Constitution on the Church)
  approval of, 35, 106
  on bishops, 108
  on catholicity, 110–11, 110n29, 125
  chapter titles, 39n142
  church as pilgrim people of God, 39–41
  church as sacrament, 38–39
  episcopal collegiality, 48
  on Eucharist, 107–10
  on laity, 47
  on local churches, 105–6, 108–9, 112–15, 135, 139, 143
  on social structure, of church, 88, 89
  vision of church, 73

magisterium, 25, 32, 159–161, 162n40
Mannion, Gerard, 98n140, 156
manualist theology, 21
Markey, John, 44
McBrien, Richard, 8
McCarthy, Timothy, 44–45
Mersch, Émile, 23–24
Method in Theology (Lonergan), 57
methods, in ecclesiology, 66–67
missionary activity (*Ad gentes*), 45, 106, 111–12
model approach to ecclesiology
  church as mystery, problem with, 70–71
  Dulles's approach, 69–70
  systematic ecclesiology, decline in, 68–69
Models of the Church (Dulles), 69, 77
modernity, 44–45
Moeller, Charles, 105
Möhler, Johann Adam, 15, 17–22, 75, 88, 104
Montini, Giovanni Battista (later Pope Paul VI), 2

Mortalium animos (Pius XI), 33
Murray, John Courtney, xvi, 54
mystery
 church as, 37, 69–71
 God as, 37
 senses of, 37
 as surplus of intelligibility, 92
 "The Mystery of the Church" (Vatican II schema chapter), 34
mystical body (church), 28
Mystical Body of Christ, 21–24, 26, 58–59
Mystici corporis (Pius XII), 22, 23, 25–26, 25n93, 65

"The Nature of the Church Militant" (Vatican II schema chapter), 33
Newman, John Henry, 54
Niebuhr, H. R., 69
Nostra aetate (declaration on non-Christian religions), 45
Nouvelle théologie (new theology), xvn1, 2, 36

Oakley, Francis, 6
obedience, magisterium and, 161–62
Ormerod, Neil, 70–71, 98n140, 100

Pannenberg, Wolfhart, 67
papacy
 church unity questions, 6
 infallibility, 7
 ministry, 137–39
 primacy, 7, 137–39
 see also specific Popes by name
particular church, 106, 116–19
Pascendi dominici gregis (Pius X), 16, 45
Passaglia, Carlo, 21
Pastor aeternus (Vatican I document), 12, 12n44
"The Pastoral Constitution on the Church in the Modern World" (*Gaudium et spes*), 35, 45, 47
patriarchates, 106
patristic era, 3
Paul VI, Pope, 2, 37, 152
Pelz, Karl, 24n90
people of God, 24–25, 39–41, 72

perfect society ecclesiology, 10–16, 37
Perrone, Giovanni, 12, 21
Peter, Second Letter of, 41
Petrine ministry, 137–39. *See also* papacy
Phan, Peter, 162
Philip IV, King of France, 5
Philips, Gérard, 34
Pius II, Pope, 7
Pius IX, Pope, 45, 138n132
Pius X, Pope, 14, 45
Pius XII, Pope
 Humani generis, xvn1
 Mortalium animos, 33
 Mystici corporis, 22, 23, 25–26, 25n93, 65
Pontifical Commission on Birth Control, 152
post-Vatican II ecclesiology
 church, as community of disciples, 77–78
 church, human and divine dimensions of, 59–60, 63, 75–76, 79–80
 church, meaning of, 71–74, 76–78
post-Vatican II ecclesiology *(continued)*
 church as mystery, problem with, 70–71
 Dulles's models approach to ecclesiology, 69
 Extraordinary Synod of Bishops (1985), 72
 local church, 102
 in model approach to ecclesiology, 68–69
 theological reductionism, 62, 63, 74, 165
 see also Vatican Council II (1962–1965)
practice, theory and, 94–95
pre-scholastic ecclesiology, 3–4
Protestant Christians, as separated brethren, 30
Protestant Reformers, 8

Ratzinger, Joseph, 71–72, 83, 131, 133–34, 133n108, 137, 140, 146. *See also* Benedict XVI, Pope

Rautenstrauch, Franz Stephan, 11–12
real body (Eucharist), 28
reciprocal recognition, of churches, 136–37
redemption, and four Aristotelian causes, 58–59
redemptive community, 87
reification, of the church, 86, 97, 157
religious liberty, declarations on (*Dignitatis humanae*), 45
ressourcement, xv, 2
revitalization, prior to Vatican II
  church and the Eucharist, 27–28
  church as sacrament, 26–27
  Congar's contribution, 28–31
  generally, 16–17
  Möhler, 17–22
  mystical body of Christ, 21–24
  Mystici Corporis, 22, 23, 25–26, 25n93, 65
  people of God, 24–25, 72
Richardson, Cyril, 54
Rikhof, Herwi, 70–71, 98n140
Roman Catholic Church
  authority in, 152–163
  catholicity of, 110–12, 110n29, 125–29
  as communion, 38–39
  as community of disciples, 77–78
  Eucharist and, 27–28
  genesis of, 81–84
  as hierarchical, 15–16
  as historical subject of its self-realization, 79–80
  human and divine dimensions of, 59–60, 63, 75–76, 79–80
  on local churches, 102–3
  meaning of, 71–74, 76
  modernists, 44
  as mystery, 37, 69–71
  as mystical body of Christ, 21–24, 26, 58–59
  as one true church, 15
  ontology of, 84–86
  question of who belongs, 56–57
  as sacrament, 26–27, 37–38
  societal and transcendent aspects, 100
  as a visible institution, 8–10
  the world and, 43–46, 46n178
  young people and, 101
Roman School, 20–21, 21n75
Romans, Letter to, 22n84, 41
Roncalli, Angelo, 31. *See also* John XXIII, Pope
Rosato, Philip, 19–20
Routhier, Gilles, 122
Ruddy, Christopher, 105, 150

sacrament
  compared to the church, 89, 134
  Roman Catholic church as, 26–27
Sacrosanctum concilium (Constitution on the Sacred Liturgy), 35, 39–40, 40n144, 47, 106, 110–11
Sales, Francis de, 9
Scheeben, Matthias Joseph, 22, 22n82, 75
Schick, Edward, 105
scholastics, of twelfth and thirteenth centuries, 4–5
Schrader, Clemens, 12, 21
Searle, John, 64
Second Letter of Peter, 41
self-realization, community of believers, 79–80, 94–95
Sentences (Lombard), 4
Sesboüé, Bernard, 152–53
Smedt, Émile-Joseph de, 33
social reality of church, 80
social relationship, authority and, 154–57
social sciences
  ecclesiology and, 63–64
  influences on Komonchak, 63–64
societas perfecta, term described, 11. *See also* perfect society ecclesiology
Spanish summa, 14n54
special categories, 96
spiritual principles, 1, 100, 116
Suenens, Leo, 35, 39
Sullivan, Francis, 55
Summa de ecclesia (John of Torquemada), 6–7
Summa theologica (Aquinas), 4
Supremi pastoris (Vatican I document), 12–15, 12n44, 21
Syllabus of Errors (Pius IX), 45

Symbolism (Möhler), 19
synodality, 151
systematic ecclesiology, 3, 17, 38–39, 89–97

Tametsi Deus (Vatican I document), 12–13, 12n44
"Theological and Juridical Status of Episcopal Conferences," 137n129
theological order, 117
theological reductionism, 62, 63, 74, 165
theological significance of locality
  ascending approach, 119–124, 132
  descending approach, 116–19, 132
theory
  as goal of systematic ecclesiology, 90–93
  and practice, 94–95
Thomas, of Aquinas. *See* Aquinas, Thomas
Tierney, Brian, 6
Tillard, Jean-Marie Roger, 128–29
Tracy, David, 51–52n2, 51–53, 58, 67
transcendent, spiritual dimensions, 1, 100
transubstantiation, 28
Treasure in Earthen Vessels (Gustafson), 61
Tromp, Sebastian, 23
True and False Reform in the Church (Congar), 30
truth, voluntaristic conception of, 161

Unitatis redintegratio ("Decree on Ecumenism"), 35, 41–43, 45, 106, 110–11
Unity in the Church or the Principle of Catholicism (Möhler), 18–19
universality, 43, 120, 129–150

Vatican Council I (1869-1870)
  church as a perfect society, 11–12
  on local churches, 103–4, 138, 138n132

papal primacy and infallibility, 7, 137–39
Pastor aeternus, 12, 12n44
Supremi pastoris, 12–15, 12n44, 21
Tametsi Deus, 12–13, 12n44
Vatican Council II (1962-1965)
  ecclesiology at, 31–36, 49–50
  goals of, 32
  Preparatory Theological Commission, 32
  see also post-Vatican II ecclesiology; revitalization, prior to Vatican II
Vatican Council II (1962-1965), documents of
  Ad gentes ("Decree on the Church's Missionary Activity"), 45, 106, 111–12
  Apostolicam actuositatem ("Decree on the Apostolate of the Laity"), 47
  Christus Dominus ("Decree on the Pastoral Office of Bishops"), 106, 108, 115
Vatican Council II (1962-1965), documents of *(continued)*
  Dignitatis humanae (declarations on religious liberty), 45
  Gaudium et spes ("The Pastoral Constitution on the Church in the Modern World"), 35, 45, 47
  Lumen gentium (*See Lumen gentium*)
  Sacrosanctum concilium (Constitution on the Sacred Liturgy), 35, 39–40, 40n144, 47, 106, 110–11
  Unitatis redintegratio ("Decree on Ecumenism"), 35, 41–43, 45, 106, 110–11

Wang, Lisa, 28
Welch, Claude, 59–61, 59n22, 79
Whitehead, Alfred North, 145
world, church and, 43–46, 46n178
Wyclif, John, 8

www.ingramcontent.com/pod-product-compliance
Lightning Source LLC
Chambersburg PA
CBHW052340230426
43664CB00041B/2567